The Franchise Affair

THE
FRANCHISE
AFFAIR

Creating fortunes and failures in independent television

Asa Briggs and Joanna Spicer

CENTURY

LONDON   MELBOURNE   AUCKLAND   JOHANNESBURG

First published in 1986 by Century Hutchinson Ltd,
Brookmount House, 62–65 Chandos Place, Covent Garden,
London WC2N 4NW

Century Hutchinson Publishing Group (Australia) Pty Ltd
16–22 Church Street, Hawthorn, Melbourne, Victoria 3122

Century Hutchinson Group (NZ) Ltd
32–34 View Road, PO Box 40–086, Glenfield, Auckland 10

Century Hutchinson Group (SA) Pty Ltd
PO Box 337, Bergvlei 2012, South Africa

British Library Cataloguing in Publication Data
Briggs, Asa
The franchise affair : creating fortunes and
failures in independent television under the IBA.
1. Television stations—Great Britain
I. Title II. Spicer, Joanna
384.55′453   HE8700.9.G7

ISBN 0–7126–1201–7

Typeset by Inforum Ltd, Portsmouth
in 11 on 12 Linotron 202 Baskerville
Printed in Great Britain by
St Edmundbury Press Ltd, Bury St Edmunds, Suffolk
Bound by Butler & Tanner Ltd, Frome, Somerset

Contents

'Thank you for coming to tell me about The Franchise affair,' Robert said, returning to sobriety.

Josephine Tey, *The Franchise Affair*, 1948

1

Why a Franchise Affair?

DURING THE MORNING and afternoon of Sunday, 28 December 1980, leading representatives of thirty-four television companies reported for interview at the headquarters of the Independent Broadcasting Authority, 70 Brompton Road. They were to be told whether or not they had been awarded television contracts and on what terms.

Fifteen companies were incumbents: they had been presenting programmes to the public for periods of between thirteen and twenty-five years, and their names were well-known locally and nationally. Nineteen companies were aspirants applying to replace one or other of the existing fifteen; in this case, it was the names not of the companies but of some of the individual members of the consortia which backed them that were locally and nationally known.

In addition, interviews were held that day with eight applicants for a new contract for the much publicized national breakfast service. And here, with individual names as prominent – and as different – as those of David Frost, Peter Jay and Harold Lever, and with all the glamour of a new operation, there was ample scope for what the Authority itself called 'drama'.

The way the Authority behaved – if not what it decided – on Sunday, 28 December, was subjected to general criticism at the time. 'The IBA . . . and its mandarins,' wrote the *Daily Telegraph* the day afterwards, 'like to award television franchises in a grand manner. . . . All of this will be of great significance to their shareholders . . . but none of it, with the possible exception of breakfast-time, will change life much for the rest of us.'

1

This was a simple, succinct and telling verdict. Leaving style on one side, however, that was certainly not how the twelve members of the IBA or its officials saw their task. Nor was it the way the people who had set up the Authority – i.e. Members of Parliament – saw its task. Moreover, it was not just a few shareholders, scattered throughout the country, who watched what was happening with interest and concern. The management and staffs of the incumbent companies, most of them far removed from the glamour, certainly knew that they were affected by what was decided at 70 Brompton Road; and in at least some of the programme areas – in Birmingham, for example, in Bournemouth, in Southampton and in Leeds – there was interest among viewing members of the public in the outcome. For them it was not just a matter of ins and outs. They had their likes and dislikes. They hoped to see them register, and they had been encouraged to believe, not least by the Authority itself, that they would.

There is a particular fascination about the events of 28 December 1980 in that the rituals of the IBA, which undoubtedly had a touch of absurdity about them, got mixed up with the rituals of Christmas and more especially of Holy Innocents' Day. Separate summonses, sealed envelopes, dispatch riders carrying the secret news from Brompton Road to Whitehall . . . all at a time when chairmen, directors, Ministers and Members of the Authority themselves would usually have been sitting before their own firesides. And more profoundly, the sense of oracles, of sacrificial victims, even a female deity, Lady Plowden, the Chairman of the Authority. 'Marvellous, isn't it,' the *Sun* mused expansively, 'the way we can turn a simple commercial transaction like the distribution of TV franchises into a ceremonial occasion.' The *Spectator* was less generous. 'It is difficult to think of anything quite as preposterous as the pantomime last Sunday.'

Whether or not the events of 28 December 1980 represented a 'simple commercial transaction', as the *Sun* took for granted, is as much a matter for examination as the verdict of the *Daily Telegraph*. Indeed, the question this poses is one of the main themes of this book. If the *Sun* was right, by far the simplest mode of dealing with a simple commercial transaction would have been an auction of the separate contracts to the highest

2

bidders. But the matter was not seen in this way. The Authority was aware of the fact, as were the people who brought it into existence, that it was disposing not only of money, but of access to the air, 'programme time'. It had been called upon to make its decisions behind the scenes about who could best make use of the franchises in terms not of profits but of programmes. There was a further problem there, of course. It was succinctly described by Philip Purser in the *Sunday Telegraph* (28 December 1980) when he described the IBA's investigation into programming as pitting 'someone's unkept promises against someone else's unkeepable promises.'

December 1980 was not the first time the Authority had distributed or redistributed contracts. After what Sir Robert Fraser, the first Director General of the Authority, called the 'delicate and laborious task' of issuing the initial contracts in the mid-1950s, there had been further decision-making processes in 1963 and 1967, with one incumbent company losing its contract in the second of these years and another being forced into a shotgun marriage. The pantomime element had been completely missing then, however, just as it had been missing during the 1950s when the BBC's monopoly was broken and the Authority was brought into existence explicitly to safeguard future broadcasting standards in a new system of competition.

It was during that first period, when much seemed to be at stake, including the success of the new system as a whole, that the *Spectator* (4 July 1958) described the issue of contracts as 'an unprecedented exercise in state patronage,' adding that 'it is extraordinary that there should have been so little interest in how they were awarded.' Nearly ten years later, when the Authority returned to its task, the *Financial Times* (21 June 1967) was complaining that 'in effect arbitrary power whose exercise affects the lives of millions' was being handed over to a small group of men; 'in its own field', it observed, the Authority had greater power than many courts of law. 'Judges must explain the basis for their decision and defendants always have the right to appeal.' Bernard Hollowood went further still in *Punch* when he described the distribution of franchises as 'one of the most squalid operations ever to deface the fair name of private enterprise.' Sir Sydney Caine, Deputy Chairman of the ITA at the time of the 1967 awards, wrote twelve years later

3

that while he had 'no doubt that the decisions were taken entirely on the grounds of public interest as seen by Members of the Authority, and had regard, in particular, to the objective of securing the best possible programmes,' he equally had no doubt 'that the decisions as a whole, coupled with later decisions about more detailed programming, were wrong.'

There is a case, therefore, for examining not only the particular outcome of the Authority's decisions in December 1980, the pantomime of the last act, but the drama and melodrama that led up to them, a drama and a melodrama with a long prelude. The pantomime itself, after all, is now part of history. Time marches on. There is now a new Chairman at Brompton Road and alongside him a new Director General and several new Members of the Authority. Two incumbent companies gave way at the end of 1981 to new concerns as a result of the Authority's decisions, and it is the latter who are now the well-established programme providers. Three incumbents retained their contracts only on conditions which required major restructuring of shareholdings and management to be performed within one or two months. These were carried through, though not in the way the Authority first contemplated, and changes in shareholdings which might have been completely unpalatable to the Authority in 1980 have been made more recently without fuss. Seven companies formed to apply for the tempting new breakfast contract were disappointed. The one winner was to face losses on an unanticipated scale. Indeed, it has hit the headlines more since it secured the contract than when it was pressing its claims to secure it. Finally, new elements have entered into all the equations since Lord Thomson, the new Chairman of the Authority, stated in 1981 that there must not be a repetition next time of what happened in 1980.

For all these reasons, it is worth trying to penetrate beneath the surface of what Lord Thomson called in the Authority's Annual Report of 1980–81 'the single most dramatic event of 1980–81 from the point of view of the television companies and the general public' and to present the event in perspective. There is now a quite different reason in addition. The question of 'franchising and licensing' has now arisen in a new context, in relation to cable television. The word 'franchise' was not employed in the Television Act of 1954. Nor was it employed in

4

the Act of 1980. Yet in the 1982 *Report of the Inquiry into Cable Expansion and Broadcasting Policy*, presided over by Lord Hunt of Tanworth, the key section on policy, chapter 3, is called 'Functions in Cable and the Case for a Franchise System'.

New technology is all the time changing communications perspectives, so that we have no secure vantage point from which to look at the past, least of all in 1985. Other factors are changing too. The Government itself in the 1980s has a different set of attitudes towards market competition from those current in the 1950s and 1960s, whatever Government was in power, and these are reflected in other areas of telecommunications policy which remains a controversial topic of debate. Moreover, outside the whole field of telecommunications the subject of 'franchising' of other kinds of business transactions, along with 'privatization', is now a regular topic in newspapers and colour supplements. There is one serious academic article in *Fiscal Studies* (February 1985) by Simon Domberger and Julius Middleton on 'Franchising in Practice: the Case of Independent Television in the UK' which notes that, while most of the experience of franchising comes from the United States, there is already a general theory of the subject.

Which?, the Consumers' Association magazine, selected the topic for an in-depth survey at the end of 1983, cautiously warning those of its readers tempted to acquire 'franchises for selling these things or those things' that they should not expect them to provide a quick fortune. Are we to assume within this new context that the granting of 'franchises' to television companies or to local radio companies – and these have also been granted by the IBA since 1972 – or to cable companies – and these are to be granted by a new Authority – is no different from granting franchises to catering companies on the motorways or in the airports or by international businesses to retailers of fast foods or flowers? Can everything be left to the market? Domberger and Middleton conclude that television broadcasting is an activity which is inherently difficult to franchise, mainly because the service 'defies precise specification'.

It is interesting to note that the Hunt Report, which puts its trust more firmly in market forces than any previous official committee report concerned with television, urges that 'cable systems should operate under minimum restraints', but states

5

firmly (clause 85) that, since 'a cable operator will have an effective local monopoly,' this should be conferred 'only after an opportunity for *judging* any competitive bids and for securing the provision of the best service for the area concerned'; and it goes on to list six items which a new 'franchising body' should take into account before issuing franchises. These include not only the structure of business interests and the 'proposed financing arrangements' but 'the range and diversity of the proposed programme channels' and 'the arrangements proposed for community programmes and local access.' We have not disposed, therefore, of the idea of some kind of examination.

The word 'franchise' looks simple enough, but, given the themes of this book, it has an appropriately complex history, even more complex than the word 'contract', which figures along with 'tort' as the title of examination papers for law students, or the word 'licence', which was subjected to careful examination by John Milton as long ago as the seventeenth century. The seventeenth-century use of the word 'franchise', the first use picked out by the *Oxford English Dictionary*, reads simply 'exemption from servitude or subjection'. (Other dictionaries add the word 'restraint'.) A recent article on the activities of business firms like Budget Rent-a-Car, Burger King and Exchange Travel was given a title in the same vein – 'Franchising for Freedom'. A second use of the word 'franchise' is also picked out, however, in the *Oxford English Dictionary* and it is described as being in wider use in the twentieth century – 'a privilege granted by the sovereign power to any person or body of persons.' It was only when people became aware of the privileges and profits that television could bestow that the word 'franchise' began to be used in relation to British television after the initial period of expansion was over.

It is on the basis of the second *Oxford English Dictionary* definition that questions focusing on the relationship between the private and the public interest arise. How the IBA does – and should – answer such questions is a matter of obvious public and private concern. So, too, are the questions: What is 'an Authority'? What are its credentials? How are its members to be chosen and what particular areas of expert knowledge are necessary? Why did the Hunt Report at the same time recognize the need for an Authority to establish criteria for issuing

6

franchises and express suspicions that 'the IBA might have an overprotective attitude to public service broadcasting' which could deter potential investors in cable?

An extra dimension is given to such questions when it is recognized that in the last resort it is not the 'Authority' but the Government through Parliament which has to answer them. There are differences of outlook behind the answers within political parties as well as between them. There are also ebbs and flows of concern and involvement at different times. All governments (and oppositions) have been tempted to criticize the media or to intervene in their affairs when they have felt that their own role was being misinterpreted or challenged, and there are no signs that they will resist the temptation in the future. There are some programmes too, that governments and oppositions, occasionally in unison, watch more carefully than others. There is a great deal of ignorance about technology and finance, but there is no disposition to ignore questions of power and influence. Broadcasting operates, therefore, in what Lord Windlesham has described as 'a condition of semi-freedom'. From the 1970s the boundaries have been 'narrowing rather than broadening'.

Communications issues cannot be reduced to technical and financial issues, although the finance, difficult to unravel, is of great importance in any analysis of broadcasting, whatever the system. It deserves far more attention than it gets. The Government's part in the present picture is to set the amount of the BBC's licence fee and the size of the levy on ITV profits. The Authority, which itself does not raise capital or revenue for the ITV system, is the collecting agent and administrator of the levy and has other wide-ranging financial powers. It determines who shall have access to profit (or loss), it controls financial clauses in contracts, and it sets rental costs and Channel 4 subscriptions which contracting companies have to meet from their revenue. Voting shares in the companies cannot be bought, assigned or sold without its prior approval, and holdings above 5 per cent must be notified to it. Finally, its approval is required also for the terms of supply of programmes from one contracting company to another.

In a newsworthy industry which as a whole is not highly capitalized and where profit rates vary from one part of the country and from one year to another, these are formidable powers, and there is considerable evidence that the IBA was determined to use them in 1980, although it had inadequate financial expertise to guide it. It used its powers therefore in a way which itself generated suspicion. The word 'franchise' has another more ancient meaning than the two meanings already mentioned. Another definition is 'frankness', 'plain speaking', and there was very little of this in 1980 either in public or in private. If more explanations had been given by the Authority after its allocation of the new contracts, this book might not have been necessary. Certainly it would have taken a different form.

Josephine Tey's well-constructed detective novel *The Franchise Affair*, from which the title of this book is taken, is not concerned with any such intricate questions. The Franchise described in it is the name not of an exemption or of a privilege, but of a house. Yet our borrowing of a title and a motto from Miss Tey, one of the most ingenious of detective novelists, seems particularly appropriate for this volume on communications issues and procedures. Will there always be an 'affair' when the Authority distributes valuable franchises and when some win and some lose? How much mystery should there be? In 1980 there was plenty, and it requires the counterpart of a detective novel to unravel it. Detective novels usually leave much in the way of resolution to the last chapter. In this book there are no final solutions, only continuing mysteries.

2

Law and Policy

OUR BOOK TAKES the form of a narrative, but it tells several stories, not one. They are all interconnected, and they are all very British stories, for there is no other television system quite like the British. Before the IBA was the BBC; and there are elements of continuity, particularly in the idea of 'public broadcasting', which go back long before the Television Act of 1954 which set up the Independent Television Authority. Sir Brian Young, Director General of the IBA in 1980, called it an 'additional public broadcasting service . . . financed by the sale of advertising time . . .' and two years later, now in retirement, he referred in a lecture to 'a paternal tradition, reaching back to Reith and now needing to be defended.'

Of course, there is some telescoping in such versions of history. There were fierce arguments and exciting events before the Television Act of 1954 reached the statute book, when the BBC was on one side and the would-be commercial broadcasters on the other, and these influenced the pattern of the 'franchising process'. It was the 1954 Act which set up the Authority, and the terms of the Act represented a compromise, with Parliament quite deliberately delegating authority to the new body as authority had previously been delegated (by Royal Charter) to the BBC. The Government showed no inclination to manage television more directly, but it did not want to leave it entirely to commercial interests or, to use a later and better-known phrase, to the broadcasters.

The fact that authority was delegated meant that it was left to the ITA to evolve its own policies in the light of experience and opinion. The law provided a framework, not a blueprint.

9

An excursion into history is an essential prelude, therefore, to any thorough investigation of what happened in December 1980. The Independent Television Authority of 1954 was to change its name in 1972 to the Independent Broadcasting Authority, when local sound broadcasting fell for the first time within its remit and contracts began to be awarded to local sound broadcasting companies. There is no evidence, however, that the extension of its duties influenced the manner in which the Authority handled the issue of contracts. It had already established its pattern.

The contracts it awarded were called 'franchises' in the IBA news release of 24 January 1980, which invited applications 'for future television franchises', and in the IBA's official publication *Independent Broadcasting* in January 1981, which referred to the new 'franchise holders'. Yet in line with the initial legislation of 1954, the key document relating to each television 'area' in 1980 was entitled 'Particulars of ITV Contract'. It set out in some detail the terms, many of them new, relating to the area in question.

The Act of 1954 left the making of programmes, which is, after all, although this is sometimes forgotten, *the* business of broadcasting, not to the Authority but to 'programme contractors' to be selected by the Authority. The United States model of commercial broadcasting was quite deliberately rejected by Parliament. Only if programme contracting companies were unable to do so was the Authority ('if need be') to provide or arrange for 'programmes or parts of programmes' in order to 'maintain balance' or to keep the service operating. There was a second crucial point. The companies made profits: the Authority received its income from the companies, not from direct business transactions. Finally, something more than 'regulation', the common American term, was implied within the new system. Competition with the BBC, which as a result of the Act lost its monopoly in television for the first time, was to be offered within a framework of public broadcasting, with the Authority ensuring that 'standards' were maintained.

It was also the task of the Authority, however, to maintain competition within its own sector. 'It shall be the duty of the Authority', clause 5(2) of the Act read – and it was a clause inserted into all subsequent legislation, including that of 1981 – 'to do all it can to secure that there is adequate competition between a number of programme contractors independent of each other both as to finance and as to control.'

The Act made no reference to the entitlement of a programme contractor either to a permanent or to a limited-term 'franchise'. They were certainly not freeholds. Instead, the Authority itself was given only an initial life of ten years and in consequence could not sign contracts for a longer period. Yet it was granted the power to terminate contracts before its own ten years were through. By clause 6(3) every contract between the Authority and a programme contractor had to contain a provision reserving to the Authority 'the absolute right . . . to serve on the programme contractor a notice in writing . . . to suspend . . . the Authority's obligation to transmit the programmes supplied by the programme contractor . . . if it deems it necessary to do so in view of breaches of the contract.'

In case of breach of contract the Authority had power to give notice of termination of contract if it had three times earlier demanded payment of penalties from the contractors. Such a conception of penalties, even if 'judged by arbitration', was itself as British as the conception of the Authority. Indeed, in a sense it was the Authority which was being granted the franchise by Act of Parliament as the BBC had been granted its franchise by its Royal Charter of 1926. It was as much a deliberate decision on the part of the Government in 1954 to allow the Chairman, Members and staff of its newly created Authority a choice of options in planning its own operations as it was to retain a public-broadcasting framework. As one of the Government's spokesmen put it in Parliament at that time, 'the ITA should have complete freedom to weigh all considerations in coming to a decision about allocations.'

It was through 'allocations', of course, that competition would either be secured or not secured, and delegation to the Authority on this vital point of debate was absolute. When the Postmaster General was asked in the House of Lords what 'adequate competition' between programme contractors would mean in practice – and it was a leading question at the end of the protracted debate on monopoly in Parliament and in the country – he replied, without going into detail, that there were

11

'two or three different ways' of ensuring it and that the Authority itself should choose the way it preferred before or after discussion with the range of would-be contractors.

The law, therefore, explicitly and deliberately left out much that was to prove of fundamental importance after 1955. 'We had nothing to guide us,' wrote Sir Kenneth (later Lord) Clark, the first Chairman of the Authority, 'except the Act of course. No one had ever made this kind of contract before: there was no precedent: nothing to look up. The job was one of creative legal thinking and skilful negotiations.'

The 'creative' thinking and the 'skilful' negotiating crystallized inevitably, however, into a set of procedures, and the procedures equally inevitably became part of a set of policies. Yet before the Authority was appointed part of the pattern had in effect been set, and set for technical reasons, like so much else, never fully ventilated in debate. In 1952 the Postmaster General's Television Advisory Committee had reported that frequencies which could be allocated to the new independent television service would limit it to one programme only in any one 'area', though with some overlap. There would be strictly limited consumer choices. And since it was the Authority which maintained the basic system of transmission, it was the Authority which had to face up to its limitations.

In spite of the report of the Television Advisory Committee, the Authority's first concept of the commercial channel was of at least two companies providing programmes at each station in competition with each other. Even in its first Annual Report, for 1954–55, it hoped 'ultimately' for two stations in each area, and in 1963 a new Chairman was reaffirming the Authority's resolve that 'when ITV2 came' there should be two competing seven-day companies in each area. But this hope was never realized; and the contracting companies continued to hold monopolies in their own areas. There were obvious limits to the power of creative thinking therefore; and when in the 1970s the question of a fourth channel opened up the Authority saw it as 'complementary to and not competitive with the first service.' In evidence to the Annan Committee on the Future of Broadcasting in 1974 it set out the 'arguments against disturbing the *status quo*'.

These were arguments relating to finance. In September

1954 it was programme competition which occupied the mind of Sir Robert Fraser on his appointment as Director General. He wrote that he wanted 'a network connection technically capable of giving an unlimited introduction of programmes' from any one region into any other and the stations to be in full competition in selling to each other – 'Each will be eager to sell, each to buy.' But 'the network must be optional – or it is not competition but cartel or market-sharing' (Fraser Papers). It was a long way from this early concept to the IBA's 1981 Agreements for Appointment, which turned the positive duty laid on it by successive Acts from 1954 to 1981 into a negative and limited duty laid by it on the contractors – 'the Contractor shall not so conduct its affairs as to prevent there being adequate competition between a number of contractors.' The BBC's monopoly had been broken in 1955, but at any time thereafter until the advent of Channel 4 its ITV competitors held local monopolies in the provision of commercial television programmes, as well as in their marketing and the revenue derived from it. The new contracting companies had become established elements in a structure, and ITCA, the Independent Television Companies Association, could describe the idea of a second set of contractors within the system as 'the wrong kind of competition'.

It was only after a fourth channel had been established in November 1983 that the ITV contractors experienced programme competition within the independent system for the first time from 'independent' programme makers who were neither ITV nor BBC. Their financial base was not threatened, for on both commercial channels the contracting companies continued to hold the monopoly of advertising revenue in their own areas. Yet 50 per cent of programmes for the new channel were to emanate from independent programme makers rather than the 17 per cent mentioned in debate. In September 1954 Sir Robert Fraser had anticipated a development of this kind. He wanted each producer company to be required to 'secure a proportion of its own original programmes from subcontractors' and he saw no reason why this should not be a fixed percentage. The companies would compete with each other for the best subcontractors and the subcontractors would be in competition with each other. He noted further, as he had done

13

before, that the network must not be compulsory: 'there would be only one buyer for subcontractors to approach.'

In fact, different considerations influenced attitudes to competition in 1955. As quickly as possible the Authority began the process of dividing the country into contract areas, starting with three major groupings of population – London, the Midlands and the North. As independent television increased its coverage an element of rivalry between regional programme contractors – though not an element of consumer choice – was introduced into the system by splitting these major area contracts and granting six contracts, the first three for weekday programmes, the second three for weekend programmes. No single contracting company was to be allowed to 'command' these important 'areas' all the time. The ITA presented the arrangement, which in the event ended in four contracting companies, not in six, as leaving the door open for new companies to join the system. As the seven-year process of completing the ITV map went on, areas of overlap of contract boundaries, where more than one station could be received, were inevitable, and in these at least the consumer could choose to which station his aerial should be directed. Some of these areas were sizable and their importance within the system was to grow.

Finally, it was stressed in 1955 that since there would be a multiplicity of programme contracting companies in the system as a whole, each with its own board and its own management, 'independent' broadcasting would not (and should not) depend on one powerful set of interlocking interests, for example, in show business or in the press. There would be a variety of interests, some local, some national, not a concentration of them.

It was with these points in mind that on 25 August 1955, twenty days after holding its first meeting, the Authority invited 'applications from those interested in becoming programme contractors in accordance with the provisions of the Television Act.' Applicants were asked to give a 'broad picture of the type of programme they would provide, their proposals for network or local broadcasting of their programmes, some indication of their financial resources, and the length of contracts they would desire.' The Authority planned to broadcast

14

initially from three stations – in London, the Midlands and the North – and, after receiving twenty-five applications 'of widely varying degrees of detail and precision', it held a series of interviews over a period of less than a month, the details of which were not revealed, before offering four nine-year contracts which were announced in the press on 3 November 1955.

The unsuccessful applicants included the Incorporated Television Programme Company Ltd (ITPC), a company formed by entertainment interests which included among its sponsors Moss Empires and the Grade Organization and was held not to have 'the breadth of interest' which the Authority sought. Another application, from the Associated British Picture Corporation, was deemed to be 'half-hearted'.

The detailed contracts with the first four successful programme companies – the Associated Broadcasting Development Company (ABDC), the Kelmsley/Winnick group, Granada (TV Network) Ltd and Broadcast Relay Service/Associated Newspapers (soon to be known as Associated-Rediffusion) – took months to work out. ABDC's financial problems were resolved only when the ITPC joined with it to form Associated Television Ltd (ATV). Finance was not resolved for another contract, that offered to the Kelmsley/Winnick group. It had to be readvertised in July and was finally offered to ABC Television, a subsidiary formed for the purpose, after personal intervention by Sir Robert Fraser, by the Associated British Picture Corporation. The story has been fully written by Bernard Sendall in the first volume of his history of the Authority. It shows how and why the Authority under the skilful direction of Sir Robert Fraser never felt that it could handle the 'franchise process' in a *laissez-faire* way.

The London weekday contract went to Associated-Rediffusion, the Northern weekday to Granada. ATV won London at weekends and the Midlands on weekdays. ABC Television took two weekend contracts, the Midlands and the North. AR and ATV set up their headquarters in London and Granada built a new studio complex in Manchester. ABC converted one of its cinemas in Manchester and for its Midland contract shared with ATV another converted ABC cinema in Birmingham. Everything depended in the first instance, however, on the work of the IBA's engineers. The first intention

15

of the Authority was to reach agreement with the BBC to instal ITV's Band III aerials on the BBC's masts at Crystal Palace for London, at Sutton Coldfield for the Midlands and at Holme Moss for the North, and it was not until after the engineers on both sides had got together in December 1954 that it was revealed that this was structurally impossible. The ITA had to go it alone, and their engineers' remarkable achievement in constructing the ITA's own separate stations brought ITV on the air as a service for the London area in September 1955 (Beulah Hill) and as a network when the Midlands service opened in February 1956 (Lichfield), followed by the North in May and October 1956 (Winter Hill and Emley Moor). It was these engineering imperatives in 1955 which substituted, for the BBC's single high-power transmitter located centrally on the Pennines, two ITA stations, one for Lancashire and Cheshire to the west and a second for Yorkshire to the east.

Subsequent awards of 'franchises', the chronology of which depended on the completion of transmitters, followed the same procedure of advertisement, offer of contract and subsequent detailed negotiations. They began with the advertisement on 28 November 1955 for the contract for Central Scotland, which went to STV, owned as to 80 per cent by Roy Thomson, proprietor from 1952 of the *Scotsman*, an investment soon to prove highly lucrative and remembered in history as 'a licence to print money'. Extensions in the North-East, South and South-West were delayed by government restrictions on capital expenditure, but by June 1961 the press reported the completion of the ITV network three years before the ITA's period of life ended under the 1954 Act. By then fifteen contracting companies had been selected, of which eleven were already operating. For one contract, that in the South-West, awarded to a group brought together by Peter Cadbury in 1959, there were eleven rival consortia. Border and Grampian were still to come in autumn 1961, Channel Islands in 1962. The last to come, Wales (West and North) (WWN), which gained the ITA contract offered in 1960 for the Welsh-speaking area, went on the air in September 1962 but lasted less than a year before its losses, inevitable but not apparently foreseen by the Authority, led to a merger with Television Wales and West of England (TWW) in May 1963.

In all this initial activity, carried through with intelligence, vigour and enthusiasm, there were echoes of the early stages of sound broadcasting a generation earlier. In the 1920s, as in the 1950s, technical conditions had shaped policies, without these being clearly explained to the public; and John Reith, like Clark, had felt that he was deciding policy without any precedent to guide him. In both cases the extension of coverage to the public was top priority, and questions of the shape of broadcasting areas – the BBC and on occasion the IBA were to call them 'regions' – assumed great importance, greater importance, indeed, than many people in London found desirable. Nonetheless, there was a big difference. During the 1920s the BBC had been both making policy and providing desirable programmes – as it was during and since the 1950s, and still is – while the Authority was concerned only with ensuring a supply of programmes of proper quality and balance, not with providing them. (Just what that meant was a matter of debate.)

By the time the basic ITA transmitter network was complete in 1962 it had become clear that while decisions about areas had to take account of population numbers and their socio-economic characteristics, it was ITA engineers, concerned with the technical problems of siting transmission stations and subject to government control, who played the key part in determining exact area boundaries. The contracting companies had to forge their own broadcasting policies in relation to the areas offered them, some more socially and culturally homogeneous than others. It was they, not the Authority, who had to establish relationships with their own local publics. The view from Manchester or Southampton was different from the ITA's view from its London headquarters. The last two contracts awarded in the long process of covering the country – for the Channel Islands and for West and North Wales – concerned areas which had little doubt of their identity. In other areas, however, broadcasters did not necessarily believe that the Authority's sense of their identity was coincident with their own.

What of the advertisers, the people who were to finance the system? In 1955 they were not given the opportunity to sponsor particular programmes as American advertisers were. They had to buy time – this had been decreed as early as 1953 (White

Paper, Cmnd 9005) – from the programme contractors who were in business to sell it. The advertisers' concern was the reach of their messages and they had to concern themselves, therefore, first with the set count – the larger the number of television households covered in an area contract the larger the potential market – and second with household spending power: in areas where consumer spending was high the higher would be the anticipated sales returns. They were concerned too with the permitted amount of daily advertising time, which was controlled by the Authority, and the ins and outs of prime-time planning for commercials which influenced the tariff schedules of the contracting companies.

There was scope here, of course, for sophisticated market research, both on the socioeconomic characteristics of television households and on their viewing habits. Advertisers were likely to spend more where consumer spending was high and the contracting companies' tariffs would be likely to be higher in consequence. Contracting companies in such areas (London and the South and South-East) could be expected to take a higher share of advertising revenue, therefore, than their set count of television homes.

The count of television households also became a complex matter of research with successive boundary surveys. From the start advertisers had to pay attention to the existence of overlap areas of dual or triple reception; the existence of such areas, a by-product of decisions about the siting of transmitters, was bound, therefore, to affect the contract process. Moreover, after the construction by the ITA of UHF transmitters in 1964 to provide for 625-line transmission for colour, the number of such overlap areas was to increase. The main heartland of each company remained, but the documents issued by the Authority to would-be contractors now included the phrase that 'most contract areas are overlapped to some extent by other areas. No contractor can be given exclusive rights to provide television broadcasting services in a given area.' By 1980 the Authority, increasingly attached to 'regionalism', was anxious through 'regional meetings' to test public preferences for the 'franchise areas' to which members of the public wished themselves to belong. It also commissioned in June 1979 a national survey, *Attitudes to ITV*, described in chapter 3. There were by then fourteen ITV regions, and the Authority was thinking of 'subregions' also.

It was thus in the light of new evidence that the Authority was to propose changes in area boundaries in the contracts from 1982. When the particulars of each franchise were advertised in May 1980, they included a map of 'the service area boundary contour of the main stations' and 'the composite main station overlap'. The Authority itself was being forced to consider carefully issues which at first had been faced mainly by advertisers and by the commercial companies themselves, since the finances of both were based on calculations of audience shares.

The weekday–weekend split of franchises had been dropped by the Authority in 1968 in all areas outside London, but already, long before then, the contracting companies themselves had evolved a line of policy of their own which was more significant in relation to the provision of the programmes which the public could view than any policy initiated by the Authority. Within two years of the launching of Independent Television, when there were still serious financial problems – Sir Robert Fraser talked of 'murderous losses' – the first 'Big Four' contracting companies, the so-called 'majors', created a networking system which entailed substantial national programme planning. Without advance sight of each other's programmes, they prepared a network schedule, placing programmes in slots and determining their mix. When new contracting companies were formed between 1958 and 1962 as television coverage was extended, the new companies, each initially on special affiliation terms with one of the 'majors', were offered the network programmes of all four in return for a percentage of their net advertising revenue in addition to a charge per hour for the programmes themselves, based for each company on the population it served. The system survived and was strengthened, although the early special affiliation terms came to an end and the 'Big Four' became the 'Big Five' after the splitting of the Granada area and the creation of Yorkshire Television. Indeed, by 1961–62 the ITA itself in its Annual Report claimed that it had worked well, having 'grown up with the system as it expanded.' It suggested, however, that there should be 'new arrangements for the next decade.'

The Authority had watched this process grow from its early

conception of competition for programme supply. It did not suggest it or impose it. 'The Authority is not entitled to interfere with networking,' its Chairman, Sir Ivone Kirkpatrick, said in 1960. It held that the contracting companies remained legally 'independent of each other both as to finance and to control' since each contracting company within the network could reach its own decisions on network offers. There were now two groups of companies within ITV, 'majors' and 'minors', even if neither group had a single point of view. But as networking evolved the Authority came to judge that the system might work against the interests of the smaller companies which, it deemed, were obliged to accept the network programmes since they had no other source of supply. They might be discouraged too, the Authority came to argue, from producing (indeed, encouraged not to produce) their own programmes beyond the minimum required in their contracts with the Authority.

This line of argument was directly relevant to the public debate which accompanied the deliberations of the Pilkington Committee, the first official inquiry (1960) into the future of broadcasting since the BBC's monopoly was broken and the Authority set up. The Committee's summing-up was that 'the total franchise divided by the Authority into and allocated to the companies by areas has in effect been reassembled by the companies: and then divided by time'; and in submissions to it the ITA itself proposed reforms. The networking system survived Pilkington, but in the 1963 Act which followed it (section 4) and the 1964 consolidating Act (section 5) the control of the system and of the network charges was put in the hands of the Authority. Bernard Sendall has described in the second volume of his *Independent Television in Britain* the five years of 'The Networking Tangle' from 1963 to 1968, when the ITA and the companies were occupied with the minimum annual hours that the Ten would take from the Four, with the maximum annual sum that they would pay for them, and with the sliding scale, which came to be based on net annual revenue after levy (NARAL), on which a company's payment would be based. In these negotiations both groups had their associations – the Four the Independent Television Contractors Association, the Ten the British Regional Television Association. In 1971 the Five and the Ten came together in the Independent Television

Companies Association (ITCA) and joint planning arrangements were strengthened.

Relatively little had been said or written outside broadcasting circles before Pilkington about the allocation of future contracts, apart from a brief statement by the Public Accounts Committee in 1959, when the main focus of public interest was unacceptable levels of profitability, that 'the rentals representing the contractors' capacity to pay should be arrived at by competition provided that the Authority judged the highest bidder to be of standing [a curious phrase] and technically and financially competent to provide the service.' 'It is always the duty of a public authority,' the *Financial Times* agreed, 'to obtain the full market price for any asset it sells.' Sir Robert Fraser, however, maintained that the selection of contracting companies by competitive tender would be 'radically inconsistent' with the discharge of the duties and functions of the Authority under the 1954 Act. There was no 'natural connection', he held, between the 'qualifications' which groups seeking contracts would be expected to possess and the amount of money that they might offer (the *Times*, 17 October 1959). 'Competitive tendering might lead to overbidding, to a defective programme performance and financial difficulties being caused by a company promising to pay more than they could afford.'

The *Times* itself noted in the same year that there was a case for competitive tender, although it was only one possible way of dealing with 'a system fashioned by legislation and organized by a statutory body' which had proved to be immensely profitable. Other ideas might be 'conjured up'. It came as no surprise, therefore, when two years later a flat-rate excise duty of 11 per cent, the television advertising duty (TAD), was charged on receipts from television advertisements, to be paid by the contractors. The first stage in television history was over.

Although the Pilkington Committee recommended toughly that after 29 July 1964 the option agreement of 1957–58 between the ITA and the four 'majors' (which gave them first refusal of seven-day contracts in areas where they held split-week franchises, subject to transmitter development) 'should be regarded as destitute not only of all legal but also of all moral force,' it was less interested in the 'commercial transaction' aspects of broadcasting than in its content and purpose. The

Financial Times, which started from quite different premises, gave the committee encouragement, therefore, when it emphasized on 30 July 1959 that the ITA had become 'too closely identified with support for the contractors it is supposed to supervise to provide a fair chance for new firms to enter the industry and to secure a fair price for the valuable assets which the public has to sell.'

By ranging widely over a great variety of issues the Pilkington Committee stimulated debate. At the same time it provoked both the ire of the contracting companies for its criticism of the quality of recent programme output and the concern of the ITA for its complaint that there had been what amounted on its part to a 'surrender of authority'; and, since the Committee appealed to principle rather than to experience at every crucial point, the ire and concern were intensified. The Committee acknowledged the efficiency of the ITA in launching a new and viable alternative television service, but stated categorically (for example, in paragraph 552) that 'as the regulatory body, charged with the duty of controlling a number of programme contractors (who are commercial companies and with separate existences of their own),' the Authority needed 'an effective sanction to compel them, if necessary, to observe its directions and instructions.'

'Formally,' the report went on, 'the relationship between the Authority and a programme company is governed by the contract. But before it is entered into the Authority has to choose the company. For each of the last contracts, a number of companies applied so that the Authority had a real choice. For the early contracts there was not the same competition.' In fact, it was the companies which had held the initiative after their contracts had been signed, and the Authority (paragraph 7) 'had no real power to ensure that they use that initiative so as to realize the purposes of broadcasting.'

The Pilkington Committee re-examined all the arguments that had been raised during the debates of 1953 and 1954 on the ending of the BBC's monopoly and, since it reached a quite different conclusion about 'the purposes of broadcasting' and the character of the 'dual system' from that which Parliament had then reached, it is not surprising that when new legislation was introduced the Committee's general line of argument was

22

rejected by the Conservative Government. Yet the re-opening of the debate had been possible in 1960 only because of the number of points left undecided when the legislation of 1954 was passed, and because there was continuing disagreement, as sharp as ever, among people interested in communications policies about the most desirable shape of broadcasting and the nature of the impact of broadcasting on society and culture. It is interesting that the then Leader of the Labour Party, Hugh Gaitskell, would have preferred to the 1955 system a second public television corporation with 'if possible, a "pay as you go" system to finance it.'

'Of the two kinds of activity – the creative and the regulatory, which together contribute to a realization of the public interest in broadcasting,' the Pilkington Committee stated (paragraph 553), 'the first is the companies' business. Because the creative activity, the positive function of programme planning is theirs, they hold the initiative.' Indeed, once contracts had been let by the Authority on the basis of the 'stated intentions' of the applicants, it was the decisions of the companies which determined output. Upon 'the use they make' of their initiatives, the Committee went on, 'must depend very largely the kind of service independent television will provide. The selection and composition of the companies appointed as programme contractors is, therefore, of crucial importance.'

The Committee maintained that in making assessments about the issue of contracts it was far easier to weigh 'the technical and financial competence' of an applicant – this was a doubtful proposition – than the honesty of its programming intentions or its capacity to achieve them. The Authority would be driven back, therefore, to 'personal conviction'; and for this reason the Committee recommended an increase in the powers of the Authority *after* contracts had been issued, including the power to call for advance information about programmes. Moreover, since the Committee was suspicious of the free and unchecked play of 'the commercial incentive', it sought to ensure that the mode of finance, advertising, would not 'unduly affect the character of the service.' There was 'an issue of principle':

On the one hand, the Authority has a financial function of selling to

23

commercial companies a public facility which is necessarily limited in amount; to that extent its duty is to get the best price it can for the public. On the other hand, the Authority's first duty remains to ensure the best possible service of broadcasting; and since the existing companies have the advantage of several years of experience, it is difficult to see how any newcomers are to be preferred to them. The existing companies are obviously firmly established; given the present constitution and organization, we do not believe that the existing companies could be seriously challenged. We conclude that, since these, as things are, are two views which cannot be reconciled, the system must be at fault.

'The choice of a company would not, of course, be crucial,' the Pilkington Committee argued, 'if the Authority held a sufficient sanction with which to enforce its directions and instructions,' and it was in the light of this argument that it pressed for sweeping reforms to secure such adequate sanctions. Although these 'organic' reforms were, not surprisingly, unacceptable to the Government, it went further, following Parliamentary debate, in imposing more statutory controls on the Authority and on the contracting companies than might have been anticipated. Its White Papers of July and December 1962 (Cmnds 1770 and 1893) stressed the importance of the Authority assuming 'a commanding position in the affairs of independent television' to be determined not by itself but by Parliament; and new legislation in 1963 and 1964 (the latter consolidating) imposed a series of statutory obligations on the Authority, including the drawing-up and implementation of codes of guidance covering violence in programmes and matters concerning standards of practice in advertising. It also introduced provisions governing newspaper shareholdings in the financial structures of contracting companies and, in place of the 1961 makeshift TAD, a levy on their gross profits before tax. In relation to the former, there was a new section in the 1963 and 1964 Acts providing that if the Authority considered that press shareholding would be contrary to the public interest it could, with the Postmaster General's consent, determine or suspend its obligation to broadcast the programmes of the company at issue. In relation to the latter, the levy, 'additional payments', was based on the part of the companies on payments on a sliding scale from advertising turnover (after an initial 'free

24

slice'). The Authority was merely called upon to collect the levy and to transfer it to the Exchequer.

One of the new obligations of 1963–64 was that future contracts should contain provisions to ensure the continuing existence within the independent broadcasting system of at least one distinctive body equipped and financed to provide news for broadcasting in the programmes put out by the programme contractors. Each contractor had the opportunity of obtaining a financial interest in this body, the chief executive of which was to be appointed with the ITA's approval. This requirement gave legal force to the principle on which Independent Television News, much praised in the parliamentary debates, had been established in 1955 after difficult discussions between the Authority and the contracting companies. At the same time regional programmes were extended to include a suitable proportion of matter in languages other than English in those areas where such languages were in common use.

Other requirements involved new patterns of relationship. Thus, clauses relating to contracts in the 1964 Act empowered the Authority to demand programme schedules and scripts in advance, to collect information about costs, and to direct any contractor to supply an item originated by him to another contractor for inclusion in his programming. (Every contractor had to put himself in a position by contract to comply with this directive.)

There were also provisions in the Act that the Authority had to ensure that a suitable proportion of 'matter to appeal especially to the audience served by the station or stations in the contract area' would be broadcast. Thereafter there was increasing pressure by the Authority on programme contracting companies to increase their 'local programme output', adding significantly to their costs without necessarily encouraging the Authority to produce more socially unified local programme areas. There were complaints from some of the larger programme contractors, who believed that the new requirements would reduce the competitive power of ITV in general vis-à-vis the BBC, for the latter had no comparable statutory restraints imposed upon it. This, of course, was the *real* competition, measured not only in comparative ratings of top viewing programmes but in 'prestige programmes' which the liveliest independent companies took pains to provide.

Within the new framework the mode of issuing contracts assumed greater importance than ever, although there seems to have been no immediate sense of this in Parliament. The Postmaster General claimed (25 February 1963) that 'the risk of non-renewal of a contract' was very slight unless the company had 'completely failed to make the grade,' and Lord Chesham stated a few months later (9 July 1963) that 'renewal of contracts should certainly follow if a contractor has faithfully carried out his duties and then there is no reason why it should not if he does.' Frederick Willey from the Labour benches stressed the importance of offering security to people working in television, and W.R. Williams argued (27 June 1963) that 'the chances of anyone getting off the ground in competition with existing companies' were 'about as great as anyone successfully launching a new national paper.'

Matters other than the franchising process – among them the form of a new commercial television channel – preoccupied MPs and peers discussing the new legislation, with Lord Swinton, among others, claiming that 'adequate competition in programme making' would not be served by introducing 'another third competing programme like the first and second', and Lord Shackleton from the Labour benches warning that 'a third television programme which would be a highbrow programme would not get off the ground at all.' Woodrow Wyatt, however, concentrated on ownership, urging that the contracting companies should diffuse it as a condition of securing further contracts.

Meanwhile, in the light of the Pilkington Report, the Authority itself, which had to deal with new contracts before the full details of the Government's new legislation were published, insisted on carefully controlled procedures. These were taken very seriously by its staff, shaken by the Pilkington inquiry, and were to influence what happened on later occasions. There was one important change in the composition of the Authority also. On 1 July 1963, the month when the first of the two new Television Acts received royal assent, Lord (Charles) Hill of Luton became the new Chairman of the Authority. The first paper prepared for him analysed 'the statutory changes in the Authority's responsibility for programmes and compared the new requirements with current practice.' And very soon after this Hill was assuring the part-time Members of the Authority that they would have powers of their own also; they wanted to play a more active role and to be less dependent on the staff. He has told his own story in *Behind the Screen* (1974).

It was within this context that the Authority rationalized the ad hoc arrangements made in the first round of the issue of company contracts between 1957 and 1962, while, in an attempt to anticipate criticisms, introducing new elements into its own set-up, including a research department, a general advisory council and a programme policy committee. In 1953 Sir Robert Fraser had sensibly condemned as 'terrifying' the imposition of any 'bureaucratic overhead that results from a preference for detailed regulation rather than broad control (let alone freedom).' That was not the language of 1963 and 1964. Television was now being subjected to more detailed regulatory instruments than any other commercial activity, except perhaps agriculture, and it was the Authority that fashioned them. As ITCA put it simply in 1974, 'during the years after the Pilkington Report, the Authority began to exercise firmer control on the balance of programming.'

The tightening-up of the Authority's procedures after 1964 – and its more searching examination of the financial pattern of the existing companies as well as of the new applicants – attracted little public debate. This was partly, doubtless, because the Authority issued all its new contracts to the fourteen existing programme companies and turned down eight new companies which applied for franchises. One new contender – for the North-East area – whose plans attracted Hill, was rejected on financial grounds. The claims of another 'star-studded' group, headed by the film producer Sidney Box and including Ted Willis and James Caine of World Wide Pictures, which applied in vain for the London weekday franchise, were taken very seriously and an attempt was made by the Authority to persuade the contract holder, Associated-Rediffusion, to take in new blood from the rival group. There would have been a 'franchise affair' in 1963 if AR had been turned down, for Sir John Spencer Wills, its chairman, told Hill – in a second interview – that, of all the contractors who had operated independent television, AR had the greatest claim to a renewal of its contract.

27

All in all the Authority hoped that the new contracts for 1964, which were advertised on 16 September 1963, would increase the Authority's income from rentals from £5·5 million to £8 million. The closing date was set for 18 November and the decisions were announced by Hill on 8 January 1964. The principles on which the Authority had made its decisions were not stated. Instead, Hill's announcement looked to the future for any significant changes. Direction of companies, he said, should be spread among a number of persons and a variety of interests, including residents and interests within the area. 'In many cases the present company pattern satisfies these criteria: in others progress towards them is being made. I mention these objectives now so that present companies and future applicants may take them into account when the time comes in three years or so to formulate applications for the next phase.' Because of uncertainty relating to future ITV services, notably the future of a new television channel, the contracts were to run for three years – and not for the six years allowed in the 1963 Act.

'In no case,' said Hill, 'had the Authority been persuaded that appointment of one of the new applicants would improve the service.' In fact, four of the existing companies had been called for a second interview to deal with questions mainly relating to their finance. Other matters were raised also then or at the first interview. Granada put up a 'robust defence' to the charge that it was not supplying enough programme information; Southern Television, which had received its first contract in May 1956, was required to appoint to its board two new members resident in its area; ATV, which applied also for the London weekday franchise, was required to appoint one. AR forestalled criticism of its share structure by a reorganization which separated its television from its non-television interests and formed Rediffusion Television Ltd as the television company, in which £2 million non-voting shares would be offered to the public. All the companies were reminded that their programme policies would in future be under closer scrutiny.

Between 1964 and 1967, when the networking system was under such close scrutiny, one new area was added to the Authority's list. Yorkshire was to be split off from Lancashire. The announcement was made one day after the Government had stated that there would be no allocation within the next three years of frequencies for a new ITV2. Sidney Bernstein is reported to have said 'if the territory of Granadaland is interfered with in any way we shall go to the United Nations.' Instead, Yorkshire went its own way in 1968, taking the Emley Moor transmitter with it. The other companies went their own way also; they were each granted a two years' extension of contracts in 1966.

It was within the framework of the new legislation of 1963 and 1964 – and the policies of an increasingly interventionist Authority seeking to interpret this legislation – that the second major re-examination of contracts, including the new Yorkshire contract, took place in 1967. This was for the award of franchises from July 1968, thirteen years after the first four programme contracting companies had begun their operations. Advertisements for the fifteen programme contracts were published on 28 February 1967, with a closing date fixed for 15 April of that year. The timetable was compressed because of uncertainty about technical developments which would affect rentals to be charged.

The advertisements made it clear that all applicants would receive full and equal consideration. There would be no favoured treatment for the original consortia as the ITA's option agreement of 1957–58, criticized by the Pilkington Committee, would have allowed. This was a crucial decision. Existing groups and new groups were free to apply for any contract, and application could be made for more than one contract provided that an order of preference was stated. No company could hold more than one contract. At the same time details were given not only of general requirements for contractors but of particular requirements applicable to each specific area.

Applications could be presented in whatever form the applicant felt most suitable, but there were a number of set questions to which answers had to be supplied. These covered the composition of the group, its financial structure, interests represented in it outside television, programme policy intentions, details of studio facilities and arrangements, and its operational timetable. Formidable though all the requested mass of detail was, there were between two and three hundred requests for particulars.

In the event thirty-six applications were received from sixteen new groups and the fourteen existing programme companies in what Bernard Sendall, official historian of ITV, has called 'the franchise trail'. The new applications were very unevenly distributed over the fifteen areas, however. In six areas the incumbent company faced no competition, but in one of the other nine, the new Yorkshire area, there were no less than ten contenders. The interview which all applicants had to undergo, even if there was no competition, seems to have played an important part in the last round, not least in Yorkshire, when the field was reduced to two. 'If the balance was finally tipped in favour of Telefusion Yorkshire Ltd,' Sendall has written, 'this must have owed much to the able way in which their written statement of programme philosophy and intentions was further developed and explained at their interview, notably by Sir Geoffrey Cox.' There were conditions attached, however, which made the arrangement 'not far short of a shotgun marriage with the Yorkshire elements in the rival group.'

In other parts of the country, including London, 'dramatic' changes were made too. Rediffusion-Television (the former AR), reconstituted since 1964 on lines 'commendable' to the Authority, lost without warning a contract which it had expected to have renewed automatically; its 'reputation had stood high' among the staff at 70 Brompton Road. It was now asked to merge with ABC, but with no majority control and, although it did this after frustrating negotiations, further disturbed by strikes, formed a new company, Thames TV, Wills was disillusioned and alienated. Lew Grade's ATV reluctantly relinquished its London weekend contract to a new London Weekend consortium, formed by television 'professionals', a new interest, with David Frost as one of its co-creators, but acquired instead the seven-day franchise in the Midlands. In Wales Lord Derby's TWW lost its contract to a new consortium headed by Lord Harlech, according to the *Times* (12 June 1967) 'the main surprise of the ITA's new deal'.

There was much coming and going behind the scenes as the Authority shuffled and reshuffled groups to try to secure the complete pattern it wished. But there was little explanation. An outraged Lord Derby asked in vain for a further hearing. 'I

30

have never been given a reason for the treatment accorded to Rediffusion-Television Ltd,' Wills wrote to Bernard Sendall as late as July 1981. A number of points about the Welsh situation were made public, but no explanations were given for the forced merger of two very different companies, ABC and Rediffusion-Television. In his memoirs Hill said rather more than he said at the time. The key to much of the shuffling and reshuffling, he made clear, was his – and doubtless some of his Members' – desire to bring in the talent assembled in the new London Weekend consortium. 'It had to have its chance whatever the repercussions,' wrote Hill.

At least one historian of television has been highly critical in retrospect. 'Lord Hill presided over a non-event that added nothing significant to programmes, quality or regional flavour,' wrote Peter Black in *The Mirror in the Corner* (1972), 'but it probably cost £20 million in new equipment, the writing off of existing equipment, and redundancy payments.' From the programme angle, Peter Morley commented that 'the cost to morale was immeasurable. The job [of the programme maker] was a team effort; the problem that of working in an insecure industry. It led to breaking up of loyalties, the severing of partnerships: it was no good to anyone.' Sir Denis Forman, chairman and joint managing director of Granada Television, complained also – in 1978 – of the 'distraction of effort from programme making' which was an inevitable feature of the process. 'There are at least half a dozen young men who were leading lights in television whose career was cut short either by failing to get a contract or by getting one and thereby achieving a position which was unsuited to their talents and led to an untimely exit from the scene.'

It was in relation to the set of 1968 contracts – they were now being talked of as 'awards' – that public as well as professional debate on 'the franchise affair' was sharper than it ever had been before. Indeed, in parliamentary debate many MPs of all parties who had been silent in 1963 and 1964 now became voluble. There was a sense of shock. There were many contrasting points of view, however, and when the Liberal Party selected the Television Act of 1964 and its consequences as the subject of an adjournment motion on 28 June 1967, Paul Bryan, spokesman for the Conservative Party, suggested that the debate should have been put off 'until some more dust had settled and passions had cooled.'

In opening the debate Dr M.P. Winstanley began by describing the power of the ITA 'to award or take away fortunes, to bestow or to remove influence, to say who shall or who shall not operate in this sphere.' He added, however, that the Authority was 'doing no more than discharging the duty laid on it by this House.' Surely the proceedings of the Authority should be open, not private, the bids should be described, the Authority's criteria, which now had to be deduced from its judgements, should be clearly set out, and a record should be published once final decisions had been made. The public could decide whether or not it approved of the criteria, and applicants could appeal against the Authority's judgements. The public could also assess whether contracting companies were conforming to the Authority's criteria between the franchise awards. This should not be left to a kind of 'secret censorship'.

Paul Bryan, recalling 'the explosion of seventeen days ago', also referred to the 'huge powers of patronage of the Authority' and to the disquieting impact of 'fortune making or breaking decisions being made in secret.' Yet while instinct was against a 'process of judgement behind closed doors' – and there was a strong case both for making criteria explicit and for an appeal system – a system of public hearings, he observed, would take a long time and not necessarily lead to the best results. 'Lew Grade fighting David Frost in open court for a London concession would in news value be quite irresistible, but it would not be the appropriate atmosphere in which to make balanced judgements.' In fact, while nobody was 'entirely happy about the settlement' or thought that the allocation should be done 'precisely in the same way next time', there was 'general agreement', he maintained, 'that this wide-scale churn-up and general post . . . will reinvigorate the programmes.' If no awards had gone to new companies the criticism would have been that the ITA was a closed ring and that 'if a company with the potential of the London consortium could not get an innings, no one would ever try again.'

Another speaker, Christopher Rowland, went further and, like the *New Statesman*, which referred to the 'improbably radical actions of Lord Hill', congratulated the Authority on 'the broad balance of decisions' which it had announced. The Authority had 'asserted its rights'. It had shown that it was 'interested primarily in programmes and only secondarily in the question of profits.' It was wise too, Rowland added, although he gave no reasons, that the decisions had been reached in 'absolute secrecy and confidence'.

This was a time, of course, when the House of Commons was increasingly concerned about its own relationship with the media – Tony Benn, former Postmaster General, had made much of this issue – and Dr Winstanley believed that a new system could do 'something to neutralize the effect of our lack of direct authority.' Obviously Rowland, like another Labour Party speaker, Hugh Jenkins, was more preoccupied with profit making by the companies, the older issue discussed in Clive Jenkins's *Power Behind the Screen* (1961), than about the dangers of arbitrary authority, the newer issue. Hugh Jenkins, indeed, did not believe that ITV companies should exchange their equity on the Stock Exchange: they should be trusts. The continuity of employment of their staffs should be guaranteed.

The then Postmaster General, Edward Short, observed that this was the first time since Independent Television was created that there had been any criticism when 'one of its sitting tenants' was not reappointed. If detailed reasons had to be given for the ITA's decisions 'the Act would have to be amended to set out the criteria.' The Authority was 'a balanced body of people with a wide range of opinion and experience' and was quite capable of analysing 'expert opinion' and reaching 'objective' decisions. 'My conception of a public corporation is that we should either back it up or sack it, but not muck about with it.' When he was pressed at Question Time on 15 July 1967 to introduce legislation to require the ITA to publish its reasons for refusing to renew or for renewing a licence, he reiterated his view that the ITA should be left 'as free as it would wish from obligations which inhibit it in choosing the companies it considers will produce the best service of television.' And he took the same line when pressed to ask the Authority to publish the applications of successful companies. 'We must be fair to the ITA . . . without saying whether or not one supports the present system. The fact remains that Parliament created the system and the ITA must work it.' 'The possibility of a change when contracts are reallocated is inherent in the system.' Nevertheless, as he added in the adjournment debate, he could not see 'the present kind of organization lasting for very much more than the decade ahead.' In nine years 'an opportunity would arise for a fundamental review of the whole system.'

In fact, while the contracts awarded in 1967 ran to 1974, two years before the ITA's life under the 1963 Act (and the BBC Charter) would end, the system was reviewed within three years, when a subcommittee of the Select Committee on Nationalised Industries took a close look at many of its features in a series of meetings beginning in November 1971. There was one change without public inquiry. A financial crisis in the affairs of one contractor, LWT, in 1970–71 brought in a totally new source of funding and a new management under John Freeman, ex-MP, ex-ambassador and distinguished broadcaster. There might well have been a more traditional kind of review also, following in the footsteps of Pilkington and chaired by Lord Annan, had the Labour Party won the general election of 1970. (His appointment was announced before the election, then dropped by the Heath Government.) Meanwhile there were structural changes in government titles and responsibilities. In 1972 the new post of Minister of Posts and Telecommunications replaced that of the Postmaster General, and two years later, in the year that the Annan Committee was eventually appointed, under a new Labour Government responsibilities for broadcasting policy and legislation passed with little notice to the Home Office where they have since remained.

The ITA's evidence to the Select Committee of 1971 on its existing procedures anticipated events and included the comment that a 'comprehensive review' of the kind made in 1967 would not necessarily be appropriate at the end of every contract period and 'indeed would lead to instability in the system if it were.' As to the contracts originally due to expire in 1974, the Authority told the Committee that it 'does not intend to reallocate contracts until the pattern of broadcasting has been settled'; and, on the number of contracts to be offered, it 'would keep an open mind until a year or two before 1976.' There should be no change in the private nature of the procedures, it insisted, although between then and 1976 it would further consider whether or not publicity should be given to the contract applications made to it and, if there were greater publicity, what safeguards would be required to secure the confidentiality of information of a financial or personal nature.

The Select Committee, after studying such opinions and other evidence about the 1968 awards in particular, recommended in a report of August 1972 (paragraph 39) that 'the Minister [of Posts and Telecommunications, the new office then responsible] should include the proposal of some form of rolling contract in preference to the existing fixed system in his consideration of the future of independent television in the years after 1976.' There had been 'unanimity in the industry' on this point: fixed contracts, it was claimed, interfered with long-term planning, lowered morale towards the end of the contract, and made it difficult to raise programme budgets. Yet the Select Committee felt (paragraph 40) that 'some system' needed to be found – it did not suggest how or what – 'whereby periodically and quite explicitly' it would become 'possible for new blood to compete even with companies whose performance has not been faulted,' a suggestion never made so explicitly before. 'While endorsing the need for stability of employment within the industry,' it observed that 'some instability is characteristic of all enterprise, and . . . in the case of independent television, a system favouring the sitting tenant (subject to adequate performance) would give the companies a virtual monopoly in selling advertising time in so far as there is virtually no competition between them' (paragraphs 40 and 152).

This state of affairs, the Committee observed, arose from the way the system of networking had developed. When 'the need for networking quickly became apparent, the Authority did not take part in the selection of programmes for networking' made by the then Big Four (now, with Yorkshire, the Big Five). Such cooperative allocation of time meant that in the event the only real competition was between Independent Television and the BBC. (The Annual Report of the ITA for 1970–71 had disclosed that ten regional companies had contributed only 8 per cent of network programmes.) 'Effectively the contractors held a monopoly of a highly valuable advertising outlet, doubly so since the Act had made no provision for limitation of profits.'

Leaving it to the Minister to determine just what new system should operate from 1976, the Committee put its trust in the interim on greater openness on the part of the Authority. Pending a new system, and, indeed, within any new system which might be devised, the Authority, with its great powers not only over an industry but over 'an important aspect of the public's life' (paragraph 93), should be required, the Select Committee stated (paragraph 98), to provide 'sufficiently precise information to permit the public to examine the criteria on which decisions are based on such matters as the particular regional structure chosen and the rentals charged.' Prior to major policy decisions the Authority should publish proposals and invite public debate. It had informed the Select Committee that it would be 'undesirable to parade' daily differences with the contracting companies, but 'greater accountability' was 'obviously' necessary at times of franchise awards.

'Secrecy rather than openness has characterized the Authority's activities,' one witness had told the Committee. 'The allocation of contracts in 1968 was a notorious example and a recognized public scandal at the time.' And there was a further reason for more openness at the time when the franchises were granted, Phillip Whitehead MP added. It had become apparent that some contracts had been awarded in 1967 on the basis of a number of inflated programme promises which were not thereafter fulfilled.

The Select Committee went on to suggest – in summary – that the meetings of the Authority and of its committees and its advisory bodies should in future be open to the public and that their minutes should be published; that two-yearly reports on the performance of the companies should be prepared, linked to a two-year warning period in relation to the extension of contracts; and that contract submissions should be published and interviews with applicants held in public.

When representatives of the Authority were asked whether they would favour the press being present when applications were heard (as in the case of public-house licensing) or at least for part of the hearings, they were unsympathetic. 'Applicants who know that the press and public are there,' said Lord Aylestone, Hill's successor as Chairman of the Authority and a former Labour Party Chief Whip, 'are likely to have one eye and ear on the press rather than on a secret meeting in which they can frankly report to questions. If, for example, there are five applicants for one franchise we would have to have something rather like a ballot to decide which one hears first.'

A different line of questioning had directed attention to the subject of the boundaries of the contract 'areas'. These, as in the past, were largely determined by the Authority's engineers, working under enforced limitations. Yet Lord Aylestone himself had emphasized when he opened the new Yorkshire station, which would not have been able to broadcast had not the engineers built west and east transmitters in the North, how useful it was to have areas with a strong sense of their own distinctive identity. What would have happened had there been a similar situation in the South? In any case, the Yorkshire boundaries themselves were unsatisfactory as social and cultural limits and the issue was to gain in importance in the future. Nonetheless, for the Select Committee (paragraph 150), whatever the weaknesses of the 1968 settlement, the Authority had achieved 'a greater link than ever before between a company and the region it served and made each company responsible for one region, with the exception of London which was divided into weekday and weekend concessions.'

The main criticisms of the Select Committee concerned procedures, not boundaries. The Authority neither warned the industry well in advance that 'there might be a substantial reorganization of the structure,' the report stated, 'nor gave any warning to the two contractors whose franchises were particularly affected that their performance was in any way deficient. Your Committee also felt that the grounds on which the particular regional structure was chosen and the particular applicants selected should have been made public.'

Between the appearance of the Select Committee Report and the announcement in April 1974 of the setting up of the Annan Committee on the Future of Broadcasting as a whole – the Committee which was to advise the Minister what to do after 1976 – the Sound Broadcasting Act of July 1972 renamed the ITA the IBA and the Independent Broadcasting Authority Act of May 1973 consolidated the 1964 and 1972 Acts, taking account of the new ministerial and administrative structure. A 1974 Act brought in a major change in the levy system, urged by the contractors and supported by the Authority, in the light of their deteriorating financial situation. Profits not receipts became the basis of the additional payments, with a free slice of £250,000 or 2 per cent in the accounting period and an across-the-board 66·7 per cent levy on profits above it. Most important of all, however, in the month that the names of the members of the Annan Committee were announced, a further Act extended the life of the IBA from July 1976 to July 1979.

This was a difficult time for the industry, for there was inevitable uncertainty about the future, enhanced by the knowledge that broadcasting policy did not figure highly in the Government's list of priorities. There was a sense also of pressure from inside the industry and of a conflict of opinions about broadcasting outside it. Board meetings were more uneasy than they had been before, labour relations more strained. The Annan Committee itself, in the words of its chairman, proved 'hard-pressed' to deliver its Report, one of a series of similarly commissioned but very diverse reports, going back to the 1920s, by March 1977, and even then it was a few months late.

For those reasons, therefore, the new round of programme contracting was to be delayed until 1980. It was characteristic of the time that a government White Paper following on the Annan Committee Report, which was expected early in 1978, did not appear until July, and during the intervening period there was room for every kind of gossip and alarm. It was necessary also – yet again – to introduce legislation further extending the IBA's functions, this time until 31 December 1981.

During these repeated postponements the Authority made for the first time a midterm review – 'a simultaneous full appraisal' – intended to be in preparation for the new contract period 1976–79 and launched before its decision 'in principle' in March 1975 to continue the contracts of the sitting companies. The 'substantial points' relating to each company were published in the IBA's Annual Report for 1974–75 and may have encouraged companies which took account of them to feel more secure in relation to the full-term report than events were to prove.

The Annan Committee, like all previous national committees, favoured the continuation of the tradition of 'public broadcasting'; and it recommended the creation of no less than four new authorities, including an Open Broadcasting Authority to be responsible for services on a fourth television channel, when 'the national economy permitted it.' The IBA was to be known as the Regional Television Authority, reponsible for a single service of regional television based on regional programme contractors. With the BBC, it was to be shorn of its responsibilities for local radio. All local radio was in future to be managed and developed by a new Local Broadcasting Authority.

The Committee rejected rolling contracts for the regional contractors, holding that they would give too much security to existing companies, and recommended that in future franchises should 'normally' be awarded for seven years. Like the Select Committee, it had turned its attention to the management and financial crisis in London Weekend Television in 1970–71, which in the opinion of the Select Committee had warranted the taking away of LWT's franchise, and had concluded, first, that the ITA should have used its sanctions in 1969 to force LWT into reconstruction without waiting for a 'chaotic situation' to develop; and, second, following the introduction of the new Rupert Murdoch holding, that no single newspaper group should have more than about 10 per cent of voting shares in any company. Total press interests in any company should not be above 25 per cent.

Loss of franchise at set intervals was obviously a crude and inflexible method of control. Nonetheless, the Committee concluded, the threat of loss of franchise was potent and criticisms of a company by the Authority should be made public. Indeed (Recommendation 9), public hearings in the area in which the franchise would be held should become part of the future selection procedure when contracts were being awarded, as should the publication of the non-confidential sections of the contract applications. Yet written applications should not be regarded as totally binding since, between the award of a contract and the beginning of service, a company might find 'a better way of fulfilling its intention' (paragraphs 13 and 24). The Committee noted the difficulty of judging between promise and performance; it did not suggest how to deal with it.

As to the determination of contract areas, the IBA was advised by the Annan Committee not to consider the original areas as immutable (paragraphs 13.36–38). It observed that Sir Robert Fraser had described the earlier rearrangement of areas as a necessary but 'brutal exercise' and had recognized that the distribution of areas was not simply a technical matter. The Committee also expressed its approval of the number of smaller companies, which added to the 'diversity of editorial control essential to regional television', and recommended that the number of network companies should not be above six or below four.

Examining the recent record of IBA intervention in matters relating to programme content, the Committee reached the conclusion that, while the statutory powers and obligations of the Authority should be maintained, the IBA itself should seek to intervene less frequently in the process of preparation of individual programmes. An important further recommendation, which was one of the many recommendations not implemented, was that a Public Inquiry Board for Broadcasting should be set up which would hold public hearings every seven years on how the Regional Television Authority (the proposed successor to the IBA) and other broadcasting authorities (including the BBC) were discharging their responsibilities.

Coincidentally, perhaps oddly, with the receipt and consideration of the Annan Report in 1977, the House of Commons Select Committee on Nationalised Industries had decided that its report of 1971–72 on the ITA should be brought up to date by an inquiry into the affairs of the IBA since 1972 and produced a report which was delivered to Parliament on 5 July 1978 – before the appearance of the Government's White Paper (Cmnd 7294) which followed the Annan Report.

The IBA had given evidence to the Select Committee on the serious effects on the contract-awarding process of the prolongation, pending new legislation, of its existence in 1974 and 1978; and, not surprisingly, the Committee found it 'intolerable' that the IBA had twice in five years been so close to its statutory termination that it could not proceed with its contract process. Questioned on the 'piecemeal' operation of three-year prolongations to 1976 and 1979, and on what action the Authority would take about contracts given a third prolongation to

1981 (still not announced at that time), the IBA replied that it had decided that in a period of continuing uncertainty existing contracts with the existing companies would be renewed. It would be unable to consider new applications – in fact, it had received at least one approach – until it could advertise all franchises at one time. The procedures it intended to follow would require two years to complete and, after awards had been made, newly appointed companies should have a run of twelve to fifteen months before the new contract period.

In the interplay of law and policy, therefore, it was continuing uncertainties about policy which delayed the franchise affair until 1980–81. It took time for the new Conservative Government to decide not to accept the proposed arrangements for future broadcasting structures recommended by the Annan Committee and to go ahead with its own plans for a fourth channel without producing a White Paper. All the talk this time was behind the scenes. Meanwhile existing IBA contracts were extended without advertisement – with some undisclosed discussion, apparently part of it dealing with matters of detail, between the Authority and the companies – so that most of the five network and ten regional companies had held their franchises since 1955 and the most recently formed of them since 1968.

One of the most experienced chairmen and managing directors of a network company, Sir Denis Forman of Granada Television, caught the sense of frustration in a lecture delivered in March 1978 before there was any news either about future legislation or about the IBA's own timetable. 'Once upon a time,' he stated,

it seems long ago, we knew where we were. We had contracts from the beginning until 1968. We had to tender for the contracts, it is true, but that was part of the game and written into the rule book. In the ensuing reshuffle two players were sent off the field, as some thought, unfairly. But the referee's decision was final, and we settled down to our new contracts until the next convulsion, dreaded but inevitable, came around. But now see what happens. . . . ITV has no writ issued, no date for its next franchise, and no certainty about its future constitution. . . . There is nothing more harmful to our trade than prolonged uncertainty.

And Sir Denis went on to describe the compounding of uncertainty because of the failure in 'the higher stratosphere of government' not to make new rules – there were different ideas of what such rules should be – but to set a timetable.

Already, however, Sir Denis went on – and his lecture was given long before the IBA announced the details of its new contract-making process – 'the canvassing and the consortia have begun and the prospect of several years of this activity is enough to make the staunchest heart quail. Last time, the process was mercifully quick, some eighteen months from start to finish.' But there could be no such degree of mercy this time. New consortia were forming and re-forming to bid for contracts and in the process inevitably 'distracting effort' from programme making. There was already a Franchise Affair.

The first two steps in the timetable were a government announcement in May 1979 that a fourth channel would be introduced and that it would be under the Authority's control and an IBA statement in September 1979 describing engineering plans for the new channel and 'provisional proposals' relating to it. The details were presented, it was stated, so that the advertisements for new contracts would give applicants some understanding of the conditions relating to the new channel which would be included in their contracts.

All the other crucial difficulties inherent in the contract-awarding process had been anticipated in Part IV of the report of the Select Committee of 1977–78 (paragraph 99):

The Sub-Committee questioned the Authority on the practical possibilities of change within the structure it had adopted for independent television, which required a limited number of companies in the large revenue-producing areas, with considerable financial and production resources, to provide the main volume of output and especially of major productions for peak viewing. In practical terms, the Authority would have difficulty in judging a new company to be better or more acceptable than the 'sitting tenant', and this situation could lead to more or less permanent tenure by the major established companies. This dilemma, between the need for stability in the industry and the avoidance of monopoly by allowing new blood to compete for contracts, was discussed in the Committee's previous Report. The problem remains and is recognized by the Authority. The opportunity for change must exist.

3

1980: The Authority Sets the Rules

I T WAS NOT until January 1980 that the IBA announced the details of what were called in a news release the 'regional franchises' due to run from January 1982 and at the same time invited applications for the contracts. It was also announced (and this had been a matter of debate within the Authority itself) that it would be prepared to consider applications from 'people interested in providing a nationwide breakfast-time service'. Detailed particulars for each area contract were available to applicant companies. The closing date for all applications was Friday, 9 May 1980 (at 12 noon).

'IBA seeks franchises in the dark' ran the headline in *Broadcast* on 14 January 1980. Originally the IBA had intended to seek applications in December 1979 on the assumption that the Government's new Broadcasting Bill would have been published. Now the announcement was made without any clear knowledge of when that Bill would be introduced and when and how it would be debated. It was as long ago as May 1979 that the Home Secretary, William Whitelaw, had authorized the launching of a fourth channel, stating that it would be under the Authority's control, but when, following a further statement of 12 September, the IBA announced proposals, including engineering proposals, it had to describe them as 'provisional'. And although William Whitelaw had told the House in November that a Bill would be put before Parliament within two months, there were rumours that in the meantime an investigation of the likely costs of a new channel had been started at the instigation of the Prime Minister herself.

In fact, a new Broadcasting Act – without benefit of an

43

anticipatory White Paper – did not become law until November 1980, one month before the IBA's decisions about future contracts, applications for which had been submitted in May. By then, therefore, the contract-awarding process was almost over.

The main clue to the Government's attitudes at the beginning of 1980 was a statement by the Home Secretary on the report of the 1977–78 Select Committee on Nationalised Industries, many of the proposals of which were by then out of date. The statement related mainly to local radio franchises. Three points stood out. First, there was to be no ministerial department to oversee all aspects of broadcasting, as the Committee had recommended. Second, the IBA alone was responsible, the Government stated, for the day-to-day conduct of its business, and the award of contracts was a necessary part of that business which it should be allowed to handle flexibly. The Government, notwithstanding, was 'considering . . . the need for additional provisions regarding the procedures governing contracts between the independent local radio contractors and the Authority.' Third, it was stated, 'the qualifications and experience of persons considered for membership of the Authority receive the most careful consideration with the object of ensuring that a person appointed is of a calibre that entitles him or her to make a positive and distinctive contribution to the counsels of the Authority.'

The Authority, therefore, was largely left to its own counsels in the autumn of 1979 and January 1980, and it had to sort out its own timetable, conscious, as perhaps the Government was not, that however quickly it acted its decisions could not take real effect until January 1982. It had to amend its proposals slightly in March and April 1980 in the light of government statements summarizing the context of the Broadcasting Bill which would become law later in the year. In particular, it was now laid down in an amendment that the contracts for the new franchises would last for eight years. (In 1964 they had been issued for not more than six.)

In its yearbook, *Television and Radio 1979*, written in the period of greatest uncertainty about future government policy, the Authority had emphasized that its own function was 'not merely regulatory': 'it is closely involved in all aspects of planning and the formulation of policy, and is ultimately responsible to Parliament and public for the content and quality of everything transmitted.' In an accompanying insert on the same page it was pointed out that 'the IBA selects and appoints the programme companies.' 'The Authority,' it stated, 'has preferred a diversified and multiple control of programme companies to a concentrated or single ownership, and has further preferred that regional and local companies should contain strong local participation.' In line with its evidence to the Annan Committee, which had talked of 'a good blend of central strength and local responsibility', it identified as a policy objective of the Authority that of 'seeking to shape the institutions of Independent Broadcasting in such a way as to increase the diversity and number of the nation's means of communication'. 'Generally in its selection of companies,' the statement went on, 'the Authority has sought to provide a broad balance of interests within the system as a whole and to ensure that the control and ownership of each company forms an identity and character likely to provide a balanced and high-quality service and genuinely reflect the area served.'

The 'creative content of television programmes', the Authority pointed out, was the concern of the contracting companies, but each company 'plans and decides' its programmes 'in consultation with the IBA, which may require alterations before they are approved for transmission.' The Authority also required 'specific periods of time to be allotted to special classes of programmes such as education, religion, news, documentaries, and programmes serving local tastes and interests.' Each contract (the word 'franchise' was not used) required the company 'to accept responsibility for the observance of the relevant provisions of the IBA Act and the specified additional requirements of the Authority. Formal consultative machinery ensures the close liaison which is necessary at all stages of programme planning and presentation.'

The emphasis on consultative machinery and new proposals relating to it, which were eventually and belatedly to figure in the government legislation of November 1980, had been communicated to the Select Committee in 1977. So too had what J.F.X. Harriott, with the IBA title at this time of Chief Assistant (Television and Contracts), called in August 1979 'a bias

45

towards publication and away from confidentiality'. Indeed, almost all the rules of the game for 1980–81 were communicated at that time (Select Committee Report, paragraphs 96–8) when there was still considerable uncertainty about structures. Only the exact timetable was to be substantially different:

The new procedures would start with surveys carried out by the Authority of public attitudes to the ITV service in each contract area, and invitations to the public for written submissions. Public meetings organized by regional officers in many parts of each area [and an important part of the duties of regional officers, it was stated in the IBA evidence, was liaison with the public in their areas] would lead to special meetings in main centres of population. Contracts would be advertised in autumn 1979, and applications would be required by March 1980. Substantial parts of the applications, including programme policy and the amount and sources of finance, would be published and the IBA surveys would also be published by this time. Written comments would be invited from the public.

After a period, final meetings (described in the IBA's evidence as 'main meetings' of a 'carefully structured' kind) 'would be held in the main centre of each contract area, chaired by a member of the Authority and attended by two others.'

The Authority would interview all applicants in private session and would announce its decisions within two months. The contract awards would be followed by a fifteen-month run-up period, during which existing contracts would be extended on an interim basis and any new companies would prepare to come into operation. These processes, the Select Committee concluded, 'go some way towards the greater public accountability recommended in the Committee's previous report.' The subcommittee had suggested that the Authority might consider publishing, after the event, the reasoning on which the contract awards were based. The Authority agreed to consider this, but felt that it would be difficult 'to particularize and make public the points which led to its decision. The actual selection interviews would be in private.'

Even given this new stress on publicity, expressed also in a statement on 'longer term' intentions to 'take the public's mind' later during the 1980s, there were bound to be continuing difficulties about the penultimate point in the IBA's statement of approach – 'The Authority . . . had thought that it would be difficult to particularize and make public the points which led to its decision.' In 1977 the IBA's Director General Sir Brian Young had referred in evidence to the Select Committee to the 'aching dilemma' involved in the selection of contractors and had made it clear that the Authority recognized the 'hazards', but critics were likely to continue to raise the whole question of the capacity of the Authority not just to select but to set criteria, and to ensure that promise and performance would match. There were financial issues too which were entangled in the whole process: how far should the Authority itself become involved in the process of safeguarding adequate finance for the franchise holder to meet his obligations? Two other points which had already been raised were not covered in the new procedures – an early-warning system of shortcomings in performance to existing contractors, and an appeal against the Authority's decisions once they had been announced to them.

As early as February 1979 the Authority issued a statement 'Future Contracts and the Public', adding that the statement was 'subject to government legislation on the future of broadcasting after 1981.' It announced two steps to be taken in 1979, before any contract details were advertised, in order to prepare the public for the contract-awarding process. First, some two hundred public meetings were to be arranged in the contract areas, at places chosen to take account of local facilities and interests, to be chaired by the regional officers and supported by members of the IBA's staff. These meetings were designed to discuss questions relating to the size and shape of contract areas, the appeal of the existing service to people living in its coverage area, the contributions made by the existing area company to the network, the standards of service, and the general quality and balance of past and present programmes. The object was to help the IBA draw up detailed contract specifications. Second, a survey on public attitudes towards the ITV service was to be carried out in each area, broadly similar to an earlier survey of 1974, but with about 8000 respondents involved, twice as many as in 1974. There was also to be a general invitation to ITV's audience, to be backed by announcements on the service, to send in written comments.

47

The number of the IBA's staff had grown considerably since Young had succeeded Fraser as Director General in 1970, after twelve years as headmaster of Charterhouse and two as director of the Nuffield Foundation. The mix of the staff had changed too and it felt itself well prepared to undertake these two exercises, the first of which was well described in an article by Harriott on 'Taking the Public's Mind' in *Independent Broadcasting* (August 1979). By then over seventy preliminary public meetings in the contract areas had already been notched up. Yet how successful – or representative – they had been was already a matter of debate. A 'variety of discordant voices' had been heard in meetings of varying sizes, but they had seldom brought to light 'feelings and opinions wholly unsuspected by television administrators and producers.' In any case, it was difficult to separate 'feelings and opinions' from vested interests, often intensely local, of particular pressure groups.

There was a greater difficulty. 'Heavy viewers, non-joiners and the inarticulate' were almost entirely absent from the meetings. Indeed, the people who attended them had likes and dislikes very different from those registered in audience ratings figures. Harriott believed, therefore, that the points raised at the meetings were 'a better guide on local matters such as regional affiliation' than they were to 'popular tastes'. Such a distinction was valid. Yet there was no guarantee that these meetings were a particularly reliable guide even to attitudes towards regional affiliation. New contractors were likely to find it easier to exploit grievances on this score than existing contractors to explain them. The existing contracting companies which carried out their own local research were probably better informed. Moreover, at the meetings as much interest was expressed in programme matters as in the reshaping of contract areas, more, ironically, than at public meetings in 1980 *after* the Authority had determined what the areas would be.

On one point – and it was not a new one – the IBA itself was uneasy about the sociology of 'regional affiliation'. It could not resite transmitters 'at the wave of a wand' and was forced, in consequence, to explain that existing transmission areas were 'largely influenced by the nature of the topography' and could not always 'correspond with areas of social affinity'. Economics came into the picture as well as technology. 'Television is a costly business,' it stated, 'which means that if ITV were fragmented into too many regions, none would be large enough to pay its way, while if there were only a handful of very large regions the intimate regional character of the system would be lost.' Clearly there were limits to giving the public what it wanted even if the public could agree what it was.

'The same financial considerations,' Harriott went on, 'determine the need for a certain number of companies to be large enough and prosperous enough to provide a steady supply of the more expensive programmes required by the network.' Networking was thus conceived, as it had been in the IBA's evidence to the Annan Committee, as being 'at the centre of the system', although the Authority had neither devised it nor controlled it. Networked programmes, 'supplemented by the more ambitious programmes coming from the regional companies,' enabled ITV to provide 'a true alternative service to the BBC' – with 'a geographical balance' – and 'it would be destructive to neglect this through enthusiasm for the diversity and local attachment which the regional system provides.' How much the public knew of the networking system before or after the public meetings is problematical. There was no prospect, however, in 1979 that, even if there had been pressure for change, the system would have been changed in such a way that non-network company contractors, old or new, could join the inner group of network companies.

As it listened to grumbles at the public meetings or was subjected to local pressures, the IBA was forced to take up a somewhat defensive position. Yet it was also in a position to explain its own difficulties (and what it called its role) more fully than the limitations which it imposed on the services provided by the existing contractor companies, which were locally often held responsible for problems arising first out of the IBA's existing pattern of coverage and second out of networking. For their part, the existing contractor companies were not in a good position to criticize the Authority on which they ultimately depended. Some of the bigger networking companies may have been in a stronger position vis-à-vis the Authority than the smaller companies, but the restraints were general. Moreover, when IBA officers announced that 'securing

49

the delicate balance of the system of companies of varying size, in which the strong support the less strong, is an important consideration which will affect the final decisions on contract areas later this year,' there were bound to be different reactions – and apprehensions – on the part of existing contractors. 'Like the technical considerations,' the public was told, securing this balance was 'a significant restraint on a general policy of responding to public preferences.' The qualification meant that in trying to fit the pieces together local opinion would by no means represent the only relevant factors.

Awareness of the role of the IBA, wrote Harriott, may have 'gradually percolated' as a result of the public meetings 'beyond the comparatively small circle and limited numbers of those attending meetings to the wider public beyond.' What then of the survey *Attitudes to ITV*, commissioned from the British Market Research Bureau Ltd and published in November 1979 (not June 1979, as the survey states)? It had been designed to examine the attitudes of viewers all over the country towards ITV in general and 'towards the service they are provided with at a local level in particular.' All fourteen ITV regions were covered in a series of interviews with members of 7697 households, fifteen years old and over, a bigger sample than had been chosen for the midterm report in 1974–75; and particularly relevant to the Authority's decisions about new contracts, the second, third, fourth and fifth topics investigated were 'awareness of individual ITV companies and associations with them', 'interest in local news and viewing of local news programmes', 'awareness and evaluation of programmes made by the local ITV company' and 'overall evaluation of the local company'. Observers noted that in the maps produced by the Authority during the autumn of 1979 the fourteen regions had been divided into thirty-nine. There were three broad divisions – areas which did not receive ITV, areas of ITV overlap and ITV non-overlap areas.

The existing contract holders might well have been as interested as the IBA in local awareness of their services and the extent to which its survey disclosed what the public knew about technical limitations on transmission areas, and they were bound to take account of its findings; and although they carried out programme surveys of their own, they were also bound to be interested in the IBA survey's first section which dealt with 'viewers' evaluation of different types of programmes shown on BBC1 and ITV' and with the answers to questions about overlap areas. Nearly one in five viewers (17 per cent) lived in areas where they could receive transmissions from more than one ITV company. Southern was doubtless not alone in producing an internal note on the IBA's findings, choosing for comment not only sections dealing with its own image as compared with that of other existing companies but general points like the influence of demography and the social structure of the population on ITV/BBC programme preferences.

Southern noted, for example, that it came third out of the contractors – after Yorkshire and Anglia – in terms of its image rating and that it had an outstanding score for 'local news' and for 'programmes about local people and places'. The survey showed that among the contracting companies Granada achieved the highest level of 'spontaneous awareness', with Channel and Ulster (surprisingly perhaps) the least. The concept of 'spontaneous awareness' itself, however, is suspect: HTV and STV were the company names most likely to be used spontaneously in conversation, a different test. As far as news was concerned, Lancashire and Central Scotland were the areas besides the South and Southeast where the local news introducers were best known. Most viewers in all regions were satisfied with the proportion of local interest programmes, although one in three on average would like to have seen more. This pattern was common to all regions. There were the usual shocks thrown up in any response to a survey. Thus, only a minority (31 per cent of respondents) said that they knew of any programmes made by their local ITV company. It was people living in areas covered by Border, STV and Westward who were most likely correctly to ascribe programmes to their local company.

Three out of ten of the respondents thought that their local company provided a 'fair and rational coverage of controversial issues,' while ITV as a whole took a big lead over the BBC in reply to the general proposition that Independent Television 'showed a great deal of interest in the people of this area.' Figures for regional differences showed in general – and not surprisingly – that those districts which were farthest away

51

from the regional studios had least awareness of the local contributions made by the existing companies. In some of these, as in the Oxford area of ATV, the majority of viewers said that if there were only one channel (a highly hypothetical situation) they would choose BBC1, with its different regional news provision. Differences in viewing reactions in the east and west of the Southern area were somewhat doubtfully attributed to 'some inherent difference in the nature of the two audiences.' Nothing was said about the technical history of the area. In Northern Ireland, the east and west were compared but no consistent pattern of difference between the two could be observed.

It is not clear what weight was attached to this evidence by the members of the Authority, who were guided in their analysis by the Authority staff. According to Lord Thomson of Monifieth in November 1982 – and by then he was Chairman of the IBA – 'Sir Brian and his staff had briefed the IBA with information presented with insight and yet total impartiality.' This was a general comment made on the occasion of the retirement of Sir Brian Young, but it is clear that Young and his Deputy Director General, Anthony Pragnell, were the sort of men who appealed to the Chairman and fitted in with her outlook and strategy. They prepared the way for a crucial 'Grand Design' meeting at Great Fosters, a large road house near the Thames at Egham, in October 1979 (Ginger Rogers had once stayed there) at which the shape of particular contracts were discussed within 'the mosaic of Independent Television', an interesting term. The idea of 'dual contracts' for the East and West Midlands and South and Southeast England was propounded by the officers. It was then too that ways of questioning would-be programme contractors about the range of programmes, 'especially of a regional character', were settled; details were set out in a draft plan provided by the IBA's officers on 2 November. It was not until later, however, that a separate breakfast contract, 'something fresh', was agreed by the Members of the Authority, apparently against the advice of at least some of their officers. The two main IBA documents released in January 1980 were clearly the result of careful staff preparation: *Statement – The ITV Franchises from 1982* and *IBA Invites Applications for Future Television Franchises*. There were also 'Particulars' documents for each franchise available for the applicants, much of their contents common to all the contracts.

The Egham meeting, which lasted from Friday dinner to Sunday lunch, was attended by John Thompson, Director of Local Radio, who was able to give evidence about the way in which the franchising of local sound broadcasting was organized; and there was further discussion between Members and officers in Manchester in November 1979 and London in December. Before turning to these documents it is important to examine the way in which Members of the Authority saw their own role. This in turn depended, of course, on who the Members were – and that depended, as the Home Secretary had said, on the Minister's choice – as well as on their formal powers or on the advice given to them by their staff. In 1980 there were twelve Members of the Authority, more than there had been in February 1979, when the document *Future Contracts and the Public* was completed.

The Chairman of the IBA, Lady Plowden, a former governor and vice-chairman of the BBC, had served in that office since 1975 and her term was extended to enable her to preside over the allocation of contracts. She was a well-known and forthright public figure, whose name was associated in particular with the Plowden Report, *Children and their Primary Schools*, published in 1966. She had been a director of Trust House Forte from 1961 to 1972, and her recreations included long walks and deer stalking. She was sixty-nine years old in franchise year, which it was known would be the last year of her office. The Vice-Chairman, Lord Thomson, who was to succeed her, was then aged fifty-nine. A Scotsman from Dundee, he was a former Labour MP and Minister, and had served at Brussels as an EEC Commissioner from 1973 to 1977. He had been Chairman of the Advertising Standards Authority from 1977 to January 1980. A month later he became Vice-Chairman of the IBA, although he is said at his own insistence to have played little part in the franchise decisions of that year. Christopher Bland, who apparently did, had left the Authority before the end of the year.

Mary (now Baroness) Warnock, aged fifty-five, was the longest-serving Member of the Authority; she had been appointed in 1973. A well-known writer on philosophy, she too was associated with a report on education, the *Warnock Report on Special Education* in 1979. As a Fellow of an Oxford College, with six years' experience as a headmistress, she was one of three academics on the board. Professor James Ring, aged fifty-two, was Professor of Physics at Imperial College: he was keenly interested in communications technology and was in close touch with the IBA's engineering division. Professor Huw Morris-Jones, aged sixty-seven, Member with special responsibility for Wales, was now Professor of Social Theory and Institutions at Bangor. The Marchioness of Anglesey, aged fifty-five, daughter of the novelist Charles Morgan, also had Welsh interests, while the members with special responsibility for Scotland and Northern Ireland were the Revd William Morris DD, minister at Glasgow Cathedral since 1967 (he was a graduate of the University of Wales), and Mrs Jill McIvor, a law graduate, who was married to a former Minister in the Northern Ireland Government. They had both been appointed Members recently, the former in August 1979, when the size of the Authority was increased, the latter in January 1980.

Mrs Ann Coulson, a Midlander, a Labour councillor and an assistant director of Worcester College of Higher and Further Education, had been appointed to the Authority, like the Marchioness of Anglesey, in 1976. So also had A.J.R. Purssell, aged fifty-three, a former rowing blue and Olympic oar and since 1975 managing director of the Guinness group with which he had spent all his working life. He and George Russell, assistant managing director of Alcan, aged forty-five, were the only two businessmen, however, so that on financial, as distinct from programming, questions there was only limited expertise. Anthony Christopher, aged fifty-five, the statutory trade unionist, was general secretary of the Inland Revenue Staff Federation and a member of the TUC General Council. He had been made a Member of the Authority in September 1978.

Neither the Chairman nor the Members of the Authority have written of their own decision-making experiences in 1980. But the long *Statement – The ITV Franchises from 1982* obviously reflects their general approach before the decision-making began. Already 20,000 people had attended the public meetings, and some Members as well as staff had been present at

54

them. 'Satellites, fibre optics and other technological advances,' the statement noted at the outset, 'may not bring about major changes in the structure of British broadcasting before the end of the 1980s, but for Independent Broadcasting the time will be one of development and expansion.' At the same time there might well be 'a harsher economic climate than even that of the last decade' and the framework of Independent Television would have to be robust. 'Money would be tight' and there would have to be financially strong contractors. 'To break the system into too many small pieces would diminish the strength it needs to have.'

No changes were proposed by the IBA, therefore, in relation to the networking system, the viability of which obviously depended on the resources of the five major contractors. Nor were there direct references in the statement to the full financial implications of the further development of the system which clearly would have to be considered carefully by both network and regional companies. 'The actual amount and the component categories of programmes provided by the contractor,' the contract specifications went on to state, 'must depend on the outputs in practice of the different companies in the system and the extent to which their programmes are taken by other companies.' Such a specification was both purely descriptive and extremely general. In fact, the particular pattern of networking arrangements influenced not only what viewers could see on their screens but the shape of the balance sheets. Non-network companies who sought outside markets had to relate the content, cost and scale of their production schedules to the chances both of network placing and of foreign sales.

The IBA itself, however, had no control over the answers to such questions. The machinery for programme planning lay within ITCA through the Programme Controllers Group, which planned network schedules, and the Regional Controllers Meeting, which received them in draft. The Live Network Agreement, arrived at by negotiation between the network and regional contractors, set the number of hours to be taken of networked programmes and the payment for them, calculated in relation to the net annual advertising revenue of each regional purchasing company and a scale of per-programme charges. No payments passed directly between the network companies themselves. Programmes made by the 'minors' were bought and sold by companies after they had been canvassed for their more general appeal. There was no guarantee of network placings for them, even for a company such as Anglia with a successful record of network showings (and overseas sales).

The full financial and programming implications for the companies of a new fourth channel were not clear when the statement was drafted, and there was only one paragraph in it on the most innovatory development – breakfast-time television – a paragraph which was cautiously rather than boldly phrased:

During the consultations which took place in 1979, it became apparent that there were those who believed that a separate breakfast-time service, primarily of news, information and current affairs, would inject a new element into Independent Television, would meet a public need, and would be viable. The Authority has decided that it would be prepared to consider applications from those interested in providing such a service on a nationwide basis. The service would need to be self-financing and to pay the Authority a realistic rental. In considering applications, the Authority will pay particular attention to the content of the programme services proposed, to the soundness of the estimates of revenue and costs, and to the implications which particular proposals may have for the Authority's other broadcast services. The Authority gives no undertaking at this stage that a breakfast-time contract will be awarded or that, if awarded, it would necessarily run from the beginning of 1982.

The general sections on the number and size of contract areas were longer and the respective arguments for 'more and smaller companies' and 'fewer and bigger companies' were spelt out at some length. So too were the technical constraints on the IBA. The UHF transmitters, co-sited with those of the BBC, would have to be placed 'so as to achieve maximum coverage' and in the light of that objective, the subject of the Crawford Committee Report of 1974, and the decisions taken at an international telecommunications conference at Stockholm in 1961, 'transmission areas' could not 'be neatly tailored to match social boundaries.' The transmitter network was based upon 'an intricate and interlocking frequency plan. . . .

The Authority cannot replace the whole network or redraw the original map at will.' The Home Office had been little interested in 'fine tuning': its main concern, like that of the IBA, had been in extending coverage.

In fact, the IBA made the most minor adjustments in 1979, deciding firmly not to introduce any new areas at all and in essence to stick to the status quo. The farthest it went was to create two new 'dual contract' areas in the Midlands and the South, the former requiring no changes of transmitter use, along the lines of the Wales and the West contract. Nor was that contract area itself changed, despite pressure for Gloucester and Swindon to join it and from Plaid Cymru in Wales to split it. Conflicting local evidence was cited in relation to dismissing the first, and more general issues of policy in dismissing the second. Already since 1976 part of the Swindon area had been geared to the West; 'the only way in which the rest of Swindon could be included' in the same ITV region would be by reallocating the Oxford transmitter and thus transferring the whole of that transmitter's coverage area to the West of England. 'Since the transmitter's coverage extends northwards and eastwards into Buckinghamshire and Northamptonshire it would obviously be anomalous as part of a West of England region.'

As for the Welsh pressure for a separate Wales contract area, it was never likely to be conceded, although several paragraphs in the statement were devoted to exploring why and also why there could be no commitment to amalgamation of the West and Southwest of England contracts. 'Even if it were possible for Wales to be a separate contract area,' the statement read, 'the Authority sees no compelling reason in the Southwest for departing from its policy against amalgamation of existing contract areas.' It did not mention the possibility of a fourth channel for Wales, ultimately to be won by pressure, but, rather, quoted the Annan Committee's conclusion that 'though some of us would have liked to see a completely Welsh ITV company, we all recognize that for financial reasons the dream must fade. We have no doubt that the ITV franchise in Wales must be linked to a franchise in England for the present. It benefits broadcasting in Wales.'

In the North too the contract crossed boundaries, and there

the addition of the Southern Lakeland district to the old and very diverse Borders area increased the share of the English as distinct from the Scottish audience. There were 'divided loyalties' in this area, the statement conceded, and wishes had been expressed in the Isle of Man, part of the Borders area, to be served instead by the Northwest of England (formerly called the Lancashire) contractor. In Merseyside, where there had been pressure for a separate area company, no concessions were made either; indeed, on a visit to Liverpool in the autumn of 1979 Sir Brian Young had already made it clear that there could be no such separate contract 'in the foreseeable future'. Across the Pennines one 'minor adjustment' was calculated to appeal unequivocally, however minor it might be, to Yorkshiremen. Relays for Cornholme, Todmorden, Walsden and Walsden South, which served 17,000 people all on the Yorkshire side of the Lancashire–West Yorkshire boundary, would be transferred from the Lancashire ITV region to the Yorkshire region. York, however, to the disgust of the *Yorkshire Evening Post* was left, the newspaper said, for 'best reception' with Tyne Tees.

For Scotland the idea of a national contract area, canvassed in many circles, was explicitly rejected and the existing Borders region, crossing the boundary with England, was confirmed. Nor were changes made to the Central Scotland ITV region. London too was basically a no-change area, although a number of transmitter changes were made which affected it. The press attributed the no-change policy in this case largely to the desire of the IBA to maintain a firm financial footing for the new fourth channel, to which the two London companies were expected to make both substantial financial and programme contributions; and the three changes which were made had little to do with profitability, although they may have forced new thinking on the part of the existing contractors.

First, the Bluebell Hill main transmitter, opened in 1974, was transferred from the London area to the South-East part of a new Southern 'dual area'. There was to be no new Kent area, therefore, as had sometimes been suggested. The consequence was a possible increase of half a million Medway viewers (11 per cent) for the successful Southern contractor and a possible loss of 4 per cent for the London contractors. From the time the announcement was made there were arguments, however, about the reliability of those estimates, with the likelihood of a future battle for viewers between the successful bidders from the neighbouring franchises.

The rationale was set out as follows: 'Local authorities in the parts of Kent served by the [Bluebell Hill] station have indicated a desire for their area to be served by the contractor covering the rest of the county.' And while it was unlikely that all the contractor's potential viewers would cease watching London television, in any case, 'the loss of revenue would not be likely seriously to weaken the London companies; and the loss for them would be partly offset by saving the costs of providing local coverage to the Bluebell Hill area.'

Second, while the splitting of the London contract was retained, the London weekday/weekend division was altered in that an extra period from 5.15 p.m. to 7 p.m. on Fridays was added to the weekend contract (after children's programmes had finished). Before this change was suggested the weekday contractor had benefited far more than the weekend contractor from the Government's de-restriction of broadcasting hours, but the effect of the change was for the weekday contractor to lose one local news programme. The Authority did not seriously consider a seven-day franchise for one company: 'to offer the franchise area as a single seven-day contract would be to give the successful applicant twice the value of any other ITV contractor and, consequently, the power to dominate the network.' Likewise, but in this case for technical reasons, a split between North and South London was ruled out, 'since both northern and southern parts of the area are served by a main transmitter at Crystal Palace.' Finally, a split between a daytime and an evening contractor was rejected: 'to give the daytime franchise throughout the week to a separate company would put in jeopardy the ability of the network to sustain at least some of [its] service output.'

Third, however, the IBA asked London applicants to state how they might provide, possibly jointly, 'an improved regional news service in London seven days a week.' This left applicants free to consider the extent of possible cooperation – from news gathering, a limited operation, to news presentation.

Perhaps most attention was paid in the discussion of the

future mosaic not to London but to the 'large area' of the Midlands. The latter was served by five transmitters in places as distant from each other as Oxford, Ridge Hill, Sutton Coldfield, Waltham and the Wrekin There was minimum 'social affinity' in an area which included Stoke and Swindon, not to speak of Oxford and Nottingham. Yet it was the distinction between east and west rather than that between north and south which most struck the Authority, and it had even considered, however briefly, the claim of the east to include South Yorkshire as well as Derby, Leicester and Nottingham. The Authority considered it important 'to maintain the size and strength of the East of England and Yorkshire ITV regions' and rejected the idea of either a big or a small separate East Midlands contract area. It was left, therefore, with the idea of a new 'dual contract' area.

It laid down:

There will be separate programming requirements in respect of each part of the area. The company awarded the contract will be required to operate two studio centres, one in the East and one in the West. Its board structure will be expected to represent the dual character of the area; and it will be required to appoint executive staff based at the [new] East Midlands studio centre of sufficient strength and status to ensure a satisfactory service of regional programmes independent of the rest of the company's output, as well some programmes which would be broadcast as part of the company's output for the area as a whole and perhaps [the insertion of the word was strange] for the network.

Having decided on dual areas, largely on grounds of elimination, the Authority introduced a note of flourish into its case. 'There is always likely to be tension between meeting the wishes and needs of individual regions and preserving the strength of the ITV network. A dual region provides opportunities for the tension to be resolved.'

There was a touch of flourish too in the references to the changed allocation of the Bluebell Hill transmitter, which extended the South of England contract area to the east and gave it the status of a dual region covered in one contract. 'Although there are social and cultural differences between the western and eastern parts of the South ITV region, they do

60

have much in common.' In addition, two separate companies, though both viable, would be less able than one company covering the whole region to 'make a strong contribution both to the existing network [how strong was not specified] and to the fourth channel when it comes on the air.' It was left to the Brighton and Sussex *Evening Argus* to point out that the dual contract ignored the interests of the middle. 'Brighton, and much of Sussex, will be perched uncomfortably on the edge of the new divisions. The IBA has not been kind.'

The financing of the fourth channel did not figure prominently in the statement. Nor, indeed, did finance as a whole, although it was stressed that 'finance must be a major factor in any ITV planning' and it was known that detailed contract particulars would specify rental and fourth channel figures and the level of levy payments. A rather earlier IBA discussion document had publicly stated that in order to fund the fourth channel 'the profits received by the ITV companies will be diminished for the first year or two at least.' Companies would have to pay an annual subscription to the channel which would average out at £5 million each, with Thames and ATV at one end of the scale paying far more than the 'minnows' at the other.

Such suggestions did not prevent new consortia being formed even before the appearance of the IBA's invitation to submit applications for the 1982 contracts, each of which included detailed Particulars. Nor did complaints by existing contractors about soaring costs, falling revenue and the minefield of industrial relations. In Northern Ireland, for example, a rival to Ulster TV had published in the autumn of 1979 a fairly detailed account of its staffing and programme plans. There was talk in Lancashire of a 'Lancashire TV' and in Yorkshire of a 'White Rose' company. Not least, there was at least one consortium seeking the breakfast contract, and ITN, which noted that when Yorkshire had unsuccessfully tested the idea it had lacked a 'hard' national news and current affairs ingredient, was showing interest in it.

The IBA explained in Part V of its contract Particulars in January 1980 that information about business activities or the names of individuals connected with consortia which was held by the applicant to be private would be kept to a strictly necessary minimum, and this point was elaborated further in two amendments to the detailed contracts issued in April 1980, Amendment 2 listing the information on income and expenditure to be provided for publication, and Amendment 3 requiring from existing contracting companies for publication full financial details for the last three completed financial years. Applicants' three-year financial forecasts were required but were to be presented, if desired, only to the Authority. The Government had by this time made it clear that it approved of the Authority's intention to make public a substantial element in the contract allotting process; these amendments followed the Authority's 'further full discussion in the light of the letter from the Stock Exchange and an opinion from Queen's Counsel on the publication of financial information.'

Part I, the General Introduction to the contract particulars, began with a statement of the legal position, to be amended in minor ways in the light of the subsequent legislation of 1980. Part II, which dealt with General Conditions of ITV contracts including programme requirements, referred back to the terms of the 1973 Act and the general and specific powers of the Authority in this field. The conditions included a limitation to 14 per cent, not more than five and a half hours a week, of non-British (which included Commonwealth) material, and willingness on the part of the contractor to cooperate with the other contractors in such collective programme planning and off-air support of educational programming which the IBA might invite or which might be in the interests of ITV as a whole. Arrangements for the buying and selling of programmes, it was pointed out, were subject to IBA control and to regular review, and if companies could not reach agreement the dispute would have to be referred to the Authority. The contracts, it was stated, would incorporate provisions to meet not only all the requirements of legislation but to comply with the IBA's current *Ccode of Advertising Standards and Practice* and the current edition of *Advertising Rules and Practices (Television)*. The charges to be made for advertising time, the key element in the business operations of the contractors, were a matter for the programme contractors themselves. Yet they might be required to accept special conditions to avoid the imposition of 'inappropriate terms' through their responsibility for selling time both on ITV and on a fourth channel.

The General Conditions continued with two pages on the subject of the composition of programme companies. The IBA's policy, it was stated, was to prefer diversity of ownership and an appropriate degree of local ownership. (Amendment 1 of March 1980 brought up to date the disqualifications for ownership specified in the IBA Act of 1973.) Before completing negotiations for a contract the IBA was to approve the constitution, proposed directors and financial structure of a company and to receive full particulars of any associated companies and of registered holders of share and loan capital. It reserved the right to withdraw an offer if the composition of a company changed without its approval before the contract was signed. To carry out the duty of the Authority under the Act of 1973 to secure 'adequate competition between a number of independent programme contractors', the contracts disallowed financial interest in another television company and control over sound broadcasting in the same contract area, and restricted directors and holders of voting shares from having financial interests or voting shares in another company. Applicants were required to give information to the IBA concerning any connection between their group and another applicant group for a television or independent local radio contract or with a television or radio company associated with another applicant. They might be required to give up such a connection as a condition of a contract and had to be able to comply.

Conditions regulating changes in or diversification of activities of programme companies were also stated. Under the 1973 Act, it was pointed out, the prior written consent of the Authority was required for any activities not directly incidental to those of a programme company or interest in companies conducting them. Funding, management and personnel resources had to be fully adequate to meet the obligations of the programme contract (a matter of judgement rather than of law) and any proposed diversification had to be backed by adequate resources and controlled by the programme company itself. It was added that the IBA's approval was required also before a company could engage in certain 'prescribed' activities; the list included pay television, large-screen television, subscription television, talent agencies, video discs and cassettes, and satellite

63

distribution of programmes. Even the name of the company was to be subject to the IBA's approval.

The companies' responsibilities towards ITN, the body designated as providing the international and national news programmes, were also stated. The programme contractors were to share between them the capital of ITN and to provide basic annual financial support. An applicant for a programme contract had to be prepared to acquire its due interest on terms which would be a matter for discussion between the IBA, ITN and the contractor. It was added, however, that this condition would not be necessarily applicable to a programme company appointed for a breakfast-time contract.

The financial paragraphs which followed referred to the rental arrangements for each contract (set out in Part IV of the document) and to the additional payments required of the contractors. The IBA reserved the right to revise rentals at any time between 1984 and 1985 in the light of movements in the retail price index, and stated that it would be likely to make a second revision if the contracts were to run for longer than six years. (In the event the 1980 Act was to allow for eight-year contracts.) Under the Act of 1973 the Authority had a right to inspect all accounts and records of the company and of any associated and subsidiary companies. The actual amount to be paid as levy would be notified before the contracts were completed.

Notice was also given that the conditions of offer would require the programme companies to undertake programme and audience research and adequate engineering research activities in fields in which they had an interest. Provisions requiring adequately financed arrangements for staff training would be included in the contract.

The technical standards required by the Authority, as set out in the IBA's Technical Codes of Practice for studios and outside-broadcast equipment, would have to be met, with UHF as the primary transmission medium. Closure of VHF transmissions, or any change in their use, would be at the sole discretion of the Authority and would not affect the level of rental payments. Details of the national linking system for vision and sound provided by the IBA were appended in a schedule attached to the draft outline contract: the companies were to order and provide links between their studio premises and the Post Office network switching centres.

All successful applicants were to take a financial part in the production of *TV Times* and to provide full programme details for it. The existing shareholding arrangements in ITP (Independent Television Publications Ltd) were set out: any new group would be required to purchase shareholdings at a price to be agreed with the directors of ITP. These arrangements would be reviewed if a breakfast-time contract were awarded.

Finally there was a concluding paragraph in Part II on provisions to be included in programme contracts for collective promotion and support by the contractors of artistic and scientific activities.

Part III dealt with 'General Conditions of ITV Contracts relating to the Fourth Channel (excluding any breakfast-time contract)' and was included subject to pending legislation. It extended the monopoly rights of each contractor over the sale of advertising time in his area to advertising on the new channel, an invaluable exclusive privilege sharply contested by the advertisers and advertising agencies.

The financial needs of a fourth channel could not yet be forecast, it was stated, and the document could give only a general indication, therefore, of the subscription required of each company. The total requirement was seen as a sum between £60 million and £80 million. The presentation of fourth channel programmes, the insertion of advertisements and possible future regional opt-out arrangements were to be discussed with contractors when more was known. It was, to use the language of the IBA's contract offer, the 'duty' of the contractors to sell advertising for the new channel in the areas in which they operated, from which they would receive the revenue; they needed to have facilities to provide for advertisements locally. Arrangements for the supply of programmes for the fourth channel by ITV companies would be discussed in due course between them, the IBA and the fourth channel company. The intention was that the fourth channel would offer financial terms to programme suppliers which would provide a production incentive. The IBA reserved the right to include provisions in the new contracts as appropriate after the discussions had been completed.

Only Part IV of the Particulars documents was specific for each contract area. It stated that for these contracts transmissions would be in UHF 625 lines colour and a map was attached showing for each contract the service area boundary contours, the main transmitters, main and supplementary coverage areas and any 625 UHF coverage overlap within the area from another contractor's main station. The text was careful to state that the maps did not indicate the actual extent of viewing from stations in or outside the area and reminded applicants that they could be given no exclusive broadcasting rights in an area.

Details specific to each contract area were then given for transmission days and hours under the contract and the technical characteristics of the main stations and their independent relays; for dual regions the stations and relays making up each service area were listed. In the section on programme production each contractor was asked to indicate the amount of regional and network programming which might be expected from him; and the document itself gave a broad guide to the likely weekly average of new regional programmes to be produced by the successful applicant in addition to any produced for the fourth channel. It drew attention to the obligation on contractors laid down in the Act to provide a suitable proportion of material of special appeal to their region.

There were a number of particular points in relation to each of the contracts. Thus, in relation to the two London areas, the IBA's right was reserved to provide in the contracts for arrangements for certain programmes 'for the advantage of the ITV schedules as a whole' to be shown 'otherwise than at times covered by the contract of the producing company.' It could also notify its intention to require a seven-day regional news service in the London area, for which a common news service was to be discussed with applicants for the two contracts. The five national network companies were given broad guides as to their respective average weekly hours but the particulars stated that the actual amount and the component categories of programmes provided by the contractors must depend on the networking system operated between them. Their weekly total excluded what they might contribute to the fourth channel, but included each company's responsibility to provide 'a suitable proportion' of programmes of interest to its area, for which the Authority indicated a minimum figure. As far as the Wales and West were concerned, the contractor had the obligation of providing five hours a week of regional programmes for the West and five for Wales in English as soon as Welsh-language programmes were transferred to the new fourth channel (Wales): it had to be a regular provider of at least seven hours a week in Welsh for this new channel.

For South and South-East England and for West and East Midlands, contractors were obliged to provide regional programmes both of interest to the region as a whole and of particular interest to the areas covered by each studio centre, exclusively to them. And there had to be separate programming (initially one or two hours a week) for audiences within the service areas of the Belmont transmitter and of Emley Moor and its stations in the Yorkshire region, and in the service areas of the Bilsdale transmitter and its relays service area and the Chatton and Pontop Pike stations and their relays in the North-East region.

In other regions the picture varied. 'New programmes' (that is programmes originated by the company) had to be 'with few exceptions regional' in South-West England, North Scotland, Northern Ireland, Channel and the Borders, and to be 'predominantly regional' in South and South-East England, North-East England, East of England and Central Scotland. In North-West England about 50 per cent of output had to be addressed to the region as a whole; and in the dual regions there were additional requirements within regional programming for minimum hours for each of their two subareas. Contractors for these regions were required specifically to recognize the dual character of their regions in the composition of their boards, in their supervisory management and, as far as possible (who could say how far that was?), in their shareholding, as well as to provide adequately staffed separate studio centres.

The detailed content of the first four parts of the Particulars seemed to leave little to be added. Part V, however, requested information in the form of questionnaires. They covered composition of the company, financial structure, programme policy, information on studio and outside-broadcasting facilities and industrial relations and staffing, although the Authority had no responsibility for the conditions of employment of the staff of the contractors or for their relations with the unions, a point which its spokesmen often emphasized. All in all, there were more than thirty questions for the applicants, sometimes heavily phrased, as, for example, how would a new applicant view 'any requirement that any incoming company should give first consideration when recruiting staff to those employed by the outgoing contractor' and how would this 'fit into its general policy for its establishment as a new programme contractor and its operations generally'?

By Amendment 2, financial information on the previous three years was reduced to cover income from advertising and other sources, revenue expenditure on programme publication, programme purchases and other items, and total capital expenditure; and somewhat belatedly it was added that the Authority would consider carefully the match between applicants' plans for expenditure and the financial resources available for meeting them within their financial forecasts.

It was explained in the contract details that while both the composition and performance of existing contractors were known to the Authority, it wanted to receive up-to-date information from them along with details of future plans. The new applicants, of course, could present their case *de novo* as they wished. Yet the questionnaires were closely followed by applicants, old or new – they were told to keep to their order – and largely dictated the contents and the arrangements of the documents which they submitted. The opportunities of offering different – or additional – material were limited largely to the introductions to the applications written by the chairmen of the companies, old or new. There was little scope for manifestos. And while the Authority was looking out, as always, for 'new talent' and for new ideas about programming in the applications, it was inevitably concerned from the start with its general ideas about the operation of the system as a whole.

Sir Denis Forman in discussing the system in March 1978 had talked in terms of the rules of football and had spoken of players being sent off. The IBA, according to the *Financial Times* (17 November 1979), was thinking of the fight for contracts rather as 'a highly structured dance for which it writes the steps'. For Peter Fiddick, who was to include a programme,

'The Franchise Game', as the last of his seven programmes in his 1980 series 'The Television Programme' for Westward Television, Snakes and Ladders seemed to provide the most appropriate games model. And in this most of the applicants, successful or unsuccessful, would probably have agreed with him. The rest might have talked about Monopoly.

What the Government said about the rules it said later. In November 1980, one month before the IBA took its decisions about future contracts in the light not only of the applications but of supplementary questions, public meetings and interviews, a new Broadcasting Act at last extended the life of the IBA by fifteen years to 31 December 1996. It further provided, indeed, that the Home Secretary might extend this period by statutory order to any date up to 31 December 2001; and it now added explicitly to the duties of the IBA (in section 33) the need 'to ascertain public opinion in the area about the steps it proposed, to invite public comment and suggestions and to take account of them.'

There is little evidence that the Government was aware of the complexities of the 'franchising process' as the Authority and the applicants saw them when the new Broadcasting Act reached the statute book. Nor was there any evidence in it of a 'towards 2001' spirit. Taking little account of new technology, which was already raising fundamental questions about future broadcasting policy, it kept essentially to the old framework, empowering the IBA, which kept the same name, to make television contracts as in the past, though now for a maximum span of eight years. While no bar was placed on successive contracts being awarded to the same applicant, under the Act extensions of the kind which the IBA had granted to programme contractors during the 1960s and 1970s would have to be granted only in the light of public consultation which had now become a statutory requirement.

In the Parliamentary debate on the Bill Phillip Whitehead, among others, opposed the extension of the contract period from six to eight years, and a number of MPs wished to substitute the phrase 'hold public meetings and take whatever other steps as appear to them appropriate' for the phrase, which was to stay, 'take such steps as appear to them appropriate, including if they think fit the holding of public meetings.'

No changes were made, however, and the discussion of Channel 4, as it had now come to be called, which influenced so much else in the general discussion, was less comprehensive – and probing – than the previous dialogue between the companies and the Authority or the public discussion outside Parliament.

The wording of the Act left the IBA free to decide whether or not to establish a second television service. It laid down, however, that, if it so decided, it was to operate the second service through a subsidiary company which would itself not produce programmes but would commission and schedule them. The IBA would hold precisely the same responsibilities for programme standards and for planning, for control of advertising and for transmission of the service as for the existing ITV channels, with the added obligation to ensure that Channel 4 was complementary to existing channels and had a 'distinctive character' of its own. At the same time section 25 of the 1964 Act was repealed, removing the requirement on the IBA to ensure that two independent television services did not show the same subject matter at the same time.

ITV companies or their subsidiaries were encouraged to be programme suppliers to Channel 4, but a 'substantial proportion' of its output had to come from other and independent sources. Finance for the new Channel 4 would come from subscriptions to be fixed by the IBA from the ITV companies, which in return would have the right to sell advertising time on Channel 4 in their own regions (section 5). The ITV company for Wales would provide funds, on commercial terms, to a new Welsh Authority, responsible for a fourth channel programme service for Wales, and would sell advertising on the service.

There were other new contractual requirements. The 1980 Act, consolidated with previous legislation in a further Act of 1981, applied to television the section which in the Act of 1973 related only to radio. It now required the IBA to give to anyone who requested it a copy of a contract made with a programme contractor, information concerning the number of applications for that contract, and a copy of the section of the successful company's application which described its proposed programme plans – although this last not until after transmission of its programmes had begun. The Act also added to the duties of the Authority a requirement to state, and from time to time to review, the principles for ascertaining the income and expenditure of a programme contractor on which his profits for an accounting period were computed. The Authority was to publish its statement and every subsequent revision of it and provide copies to the Home Office.

By section 20(8) the IBA was required to make suitable arrangements to meet any requests from a newly set up Broadcasting Complaints Commission in connection with any complaint made to the Commission, and to achieve this was required to make provision in all programme contracts for programme contractors to be obliged to hand over scripts and related documents and to allow the viewing of programmes referred to in the complaint.

If this was a tightening-up, it is fair to add that the Act liberalized those sections of the 1973 Act which banned the expression of the IBA's own views and those of the programme companies in programmes devoted to broadcasting policy subjects. It also freed IBA members and directors and officers of the companies to express their views on television concerning subjects of current programme policy and of political or industrial controversy. It left open, therefore, the possibility of broadcasting informed criticism from within concerning the contract-awarding process itself.

By then, however, not only was the franchise affair well advanced, but Peter Fiddick, the *Guardian's* television critic, had dealt with the process and its implications on the screen. And he had to take account not of the intentions of the Government but of the operations of the Authority.

4

The Contenders

O N FRIDAY 9 MAY 1980, the appointed day, before noon, sixty copies each of forty-four franchise applications had been received at 70 Brompton Road, the first of them on the previous Tuesday, most of them on the last morning. Most of the applications were weighty: most of them ran to more than 120 pages of text. Not surprisingly, therefore, the IBA had required each application to be accompanied by a précis and the name and telephone number of a contact. Each was accompanied also by confidential supplements which the IBA had promised would not be made available to the public or to the press. These related both to finance and to staffing, where some of the arrangements suggested were tentative or conjectural or when disclosure would endanger existing jobs.

By the end of the day the staff at the IBA headquarters, fortified it was said by tea and a bottle of Benilyn, had compiled and issued to the press a list of the names, addresses and contact references of all the contenders; and less than a fortnight later, on 22 May, had checked all the various précis for their accuracy in order, in particular, to guard against being responsible for publishing anything which was defamatory. This was quick work. The magazine *Broadcast*, however, had been even quicker. Its issue of 19 May included a well-informed and comprehensive article, 'Enter the Gang of 44'. And only one of the forty-four was to withdraw; the rest were to go through the franchise ordeal to the end.

The total number of applications was such as had been expected by the informed press, and many of the contenders had been in the public view for several years. In many areas, however, there were surprises for the public. There were more applications than had seemed likely a few months earlier. Fears of future financial storms – or of more damaging industrial disputes – seemed to have abated in the spring of 1980, although there was little speculative bidding based on a willingness to take a gamble. Many of the new contenders had been planning their applications for several years and monitoring the work of the existing contractors, sometimes from within. They could be as well informed as the established contenders, while less burdened by experience of management. Some, indeed, were relying on the services of creative and managerial staff employed in existing companies and looking for new openings.

From 22 May onwards the relevant documents were accessible to the public at the IBA's regional offices, in a number of public libraries and at 70 Brompton Road. There was no great rush to see them, although provincial papers, many of them well informed also, picked up new details. There was certainly none of the drama to come in December 1980. Nor was there much excitement about the projected round of public meetings planned to start in June in Jersey and in Belfast and to finish on 30 October in Aberdeen.

Among the contenders the fifteen existing franchise holders could point to their record as well as to their plans and promises for the future. Leaving on one side the eight applications for the new breakfast franchise, there were twenty-one new applicants for the regional franchises, no less than seven of them for the tempting money-making franchise in the South and South-East. Nonetheless, only one of the Big Five network companies (ATV) had to face more than one challenge. The three smallest companies, Grampian, Border and Channel, in areas with restricted populations where there was little potential for development, had no competitors. It was an open question as to whether the number of challengers indicated greater or lesser risks to the sitting company. 'A company with one strong contender,' *Broadcast* suggested, 'could be under just as much (or as little) threat as Southern in the South and South-East.' The number of contenders could be 'self-defeating'.

The number of contenders was determined not only by prospects of profits – the main reason for the appearance of seven in the South and South-East, where there was little local criticism of the company 'in possession' – but by issues which had nothing to do with finance. One issue was the location of the existing programme centre: in the East, for example, the contender wished to change the centre from Norwich to Cambridge. Another was the financial and managerial structure of the existing company: in Yorkshire, for example, some members of the staff of the existing company put in an application not for a new concern with a new management but for a new kind of board structure. Finally, there were disgruntled or ambitious members of the staffs of existing programme contractors who were seeking a change in alliance with other interests. Loyalty to the company in possession, while often evident, was not ubiquitous. New contenders could draw on experienced professional support.

In every case the contenders had to demonstrate that they would offer a better range and quality of programmes than the company in possession. It helped, therefore, not only to present new ideas for programmes but to point to alleged shortcomings in current local programming or to 'metropolitan bias' in current programmes as well as in shareholding. Yet some applications, including those of a few of the existing companies like Anglia, touched on other even more basic issues, including the power of the network and the need to give greater opportunities to smaller companies. There may have been differences of opinion within the smaller boards on this point, and the argument was muted on an even bigger point – the quality of programmes. Granada, powerful within the network, claimed that the programming pattern of independent television had become 'perhaps too settled', adding, not as a compliment, that there had been 'a substantial increase in the strength of the IBA's influence over the past decade': 'the re-think engendered by the fourth channel may result in a shake-up which will refresh ITV.' Yorkshire saw 'a danger of ITV losing its popular touch': it looked to the fourth channel to eliminate 'many' of the constraints placed on the companies and reported optimistically that its own 'present structure works well and successfully – it is not therefore proposed to make any change' – while Southern claimed that 'we have in fact done everything we said we would do – and more.'

There were references to Channel 4 in other, but not all, of

74

the applications, with the biggest of the three small companies, Grampian, suggesting a contribution of programmes 'which larger companies seem less inclined to fill': it hoped to increase its programme budgets from commissions; and with Channel, despite its name, warning that, since it did not expect any production or programme sale to Channel 4, a subscription from it to the new channel, as proposed by the Authority, would 'seriously inhibit the further development of the company.' Thames reported that its own strong pressure for the setting up of a fourth channel had arisen because of the restrictions placed on creative energy within ITV by reason of the single channel previously at its disposal; it offered a wide range of new programmes, including a 'History of the Twentieth Century'. So too did LWT, which promised 'new forms and new performers'. Thames suggested also that a new independent sports organization on the lines of ITN should be set up. Granada looked at the logic of the whole system. 'We have no desire to go broke in an attempt to prove that two channels need not be complementary.'

There were significant differences in the approach to the facts of the longer record before there had been any talk of Channel 4, in particular in relation to the production of programmes designed for limited audiences and programmes designed for export. Thus, Anglia described itself as the 'leading ITV contractor in America', while Thames, by contrast, insisted that 'no television programme has been planned or produced primarily for an overseas market, though many have been sold worldwide.' Almost all the applicants made the most, of course, of prizes received for programmes in national and international contests, as testimony to the quality of their output, although the LWT application was 'based on the premise that the Authority is familiar with the company and its record as a programme maker' and deliberately made no mention of national and international awards won. Granada argued generally that the IBA should take a positive lead in the economy of ITV by advocating self-discipline in programme expenditure.

Considerable attention was devoted to the presentation of local news and issues, for all the contenders, old or new, were aware – with varying degrees of apprehension – that any shake-up might not be restricted to a 'rethink of the implications' of Channel 4. Questions relating to networking were bound to arise even if the IBA was committed to its existence. So too were questions about finance – some felt that the IBA was fussing too much about these – and about staff participation schemes. The forty-four applications, *Broadcast* wrote, offered the IBA 'a lot of options, not just for root-and-branch replacement of one group by another, but for a whole gamut of changes, from shotgun marriages to the enforced removal or addition of shareholdings or senior executives.' It reported that 'one informed observer' was maintaining that the Authority's members were 'raring to make changes.' 'It may be relevant,' it added, 'that such a large proportion of them are recent appointees.' Would this make them 'readier to change,' it asked, 'unencumbered by the kind of natural acquaintance with the existing contractors that members acquire over the years?' Or would it make them 'more dependent on the judgement of the experienced permanent staff, who may be more conservative?'

'Is London too big for anyone to compete for?' the *Daily Telegraph* asked in May 1980. In fact, there was only one London contender, London Independent Television, which had begun by making an unsolicited application for a seven-day contract – urging the need to plan programming for the week as a whole – and subsequently developed its bid into an application for either the weekday or the weekend franchise. At least one commentator, a writer in *TV and Home Video*, treated the bid as a joke. It was a bid which had not been anticipated, yet there was considerable detail in it. LIT preferred, its application stated, not to work from Thames TV's site at Teddington, but from converted Rediffusion studios at Wembley, where a substantial outside-broadcast fleet would be housed for sport as well as for news and actuality. Its programme plans included four local bulletins and magazines a day, the first at 8.30 a.m. and the main news (an hour of it) at 6 p.m. It would 'strengthen Saturday programmes', produce a major British drama series, launch a 'British cartoon' and give wider coverage to world affairs and to those of the European Community. Its contribution to Channel 4 was left open.

Its board was described vaguely as being equally divided between representatives of financial and cultural interests and executive directors with broadcasting and managerial experience, and its best-known backer and contact man, well known to press and public, was Hughie Green, previously associated with Thames and before that (for many years) with AR (later Rediffusion Television). Its chairman was the chairman of Marconi Space and Defence Systems, General Sir Harry Tuzo, and other members included Kenneth Winkles, vice-chairman of the Civil Aviation Authority and a Lloyds underwriter (and formerly a director of Rank and Southern Television and chairman of Visnews), Dame Margot Smith DBE, for one year chairman of the National Union of Conservative and Unionist Associations, Raymond Mawby MP, a former Conservative Assistant Postmaster General, and Thomas Pendry MP, a former Labour Under-Secretary for Northern Ireland. Guy Paine of Radio Victory, and formerly a director of both Rediffusion and LWT, would be managing director, it was stated, along with John Barker (formerly LWT) as finance director and Gabrielle Beaumont as programme director. Hughie Green was described modestly as a consultant for entertainment and Eldon Griffiths MP as a consultant for current affairs.

The consortium would raise £30 million capital, it was announced, £10 million of which would be in equity and £20 million in loan stock. Its principal investors would include major business organizations, a newspaper and the displaced contractor, although 40 per cent of the shareholding would be reserved for a 'wide spread of artistic and commercial interests'. Preferential treatment would be given to London residents in future flotations – the kind of promise, difficult to implement, that it was felt the IBA would like.

The two existing companies stood by their record, with Thames, weekday contractor since 1967, pointing out that its two parent companies were 'sufficiently diversified to provide a wide and stable base', and with London Weekend Television, for which, like many other companies, 1979–80 was proving a difficult trading year, stressing its unique record as 'the only broadcasting organization in the world' with its hours of broadcasting confined to the weekend. Both companies had to concern themselves inevitably with the relationship between their local role and what might be called their metropolitan and networking role. Of 1000 hours of planned production a year

Thames offered 270 hours for the London region, promising several new programmes, including a weekday 'Thames Report' and a current affairs magazine for fifteen- to twenty-two-year-olds, and greater outside-broadcast coverage of London's 'cultural brilliance in diversity'. 'We would summarize our programme intentions as ambitious, comprehensive, eclectic and above all responsive,' it declared. LWT, particularly conscious of the need 'to beat the BBC at its own game', thought that its programme mix was right, although it too offered a new regional news magazine of one hour on Fridays.

There were suggestions in the Thames application that the two companies would cooperate not only in news selection and presentation with a view to offering 'a consistent service of local news across seven days a week', but also in 'new ways and by means of inter-company scheduling', although the latter idea was not taken up by LWT. Higher ratings and greater receipts could have been obtained, LWT pointed out, if the substantial resources available to it had been put into entertainment but, leaving on one side the IBA's requirement for 'balance', it had itself chosen to reject such concentration, which would have meant neglecting other demands from an audience 'identified as requiring programmes of all kinds'. Both companies also offered a sizable contribution to the programming of Channel 4, at the same time emphasizing the extent of their current contribution to the network. Thames proposed that 5 per cent of its issued share capital would be available for purchase by employees (how the market value would be assessed was not explained) and stated that a profit-sharing scheme would be introduced on 1 January 1982, while LWT, pointing to its excellent record in staff relations, also claimed that the possibilities of staff share owning and greater participation were being carefully investigated.

The view from London was bound to be different from the view from the provinces, and at the periphery of the national television system there was no opposition to Grampian, which had held its contract since 1959; to Border, which had lost money in 1979–80 and was reported as deciding to reapply for the franchise only because the South Lakeland district had been added to the contract area; and to Channel, which repeated that if it was expected to contribute financially to Channel 4 this would involve great financial strain. In Wales, however, there was opposition to HTV from Severn/Hafren Television, in Scotland to STV from Caledonia Television and Lowland Broadcasting, and in Northern Ireland from one new group, Northern Ireland Independent Television.

In Central Scotland the existing contractor, Scottish Television Ltd, from a difficult start in 1957 had become in the 1960s a highly profitable subsidiary of the Thomson Organization. A condition of the 1968 contract had been a reduction of the Thomson holding to 25 per cent. In 1977 the remaining holding was acquired by a number of Scottish investment institutions, and at the time of the 1980 application it was claimed that half STV's 7200 shareholders lived in Scotland, with no single institution or individual owning more than 6 per cent of the non-voting shares. Of the twenty-two voting shareholders, fourteen were members of the board, and of the others two were a former director and an original shareholder. STV described its main objective as a contractor as that of 'rounding out the total ITV output with programmes which cater for the full range of Scottish interests.' It planned to increase its sales to the network (fifty to sixty hours a year in 1980) and to other ITV companies (over 500 programmes a year in 1980) and in order to do so to inject £5 million into studio equipment. It hoped too to meet the needs of Channel 4 by providing up to sixty hours a year, for which it would recruit additional staff. Drama output, up by 50 per cent, would be a major contribution. The aim was fifty hours a year of STV drama on network or on the fourth channel. As far as Scotland itself was concerned, the company had no intention, it stated, of making distinctive programmes for 'sub-areas', but it would range widely with film and new electronic news-gathering (ENG) units to show news items of interest from all areas to the whole region. Most of the applications referred to the effects of the new ENG technology on news selection and presentation and what Thames described in London as 'the fresh dimension that will be gained from connecting disparate parts of the transmission area.'

STV had two challengers for the franchise, both well known to the Scottish press – Caledonia Television Ltd and Lowland Broadcasting Ltd, both of which placed their main emphasis on quality. The former company had been originated as early as

1977 by a group of television producers who were disturbed by 'poor service' and 'inadequate' network representation of the franchise area. It complained that TV in Scotland was 'enfeebled by parochialism, chauvinism and lack of authority.' The latter, 'a grassroots contractor', emerged in 1979 from a campaign of the Better Scottish Television Association.

Caledonia Television Ltd was chaired by Lord McCluskey, with a working board which included the Marquis of Bute, 'Britain's richest man', Derek Webster, chairman of the *Daily Record* group, Viscount Weir, Chairman of Weir Engineering, and TV producers Hugh Pitt and Richard Bates (of the STV drama adaptation of 'The Prime of Miss Jean Brodie'). The company hoped to take over STV's assets, acquire its shares and re-employ its staff. No shareholder was to hold more than 10 per cent of the shares. Information on its approaches to fill the posts of managing director and senior executives was to be given confidentially to the IBA. The company would have a programme advisory committee of non-executive board members and 'creative professional executives', an advisory council of individuals representing different interests in the contract area, and an audit committee consisting of the chairman and financier members of the board. Among the innovations proposed was a special marine unit to make programmes reflecting the 'unique beauty' of the Scottish sea coast and the industries related to it – for example, oil, fish farming and engineering – and to cover 'marine subjects' beyond the British Isles. An initial twelve hours a week of programme making (one more than STV's) would be extended in stages to seventeen, while some programmes would be made for the network and some for the fourth channel; up to fourteen hours a week would be produced for transmission in Scotland. A late-night transmission period would be added, starting at 11.30 p.m., to carry American movies and fiction series; in prime time there would be a reduction of such material. Programme-making resources would be increased in Edinburgh and out-stations would be established in Ayrshire and Oban (the latter especially concerned to serve Gaelic speakers and Celtic music).

On the board of Lowland Broadcasting Ltd there would be three members of the Better Scottish Television Association, including John Gray, a former BBC Scotland producer, to hold a watching brief on the company's programme policy. Six directors would represent the main investors in the company, and four executive directors – the managing director, the programme director, the finance director and the marketing director – would be responsible for day-to-day management in consultation with a programme and policy committee of the board. The company's Articles would require a division of shares in which the BSTA would control 25 per cent of the voting interest in deferred shares. The £7 million capital would be divided equally between voting and non-voting shares, and none of the initial investors would have more than a 10 per cent shareholding. Loan capital of about £6 million would complete the requirement. The company would make dynamic use of its resources, it stated, to produce programmes consonant with Scottish culture and social needs, to increase the contribution from Scottish talent and to involve programme makers and the public more directly in broadcasting policy. Yet it observed also that too much Scottishness would be 'stultifying'. In setting up an audio-visual workshop trust with equipment and funds for experimental work, more general programming considerations would be in view. The company hoped to achieve twelve and a half hours of programme output per week, of which five and a half or six and a half hours would be for regional news, current affairs and sport, and four hours a week for entertainment, music and the arts. There would also be a weekend family magazine, and one hour a week would be offered to the network and to Channel 4. The company hoped to work with the North Scotland contractor on Gaelic programmes for the west of the region, although 'Gaelic culture' would also be provided as an element in programmes for the whole region. The company noted that no questions had been asked by the IBA about marketing policy, and recorded that it would want to discuss new approaches to marketing with the Authority.

In Wales, where there was one challenger for the bilingual franchise, HTV offered more programmes in English. It pointed out that it already produced more programmes in the Welsh than in the English language and that a further increase in Welsh broadcasting would follow from the opening of Channel 4 in Wales. ITV programmes in Welsh should be limited to those having an obvious appeal to the majority of the viewing public. HTV Wales hoped to reach a figure of five hours a week in 1982 after opening a new studio at Mold in North Wales and developing its news facilities from there, while HTV West also intended five hours a week of programming for the area. More news, current affairs, drama and music were urgently needed. HTV's submission was a diplomatic application for the favoured treatment that only the IBA was in a position to accord; it looked, too, to coordination with the BBC as well as with Channel 4, and strongly opposed breakfast-time television as a likely drain on financial resources.

Competition for the dual contract came from an unnamed company, which would, it said, acquire HTV and offer two services – Teledu Hafren for Wales and Severn Television for the West. Its application was presented by a consortium, which included as chairman A. J. Gooding, High Sheriff of Gwent, a leading solicitor and managing director of Western Mail and Echo Ltd, and as executive directors a group of creative people who had attracted substantial financial support (although it added that it could not yet name them). The spokesman for this group at the public meeting held in Bristol (with Lord Thomson of Monifieth presiding) was Lord Hooson QC, a Liberal peer and former MP for a Welsh constituency. The company's objective would be to present regional television in the same style as a local newspaper, while taking television to all parts of the area, including each side of the Severn Bridge, which, it pointed out, served as a link for Welsh people working in Bristol. Live theatre in both Wales and the West would be encouraged through the creation of television repertory companies, offering work to local writers and actors and providing hour and half-hour plays in both areas. Documentaries in English on major topics for Wales would be as significant a part of the output as documentaries in Welsh. New young talent would be recruited for news and current affairs programmes in both Wales and the West, and a separate series of current affairs programmes would be broadcast during parliamentary sessions. Entertainment in the Welsh language would be developed, especially drawing on the development of Welsh 'pop' and record companies, in an effort to attract young viewers. A series on the work of young film makers would be offered to the network. In relation to Channel 4, the application presented proposals for a 'bold system of complementary planning' between BBC and ITV, to reach formal agreement on the types of programmes in which each would specialize and to avoid irritating time clashes.

For Wales at least, therefore, there was as much stress in both applications on coordination as on competition. This emphasis was accounted for, however, by the Government's decision to set up a Welsh Fourth Channel Authority, although the timing of the development had not yet been determined when the bids were made and both contenders had to stress that they were concerned with programmes in English as well as in Welsh.

There were no language problems in Northern Ireland, where Ulster Television Ltd, which had held its contract for twenty-one years, was faced with a challenge from a new consortium chaired by Lord Dunleath, a former BBC national governor for Northern Ireland. UTV itself had its origins in a local Northern Irish group and claimed that its voting shareholders – nearly 100 people – were a 'cross-section of the Northern Ireland public . . . spread across the four corners of the Province.' No registered holder had more than 5 per cent of either the voting or non-voting shares. Its seventeen-strong board included the deputy chairman and managing director, the assistant managing director, sales director and controller of local programmes and executive director. In 1980 UTV was in the middle of a five-year £3 million expansion plan (a new studio in Londonderry, an outside-broadcast unit, ENG units and a new master control facility) which, it was stated, would make possible increased production both for regional programmes and for Channel 4, which it was hoped would offer opportunities for the smaller companies.

The application pointed to UTV's programme innovations, among them the first UK regional magazine and the first UK adult educational programme, the 'Midnight Oil' experiment of 1962, and noted that it had five local programmes in the Top Ten. It had tripled its budget for local programmes since 1976 and had increased its local output to more than eight hours a week. New plans included an original weekly drama serial based on life in the Province and shot on location; co-production

83

arrangements to make a drama series 'The Memoirs of an Irish RM' as a major television serial; an extension of the regional news magazine 'Good Evening Ulster' to seven days a week with coverage around the Province; and proposals to revive a 'Four Companies Project' for exchange productions with Westward, Grampian and Border. The company, in a region unique among ITV areas, was committed, it said, to covering 'all aspects of life in a troubled Province'.

The consortium contending for the contract, Northern Ireland Independent Television, offered strong competition. It claimed that it was responding to 'a general desire for a fresh initiative', a very familiar phrase in Northern Ireland. Names mentioned, along with Lord Dunleath, included Derek Bailey, former producer of 'Midnight Oil', as managing director and programme director, Dr William Cockroft, vice-chancellor of the New University of Ulster, Robert Coulter, former BBC Northern Ireland controller, Olympic athlete Mary Peters, flautist James Galway, composer Philip Coulter, playwright Brian Friel and actor Colin Blakeley; and among its shareholders was Standard Broadcasting UK, which, it was stated, would make available over £6 million in capital for expenditure in 1981 and 1982 and over £8 million revenue for the first year of the new contract period.

The consortium would not want to take over UTV's facilities, it added, and would build a three-studio centre in central Belfast and an interview and report studio and ENG base in Londonderry in an effort to provide local programmes of high quality and broader range – among them a five-nightly magazine. NITV saw a danger in Belfast-dominated coverage and would seek to 'serve a wider geographical spectrum'; it would also cover local religious services in 'the most religious-minded area within the ITV network'.

One of the medium-sized companies within the system, Tyne Tees Television Ltd, the incumbent contractor, presented its application as a company wholly owned by Trident Television Ltd, which also owned Yorkshire Television. The IBA's invitation to apply for the North-East contract had stated clearly that, while the two companies then serving the North-East and Yorkshire regions were subsidiaries of the same parent company, Trident, each had a separate contract with the Authority and that the two regions would remain separate contract areas in the new contract period; and Tyne Tees, describing its objective as that of serving as 'a unifying force' in a region which ran from Scotland to Yorkshire and covered areas of much diversity, offered regional programmes as its first priority. It recognized, however, that it had also to meet the demands for local services within the region. The IBA had confirmed that its invitation required the North-East regional contractor to continue to supply, and to develop as required from 1980 onwards, an opt-out service to its viewers in the southern part of the region from the Bilsdale transmitter, which also extended southwards beyond York, overlapping Yorkshire Television's main transmitter coverage. In future, therefore, part of 'Northern Life', its new magazine, would have to go out in two versions to the northern and southern parts of the region. Meanwhile, the company promised, Tyne Tees's new studio in Middlesbrough would add to the coverage of the news crew based there, as soon as the Post Office provided a circuit from Newcastle which had been on order since 1978. It added that news film units were already being replaced by ENG units, and that it would open its fifth and largest studio in Newcastle in 1981.

In the new contract period from 1982 Tyne Tees planned to add daytime and late-night local news bulletins, to introduce local comedians to its regional audience, and to increase to sixty minutes the length of its regional Saturday-morning programmes for children, popular with 'the largest Saturday morning audience on ITV'. It would also offer 'Face the Press' as a major topical programme throughout the year. Tyne Tees had been active in arguing for a fourth channel, it went on, and hoped to make contributions up to fifty-two hours a year.

The rival Norseman application for the Northeastern contract came from a local group, 'rooted in the history, traditions and problems of the area,' a group which already in 1978 had unsuccessfully proposed to the IBA, without being solicited, that there should be a Northumbrian franchise with no links with Yorkshire. There were changes in the composition of the group, however, which had then included Donald Baverstock and Tom Margerison, who in 1980 were involved in other applications. Norseman's chairman was Paul Nicholson, chairman of Vaux Breweries, and its directors included Joe Mills, northern regional secretary of the Transport and General Workers Union and editor of its newspaper, Bill Forsyth, former Lord Mayor of Newcastle and chairman of the Northern Sinfonia Concert Society, Fred Holliday, vice-chancellor of Durham University, Robin Gill, founder of Border TV Ltd, later managing director of ATV, and Bernard Greenhead, former director of studios and engineering at ABC TV and then at Thames TV. The company, it was stated, would provide £16 million capital by share and loan stock held widely in the region, with no holdings of founders' or ordinary shares of more than 5 per cent.

The declared intention of the company was to give the North-East 'its own television service', concentrating on programmes with a specific regional identity and 'drawing collective attention to the achievement and hopes of the region.' Norseman, it was stated, would not take over the Tyne Tees Newcastle or Middlesbrough centres, but would develop its own studio complexes at Washington New Town, south of Newcastle, and in the Darlington area for the southern part of the region. It aimed at a programme output of twelve hours a week, with a full hour's news magazine from 6 to 7 p.m. consisting entirely of material of local production, which would include within it an increasing amount of opt-out material to cover the separate needs of its northern and southern areas. Special effort would be devoted to developing a new children's programme, to presenting serious popular music for young people, including programmes featuring the Northern Sinfonia Orchestra, and to popularizing further education. The company saw current affairs items, children's programmes and sport as its main contribution to the fourth channel, along with educational programmes concerned with 'leisure time self-improvement'.

The application, described in the press as a 'last-minute bid', from Television North came from a consortium chaired by Sir Monty Finniston, scientist and industrialist and former chairman of British Steel. Its programme controller designate was Andrew Quicke, former BBC Television producer of 'Panorama' and 'The Money Programme', former executive producer for Visnews and currently head of an independent film company, UFO Productions UK Ltd, and of the consultancy firm TV Trans International. Its board included Steven Keynes, director of Arbuthnot Latham Holdings, Sun Life Assurance Society and Premier Consolidated Oil, and it claimed that it would have at its disposal over £22 million of capital in ordinary shares and loan stock. The majority of its half million voting shares would be held by residents in the contract area. The names of the managing director and other senior officials were kept confidential, but the key role of a network of advisory committees, all of which had already been set up, was strongly stressed. The company would negotiate, it was stated, to take over the Newcastle and Middlesbrough facilities of Tyne Tees and to enlarge both. Its news and current affairs department would have two news rooms in these two centres and would add new reporter posts to the staff, for example, a senior industrial correspondent. It would add to the Tyne Tees studio centres a full outside-broadcast unit, would replace film units with six Electronic News Gathering units over the first two years, and would build a production studio on the Middlesbrough site and add origination points at York and Alnwick by 1984–85.

The company intended to mount a ninety-minute live magazine show at 10.30 p.m. on Fridays as the weekly centrepiece of its regional programmes, an output of 515 hours a year. Of these, about 100 hours would consist of local news bulletins and programmes on local issues, transmitted separately in the northern and southern areas, and over 400 hours would consist of programmes for the region as a whole. The network would be offered farming and nature programmes, children's concerts, church services and preschool educational series. The company also had 'in hand for the 1980s' one 'giant project', the visual history of the twentieth century, to be developed in cooperation with a well-known publisher. It hoped to be commissioned to offer seventy hours a year of output for Channel 4, and would create a new drama and light entertainment department to secure this.

Further south in Yorkshire the second company owned since 1974 by Trident Television – Yorkshire Television – was faced with internal argument as well as with outside competition. In its application YTV stressed that, while it was owned by Trident, it was an autonomous operating company in its own right with no outside interests and with no intention of diversifying. The reasons for the formation of Trident, YTV pointed out, were 'well known to the Authority' and were just as valid as they had been in 1974; any change would be damaging to YTV, seriously impairing its ability to continue as a major network company, and would be harmful, therefore, to the ITV system. To a specific question from the Authority as to whether changes in composition, structure or direction would be made if a new contract was awarded, YTV replied in one sentence that the present structure worked well and successfully and no changes were proposed. (Across the Pennines Granada held the record for the shortest answer to this question in eight words; ATV Midlands held the record for the longest.)

YTV based its application on twelve years of programme production covering 'the broadest spectrum possible of television' and its power to attract the best programme makers and to give them 'the best conditions to do their work'. In twelve years, it pointed out, it had contributed an annual output of ninety-two hours of drama to the network, 'strong situation comedy', varied documentary and innovative schools and adult educational programmes. It would build on these strengths after 1982 and, in particular, wanted to introduce to the network a new regular current affairs programme. YTV felt it had struck the right balance between local and network programme output: its 700 hours of programmes a year were about equally divided between them. YTV, alongside Anglia, believed it had 'the finest local news magazine on ITV: it is certainly the most popular produced by any major company.' Its 'Calendar' news magazine and many 'Calendar' spin-off programmes were 'big, popular and professional'. In future, however, two ENG units would be added to the 'Calendar' operation; it already covered the whole of the contract area, supported by local offices, film units, reporters, small studios and regional executives.

YTV was grateful to the IBA for solving the border problem with Anglia by the installation of relays which would give people in northwest Norfolk the choice between the two services. YTV added that it would supply more than 100 hours to Channel 4 and that it had many new programme ideas to present. When ITV was 'freed from the present straitjacket of the single-channel operation,' it too could 'start off in a new direction,' recover its audience and attract a new one.

For two reasons YTV devoted five pages of its application to the IBA question on industrial relations arrangements, policies and records. First, during the eleven-week ITV strike in 1979 its managing director and director of programmes, Paul Fox, was seen as 'heading the tough line' taken by the ITV companies. Second, the submission of a separate application for the Yorkshire contract by Television Yorkshire had been prepared for the IBA 'on behalf of the present staff of Yorkshire Television'. A riposte was necessary. YTV wanted to ensure, it said, 'that as many people as possible can obtain job satisfaction and hence high performance in their work.'

The competing application, described in one newspaper as 'a massive indictment of YTV's operations at all levels', was presented by three former YTV staff – Donald Baverstock, Yorkshire's first director of programmes (who had first made his mark with the BBC), and two MPs, one Conservative and one Labour, Jonathan Aitken and Austin Mitchell, both former presenters of 'Calendar'; it also won the support of Sir Harold Wilson, Stella Richman and Lord McCarthy, the Oxford University expert in industrial relations. It was an understood convention in 1967, the application noted, that 'nobody working in the industry should lose their livelihood as a result of changes introduced by the ITA' (as it then was). The same convention would 'prevail this year', it held, and staff recruitment by new applicants would necessarily be suspended until after the new contracts were allotted. Whatever changes were made in the Yorkshire contract 'would have to depend on the existing staff', and it was reasonable, therefore, that their views should be given greater weight than those of 'accidental conjunctions of financial interests' or of 'existing vested interests', all 'articulated by professionals from public relations consultants.' 'Yorkshire's problems stem from the fact that Trident is a financial holding company,' the contenders stated. 'The structure is quite unlike that of any other ITV company because here the Trident tail wags the Yorkshire dog.'

In fact, YTV was not alone in being part of a larger entertainment complex, and the TVY case was grounded essentially in arguments not about finance but about decision-making within YTV and its pattern of labour relations. There had been an earlier effort to set up a new White Rose Television during the strike; it drew in many of the prominent figures of 1980 and some behind the scenes.

The proposed 'reconstituted' TVY company would be more beneficial for the area, for the ITV system and for television generally, the application claimed comprehensively. 'Control from the centre' would be replaced by 'purposeful leadership and responsibility at every level' and 'financial interests would be subordinated to the purposes of good television'. The names of directors and staff and details of staff structure could not yet be supplied, but the 'company of people' who would form TVY had existed before this application and commanded 'a wealth of experience'. With no access to financial information on YTV's operation, full answers to the IBA's questions on company composition and finance could not be given. But TVY had received 'positive indications of interest' from four major financial institutions or shareholders who would provide £5 million or more capital, on condition that staff would subscribe at least £1 million, which the three spokesmen were confident would be raised.

Even with these provisos, the group appeared to have conceived of its future television operations on a limited scale. The future company, it was stated, would engage in no activities outside television contracting other than 'publishing' its own output of video disc, cassette or print. It would initially expect to continue present output of roughly equal hours of programming for the network and for the region, but it would plan to increase the latter and to improve programme quality. It would also plan to make 'a proper contribution to IBA2'. For better coverage of the region it would commit itself to 'non-preferential proportionate coverage throughout the area, irrespective of distance from the main studios' and would make the 'necessary improvements in communications' to do so. TVY's submission put emphasis on the pride which its audience would take in seeing Yorkshire locations and characters 'made interesting in network programmes' and, for good measure, 'in other countries as well'.

There was abundant pride across the Pennines where Granada, which until 1968 had provided television for Yorkshire as well as for Lancashire, faced its one challenger from the west of its contract area, Merseyside. Granada Television Ltd, never a great respecter of authority, was a wholly owned subsidiary of the Granada Group, to which it had provided 16 per cent of profits in 1980. The group imposed no financial restrictions on Granada Television, which had its own budget and made its own forecasts, and three Granada Television directors were members also of the Group board. No change was proposed to this structure.

Of the two major cities in the North-West, Liverpool and Manchester – and they were cities with rival traditions – Manchester had been chosen as the headquarters of the company at the time of the 1954 franchise, as it had been selected by the BBC and by national newspapers as the centre for their operations in the North of England. Given the distinctive identity of its rival, the Granada application specifically examined the representations of Merseyside to the Authority that Liverpool should have its own station and due share of coverage with other parts of the region. First, a studio had now been built in Liverpool to provide a centre for local news. Second, a single production centre was economical for two cities only forty miles apart. Why have two? The national television system was a regional system, not a civic system open to local pressures. Third, the Winter Hill transmitter could not be split between the two cities: a new transmitter would be necessary if there were to be parallel television services. Fourth, Granada would take further account of Liverpool interests. In future the daily magazine programme would become a two-centre programme, each with ENG unit support. Fifth, the company was in a position to back joint endeavours, for example, for the foundation of a North-West Opera Company, which had so far not succeeded because Liverpool and Manchester could not agree to join forces.

Not surprisingly, the Granada application was centred positively on its general programme record in the making of network programmes, regional programmes, many of which would have been made by no other company, and especially programmes for the network reflecting regional life and culture, a third category in which it believed it had made a significant contribution, especially in its promotion of the work of northern writers. It mentioned perhaps the best-known of all television programmes, 'Coronation Street', which fully reflected the 'personality of the region' but which was classed as a network programme in the IBA's schedules. Granada would continue its output of seven hours a week for the network and seven hours plus for the region. A new programme development would be the creation of a strong arts department, the work of which would be available for Channel 4 as well as for the network.

The contending application in the name of Merseyvision, first announced in January 1980, was put forward by a Liverpool-based group led by Dr Lewis Lesley, a lecturer in transport at the Liverpool Polytechnic, and Brian Doyles, a local builder, and it had strong local authority support. 'We are not happy viewing Merseyside through a Mancunian lens,' explained the director of the Liverpool Planning Committee, who gave the new company his full backing. It would operate, the application stated, from studios in three major population centres of the franchise areas – Manchester, Merseyside and the Preston–Blackburn area – and new facilities would be provided outside Manchester with access to ample funds. The Merseyside studio would originate the major programme output for the network – documentaries, drama, art and science programmes – but all three centres would provide a greater flow of local news and current affairs programmes for their respective areas, presenting viewers throughout the North-West with a balanced and detailed picture of the region. For Channel 4 the main contributions would be single plays and minority sports. The company could not at the time of its application divulge the exact sources of its finance or the names of its senior executives. The application was sketchy, suggesting that the sponsorship had many of the features not of a consortium but of a pressure group. One novel feature was reported in May 1980: Merseyvision shares would be 'sold over pub counters'.

There had long been a Manchester financial stake in Anglia Television, wholly owned by a holding company formed for the purpose in which the *Guardian* and the *Manchester Evening News* held a block of shares, and, like Granada, Anglia stood first and foremost on 'the basis of its established record'. Two of its best-known programmes nationally were 'Survival' and 'Tales of the Unexpected'. There was little doubt about Anglia's survival: few observers expected Anglia to fail in the franchise affair. For the *Daily Telegraph*, it was 'one of the few impregnables'. In its service to the region it was 'wholly identified' with its areas, it claimed, for its management and personnel were 'an integral component' of its audience. Over 80 per cent of its programmes were devised and produced for the East of England. Anglia's anxiety, not new in 1980, was to secure network time on a regular and assured basis.

It was as a result of an ITA decision in 1958 that the East of England contractor's studios were sited in Norwich, the city which was 'steadily becoming a bridge between this country and the cities of Europe', and Anglia was now engaged in an £18 million development scheme of studio and facilities.

The Anglia application listed the programmes in production in 1980 within its regularly scheduled categories and series and offered to contribute up to two hours a week to Channel 4, in the form of drama and drama series, children's programmes, sport and programmes drawn from the field of archaeology and anthropology. Its coverage of regional news would be enhanced, it went on, by the addition of two centres for journalists and film units in Chelmsford and Northampton to those already in operation in Luton, Kings Lynn and Peterborough, and by a changeover from film to ENG units.

As in the North-West, the challenge to the sitting company came from a group based on a different geographical centre, and in this case also it had big names to support it. Eastern England Television Ltd stated that, while it was prepared to acquire Anglia's Norwich premises, it would build additional studios at Cambridge, which was the approximate centre of the region as it had now become in the new contract; indeed, it added that, if Anglia's property was not available, it would create totally new facilities there. News operations and the mobile units deployed around the region would be coordinated at Cambridge, where a major studio for drama and audience shows would be built. There would also be links with the University of Cambridge. The company made much of its 'sense of purpose'. Moreover, it claimed that Anglia programmes had not reflected the fact that there was now less agriculture and more industry in the eastern region. It also referred specifically to 'young viewers' and minority coverage, and suggested the creation of 'watchdog panels' consisting of members of the public.

The consortium was chaired by Professor Bernard Campbell. Its managing director was Forbes Taylor (a former Anglia head of documentaries), and among its directors were Peter Fairley, one-time science correspondent of ITN, Sir Peter Hall, Lord Norwich, Jean Floud, principal of Newnham College, Cambridge, writer Frederick Raphael, and Rex Winfrey, managing director of the East Midland Allied Press. Among its advisors were merchant banker Lord Aldenham and Sir Keith Faulkner, former director of the Royal College of Music. The consortium had a planned capitalization of £10 million and promised that a proportion of the non-voting shares would be reserved for residents in the region. The only allocations of non-voting shares above 5 per cent would be to the East Midland Allied Press Ltd (12½ per cent) and to the Colne Fishing Company Ltd (also 12½ per cent).

EETV offered to produce at least ten hours of programmes a week, giving first priority to a regional news service. The half-hour from 10.30 to 11 p.m. each night would be reserved for regional magazines covering arts, science and politics and for audience participation programmes. Entertainment would include summer seaside shows, a new panel game, and variety with regional performers. Sir Peter Hall would guide drama plans, Keith Faulkner music, including production for television of Britten's operas and programmes from music festivals in the region, Lord Norwich the arts, Jean Floud adult education, and Peter Fairley science and science fiction. They would interest themselves specifically in contributions to Channel 4, on which they already had 'ideas'.

To the west of the eastern contract area, the new East and West Midlands area was bound to be the scene of as much change as that set out in EETV's controversial *A Time for Change*, for the IBA itself had already altered the pattern by announcing a dual contract. No less than three contenders put in bids for the new dual region which required the contractor to operate two studios, east and west. The IBA had set out such specific (and detailed) requirements for this contract that, in the words of *Broadcast*, 'it virtually directed the shape of any applicant's bid for the franchise.'

ATV Network, from 1978 a wholly owned subsidiary of the Associated Communications Corporation (ACC), the holding company headed by Lord (Lew) Grade, had been one of the first four founding contractors of independent television in 1954 and had remained a network company for twenty-six years. Indeed, from 1955 to 1967 it had held the London weekend contract as well as the Midlands weekday contract, and even after 1968 it had kept its Elstree studio when the company became the Midlands seven-days-a-week contractor. A new company, the application stated, had now been formed to take the place of ATV Network, with the title of ATV Midlands Ltd and based solely in the Midlands. Yet it chose to present its information to the Authority in the format applicable to an existing contractor. There was direct continuity through the chairman and managing director, Lord Windlesham, one of the best-known personalities in independent television, through the full-time executive directors and all the Midlands-based staff of ATV Network.

Two new vice-chairmen would be appointed, however, ATV Midlands stated, one for the East and one for the West, and there would be six non-executive directors, persons of standing with public and private connections in the constituent parts of the franchise area. Half the new board would consist of these non-executive directors and half of full-time executives, of whom two would be the general managers of the ATV centre in Birmingham and of a new East Midlands three-studio tele-vision centre for which sites in Nottinghamshire had been surveyed and which would become operational at the end of 1982. The new complex would cost about £20 million, and one of the new studios would be the biggest at the company's disposal. The Elstree television studios would be handed over to a new ACC subsidiary, Elstree Television Centre Ltd, with no overlap of board members or of senior executives with ATV Midlands. However, Elstree's capacity could be drawn upon by ATV Midlands until the new East Midlands centre was operational; and ATV was considering with other ITV com-panies and with independent producers its possible future use as a collective production centre for Channel 4.

ATV Midlands suggested that this 'restructuring . . . within a wholly Midlands context' would give a new impetus to fresh programme approaches. There would be an extra four hours of programmes a week, bringing the total to twenty hours, with 60 per cent of the output for the region and 40 per cent for network. The annual network output would include 39 per cent drama, 17 per cent documentary and factual programmes, 16 per cent light entertainment, 16 per cent children's programmes and 12 per cent education and religion. There were new programme ideas also. For example, a new network series, 'Earth Watch', would consider environmental problems of global concern, and the company planned to set up an Earth Watch Trust to supply material for the network and for Channel 4. Regional transmissions would increase by 50 per cent, and although much of the output would be transmitted simultaneously from the two area centres, the East and West centres would transmit four hours a week each of programmes of specific interest to their own areas.

The opposition to ATV reflected some of the same influences as Merseyside's opposition to Granada. Thus, Birmingham City Council produced a report strongly criticizing ATV, and the Coventry City Council planned to invest in one of the contenders, Mercia, if it was successful in its application. Mercia suggested a Mercia Television Trust with elected members and representatives on the board.

There were two contenders. Midlands TV, inspired by Stuart Wilson, who had been active in 1967 in the successful bid for the Yorkshire contract but later had left YTV, welcomed the IBA's decision not to split the Midlands into two completely separate areas and pledged its efforts and resources to 'one end alone – the creation of a truly regional company.' It would engage in no activities, it stated, other than the TV contract, the same point made in the TVY application. Chaired by Sir Robert Booth, chairman of the National Exhibition Centre, Birmingham, with Lord Willis as vice-chairman and Stuart Wilson as managing director, Midlands TV included as members of its main board Joe Gormley and the Duke of Rutland. It would also have two regional boards, it stated, both to be chaired by Sir Robert Booth.

Letters of intent from Midlands organizations and individuals had already promised over 60 per cent of the proposed capital of £23½ million and an overdraft facility of £10 million.

Only two shareholders would have investments of over 5 per cent. The Birmingham and Nottingham production centres would have 'twinned resources', each to be managed by a station director and head of regional programmes who would sit on their respective regional boards. Film units and ENG units would cover the needs of both East and West Midlands centres. There would also be a news and information centre at Oxford.

Midlands TV Ltd proposed an average of no less than ten and a half hours a week of network programmes, five and a quarter hours a week of news, current affairs and local issue programmes, from each regional centre, and two and a quarter hours of programming for the whole region between the centres. The names of senior staff, the majority of them employees of the BBC and ITV, were only to be revealed confidentially. There was little in detail about particular programmes. There would also be a contribution to Channel 4 of four hours a week, to include the development of new magazine formats 'especially in the leisure area'. Indeed, MTV saw itself as more committed to the success of a fourth channel than the major ITV companies, since a partnership, Independent Productions Company Ltd, had already been set up with a number of leading independent producers to create MTV programmes of quality for offer to Channel 4.

The bid of the second contender, Mercia Television, was led by two programme department heads from Yorkshire Television, John Fairley and John Wilford, who were subsequently to leave these positions and remain as producers with YTV, and its board included Brian Walden, Clive Richards and later Shirley Williams (not 'nameplate engineering', it was stressed) and the cricketer Basil d'Oliveira. On formation of the company, the bid stated, a Mercia TV Trust Ltd would be incorporated to carry out the promoters' concept of public interest in the development and output of its television service; it had a clear idea of how to do this. The Trust would be allocated a 'significant proportion' of voting shares and the right to appoint two members of the main board and three each to the two subsidiary boards. Capital would be raised by way of a regional offer of sale: voting shareholders would include the Trust, local authorities, institutions, management and the public 'in equal proportions'. Mercia's structure would incorporate Mercia Network Television, West and East Mercia TV, and Mercia Services to provide central services for all three. It would plan substantial network contributions in current affairs from the Midlands, under the present contractor 'only erratic and vestigial', drama 'of the highest international standard', entertainment, documentary, children's programmes (of 'BBC-like production standards'), religion (dealing with contemporary issues) and sport. The West and East centres would produce six hours a week of local news, current affairs and local programmes and one hour a week for the whole region, and there would be ENG facilities in nine towns. (There would be a nightly opt-out for Oxford.) Mercia would also be ready to meet from its own resources, it was claimed, around 6 per cent of the programme needs of Channel 4, and would act as an 'umbrella', it said, for independent producers to establish themselves in the Midlands as contributors to the new channel.

There was considerable public interest in the Midlands – and, indeed, outside – in the announced claims of the three contenders for the franchise. National interest, however, more frequently was to focus during the summer and autumn of 1980 on the position in a different part of the country, the South-West, where Westward, the contractor since 1961, was torn by boardroom squabbles after its application had been submitted. Led by Peter Cadbury, a controversial figure, Westward had achieved record advertising revenue of £9·12 million in 1979 and its application claimed 'a notable record of success'. Yet Cadbury, whose company produced Peter Fiddick's 'The Franchise Game' in the spring of 1980, was ousted as chairman in July and replaced by Lord Harris of Greenwich, a former Home Office Minister of State. What was described graphically in the *Daily Telegraph* as 'a shoot-out for the West' inevitably followed.

The Westward application, however, was straightforward enough. It was drawn up when Cadbury was chairman, the Earl of Lisburne deputy chairman and Ronald Perry managing director. Cadbury then held 17½ per cent of the voting shares. 'Westward is fortunate,' the application stated, 'in serving an area with a strong sense of regional identity and pride in its history. Our objective has been to become an integral part of the social fabric of the region. We believe that we have succeeded.' A commissioned poll had shown that 86 per cent of viewers in the region were very or fairly satisfied with Westward's output and that Westward scored heavily when compared with BBC South-West. Advisory panels on agriculture, education and religion had become very effective, encouraging such programmes as 'Just the Job' for teenagers.

The company promised a bigger contribution from a new studio in Plymouth, an extension of 'Westward Diary', Westward's 'flagship', to up to an hour every weekday and a 'Weekend Report'. More documentaries, including at least four on West Country themes for the network (among them programmes on Ernest Bevin and on Edward Heath as a sailor), were also promised along with more drama, including children's drama, more sport (including 'The Toughest 18 Holes in the World'), and the conversion of news units to the ENG system. 'We look forward to the chance of offering programmes to the fourth channel at the conceptual stage,' it added, 'and to obtaining a commission to produce them.' There was a note of realism, however, in Westward's approach. 'As we have no intention of making promises which cannot be justified, we must emphasize that we will only be able to embark on a number of these productions if the industry remains profitable and if we are able to recover a substantial proportion of the production costs.'

The first rival application came from West Country Television. It was submitted from Ivybridge, Devon, in the name of West Country Television, and was led by Simon Day, a forty-five-year-old farmer, who numbered among his team Bill Cheevers, a former managing director of Westward who had been fired by Cadbury in an earlier internal company dispute of 1970. His chief executive was to be Tony Gorard, who was running the Cardiff local commercial radio station – Day himself was a director of Plymouth Sound – and had previously been a managing director of HTV. Also on the board were Ted Hughes, the poet, Sir James Redmond, former director of engineering of the BBC, and Bill Ward, former deputy managing director of ATV and head of ITV Sport.

The company, which said that it would raise £7 million of initial capital with 5 million non-voting ordinary shares, at

99

least half of them reserved for people living in the region, made no reference to Westward's plant or personnel, although there was talk of an offer to take over the Westward studios. It planned to produce twenty-eight hours a year for the network as well as seven hours a week of local programmes. There would be three news-gathering teams located in the region, producing amongst other items a nightly weekday news magazine, which would lose its current air of predictability. The company would not be inward-looking, however: it would devise programmes, for example, on the influence of Europe on the life of the region.

Television South-West, TSW, first announced in February 1980, professed an 'open management' philosophy – keeping its staff as well informed as possible about the various aspects of the company's finance and its proposed pattern of activities. It also felt a moral obligation to offer employment to all existing union members of Westward's staff. It nominated as its first chairman Sir John Colfox, former High Sheriff of Dorset and chairman of the Land Settlement Association, and as deputy chairman Lord Iddesleigh, custodian trustee of the South-West Trustee Savings Bank. Its directors included Brian (later Sir Brian) Bailey, southwest regional secretary for the TUC, chairman of the South-West Regional Health Authority, a Somerset county councillor and future chairman of the company, David Johnstone, managing director of Dartington and Co., Dennis Sewell, managing director, Video Communications Division Phicom Ltd, Bernard Webster, head of the School of Electrical Engineering at Plymouth Polytechnic, Gareth Keene, secretary of the Dartington Hall Trust, and local newspaper publishers and industrialists. The company also intended to add to the board a representative elected annually by TSW staff. The first statements did not give the names of the chief executives, but behind the scenes Kevin Goldstein-Jackson, who reached Plymouth as joint managing director and programme controller via Hong Kong and Oman, was said to be responsible for the picking not only of the staff but of the board.

TSW, which did not use a merchant banker for finance, declared legally binding agreements for an investment of £2 million, offered £1·2 million in shares to the public through Barclays Bank and the Trustee Savings Bank, and stated that it would negotiate an overdraft facility of £1·5 million and obtain £4 million of lease finance for equipment and building. No investor would have been able or would be able to increase his share to 20 per cent or more of the share capital. The company's intention would be to have one class of ordinary voting shares. A share incentive scheme for staff would be discussed with the staff and the unions.

As far as programming was concerned, 'the main thrust', it was explained, would be 'to bring television to the people rather than the people to television.' From its inception, TSW had sought, it claimed, to be a 'grassroots organization' with six advisory boards – arts, agriculture and fisheries, education, industry, politics, and religion – and in January 1980 it had commissioned a British Market Research Bureau survey, complete with questionnaires, of viewers' opinions in the region which showed that 54 per cent of the people wanted to see more local documentaries and 53 per cent wanted more adventure/ thriller series.

In five main locations (Bridport, Truro, Taunton, Bideford and Plymouth) there would be single lightweight camera/VTR units, all capable of linking back by line or radio link, and there would also be a 'mother unit' for larger location productions. The entertainment offerings included 'ghost stories . . . recorded in an eerie way', 'More than Meets Your Eye', a series of six thirty-minute programmes on flower arranging, and 'Secrets of the Coast', concerned with geology and 'coastal creatures from crabs to birds'. The company wanted 'to gain a reputation for high quality comedy dramas' and planned an adventure/thriller series a year from 1983 onwards. It also suggested a new 'Teach Yourself Cornish' series, a weekly garden series and programmes by a newly formed modern dance group.

Programmes would be offered to Channel 4 'so long as the company receives an adequate financial reward' and, if no national breakfast-time service came about, TSW would consider running its own following a simple formula: at 6.30 a.m. it would start with farming news.

An 'adequate financial reward' seemed to be guaranteed, whatever the outcome, in the most fiercely contested of all the contract areas – the South and South-East of England. Only a few months before, the *Financial Times* had reported on 28 May 1980 that the burning issue in the run-up to the ITV contracts reallocation had been speculation about who would be joining the race to topple ATV. Now it said that 'it seems that the gossips were looking in the wrong direction. It is the prosperous pastures of England south and south east which have recently drawn the greatest attention.'

Southern Television, contractor since 1958, was a company owned by Rank, the *Daily Mail* Group, Associated Newspapers Ltd, and D.C. Thomson Company Ltd, the last of the three with its base in distant Scotland. In its application Southern pointed to its average of twelve hours a week of programmes for the region in 1980 and its average of two hours a week for network or part-network transmission, including its successful children's and drama productions. 'We promised the Authority to produce 8½ hours of programmes for the region each week – in fact we produce nearly 12 hours.' Indeed, 300 regional documentaries had been produced since 1968. 'We have in fact done everything we said we would do and more.' 'Day by Day' was acknowledged to be 'one of the best news magazines in Britain'. As far as networking was concerned, the link with Glyndebourne, established in 1972, had made Southern Europe's major television producer of opera.

The company welcomed the new dual contract 'as a natural development from our initiatives in the South-East in 1960 and our development of coverage since.' Pointing to the increase in its output from Dover, it stressed that following the change in the allocation of Bluebell Hill, the first priority would have to be the creation in the South-East region of a sense of distinct identity. The key to this would be the independent presentation of programmes from the South-East and the continuity between transmissions. Southampton would remain the major production studio, but Southern would now build a new southeastern studio complex near Maidstone for such independent presentation and production. It anticipated a one third rise in staff and was ready to become the central ITV training centre for some categories of production staff in order to assist the general expansion of the system. For the network 125 hours would be produced in the first year after the contract as against 100 hours in 1980, and a contribution would be made to Channel 4. At the same time, Southern pointed out, the Authority itself had to resolve important questions relating to the new channel, and for this reason the application asked questions as well as offered answers, expressing itself as 'acutely aware of the dangers of grandiose plans and hyperbole.' Some Southern programmes were already being made which were suitable for Channel 4. Would the channel accept them? Could it be used for the expansion of regional sports programmes? Could it provide local opt-outs?

As far as structures were concerned, there would remain one board, not two, but there would be 'a balanced representation of the two regions'. There would be financial changes too. The shareholders had agreed in principle to a capital reconstruction whereby staff could acquire shares and whereby educational interests in the South-East would benefit through share participation in the company profits.

There was a wide range of contenders for the South and South-East contract with quite different suggestions to make about both policies and structures. The most radical were presented by a consortium, Network South, which was chaired by Lord Weidenfeld, the publisher, with Dr Tom Margerison, a former managing director of LWT, as managing director and Peter Batty, an independent producer formerly working with the BBC, ATV and Thames, as deputy managing director and programme controller. It suggested that the future of public television would be local, not regional, and that TV should 'become less remote'. At the same time, given the development of technology, any contractor would also have to take account of the future provision of cable and satellite services which would be non-national in character. Looking beyond 1982, the proper solution for the South-East was not a dual contract, as the Authority had proposed in the contract, but the wider promotion of local interests; and this could best be achieved by subdividing the region into five sub-areas, each to be served by its own television company – Thanet TV, Estuary TV, South Down TV, Wessex TV and Thames Valley TV – each with its own small studio and two ENG units, producing their own news magazines and local current affairs programmes. The cost of each was estimated at around £1½ million and there would be reliance on a high volume of local advertising. A regional television centre, probably at Southampton, would supply programmes for the whole region and for network offer – about seventy hours a year to the network, with a similar scale of supply to Channel 4. Capital of about £10¼ million would be underwritten by Barclays Merchant Bank, and no shareholder would hold more than 5 per cent of any class of share. Voting shares would be held by the Network South directors and the five area companies and staff would be given the opportunity to buy non-voting shares.

Less radical ideas about structures but sharper criticism of the existing system and its 'tired conventions' were offered by a group which was to be dissolved in November 1980 before the interview stage – Tellecom (Broadcast) Television Ltd, trading as Home Counties Television. It had been set up very modestly by an industrial and provident society with individual share-holdings limited to £1, by a group of seven subscribers who included two television technicians and an accountant, and its structure was described as 'a deliberate departure from ortho-doxy in the industry to reflect its motivation.' Available loan capital was said, optimistically, to be 'substantial'. If the application were to be successful, two companies would be created for the west and east areas of the region. Southampton would remain the centre for the western company and Dover would be expanded for the eastern company, but a third major centre would be built at Brighton, a town 'with style and panache'. The company's headquarters would be located there along with a drama production studio. Brighton, it was pointed out, was the 'only provincial town in the country that is not regarded by London as such,' and it would be possible to attract talent there 'from Greenwich Village to Tokyo'. There would be satellite offices in four principal towns in each area, staffed to produce news and local features with ENG and film units. The Brighton studio would also be used for independent productions of national and international standing, which 'would bring advantage to the company's finances and to the stature of the region' in continental Europe as well as in Britain. In this contender's view, the existing television system had resorted to clichés, had put profit above quality, had blocked potential, and had taken no responsibility for the long-term effects of its programmes. 'We feel we are eminently more qualified and responsible to run our local television company than non-local and disinterested multinationals.'

At the other end of the spectrum was Television South and South-East (Holdings) Ltd, with Lord Nathan as chairman and Sir Freddie Laker and the Earl of March among the directors. Other names mentioned were those of cricket commentator and author John Arlott, cricketer Michael Denness and racing yacht designer Peter Nicholson. The company was backed financially – and this was its strength – by the Charterhouse Group, a 20 per cent shareholder in the London Broadcasting Company, and the Haymarket Publishing Group: the former would hold 20 per cent of both the voting and non-voting shares, the latter 13 per cent. Among the shareholders were Portsmouth and Sunderland Newspapers and the *Kent Messenger* Group. The directors and staff, however, would hold 20 per cent of the voting shares. The company would operate two sets of studios in Maidstone and Southampton and would produce no less than 500 hours of regional programmes per year for the South and 400 hours for the South-East. Each area would have its own regional programme controller, who would have 'the editorial autonomy necessary to meet the needs and aspirations of the people of his area'; each, too, would have its separate news magazine. Variety and comedy (sit-com on the lines of 'The Good Life') would be among the offers to the network and to the fourth channel, along with a 'Roots'-style series on the Tolpuddle Martyrs and programmes produced by a 'Science Today' group. 'We are a group of highly professional broadcasters who live or have worked in the South and South-East,' the précis of the application stated, although names were kept confidential. 'We wish to serve our special audience with programmes of excellence in which they will delight.'

Cresset Television, at first called Vayglen Ltd, also made much of its professional base. It had been originated by Tim Emanuel of Trilion Ltd (videorecording facilities), a former television producer, and Peter Mooney, a management consultant and former marketing head of the Thomson Organization, who had first shown interest in the breakfast contract. Among its directors were Lord Montagu of Beaulieu and Philip Reid, a former head of the National Research and Development Corporation, and the Bishop of Dover. It would have a main board and an operating board. Two groups would hold more than 5 per cent of the shares – Phoenix Assurance and Norton Warburg Nominees.

'The attitude' of the company, it was proclaimed, 'would be strongly regional – but not parochial. We shall aim for the network without compromising our regionality.' Southern's 'Day by Day' would be continued. So too would the production of children's programmes, sailing programmes and farming programmes. There would be more drama and a new 'prestige series', 'Rupert and Hugo', not to speak of a sit-com about a Brighton antique dealer, 'The Blind Date Disco' and 'The Wonderful Weekend World of Reginald Bosanquet'. Total output of the station would be around 920 hours a year, including 500 hours of regional programmes and another 170 hours of local material broadcasts.

The Southern Counties Television Consortium was also a professionally based body, chaired in this case by a film and television producer, Gerry Anderson, and describing itself as a 'consortium of programme makers', among them Barry Charington and Christopher Burr, 'The Money Man'. No one person or company would hold more than 9 per cent of the shares. There were to be two area boards, one based on Southampton, the other on Ashford, each with its own chairman and programming controller, but there would also be a main board with a separate chairman. The consortium aimed 'to exceed very considerably the 13½ hour maximum programme origination requirement.' It even proposed its own 'full symphony orchestra'. 'We hope', the consortium stated, that the proposals demonstrated 'that we are very ambitious programme makers, convinced that ITV needs a vigorous transfusion of new blood and ideas.' Neither this company nor Cresset had much to say, however, about Channel 4.

South and South-East Communications Ltd, which proposed to operate as TV South, TVS, also summed up its philosophy in one word – 'professionalism'. 'The Group's television practitioners – collectively and individually – have a wealth of experience which is widely recognized. Our senior programme executives have won, between them, over twenty national and international awards.' The consortium was chaired by Lord Boston of Faversham, with James Gatward, who had worked with Southern, as managing director and Dennis Rowland as his deputy; and it claimed that funds were already committed or agreed in principle for the £12 million capital which it required, raised substantially from companies and individuals active in the region. Only two principal investors would hold more than 5 per cent of the shares – European Ferries Ltd and London Trust Company and Associates. Keith Wickenden, Conservative MP and chairman of European Ferries, would be a deputy chairman. The company would also set up TV South Charitable Trust Ltd, which would hold 15 per cent of voting capital; it would be administered by governors 'representative of the region' and would seek to support the arts and sciences and recreational and community programming throughout the South and South-East. Finally £2 million of non-voting shares would be offered to the general public with 10 per cent of them reserved for employees. The dividend policy would be to distribute not more than 50 per cent of net profits after taxation; the rest would be ploughed back into programming. The company's main board would receive reports from the chairmen of two supervisory boards, one for TV South and one for TV South-East, each of whom would sit on the main board. An executive management board would carry day-to-day responsibilities. The names of the executive directors and senior staff, described as all experienced practitioners, were given in confidence to the IBA; all of them already lived or would live in the region.

As far as programming was concerned, TVS stated it would not be satisfied with 'important' but 'poorly viewed programmes', and that it would follow policies 'relevant to the 1980s', a decade which would witness a great deal of technological and social change. 'Young people in particular are going to need help in the next decade, and we shall supply the youth of our region with constant access to television,' with programmes encouraging them to ask the questions and to receive the information which would be 'relevant to their lives'. There would be a new science and industry unit, and one of the 'cornerstones' of the application was a news and current affairs service serving both the South and South-East areas. 'When Channel 4 commences, we should expect to provide between two and four hours a week of network material, drawn from any of the subject fields in which we are specializing. . . . We believe that our expertise will be of great value to the fourth channel when it goes on air.' The application ended with a flourish: 'We are both willing and competent to operate the television service for the South and South-East of England and we welcome the challenge it presents.'

There was one other set of contenders – for the breakfast-time contract. Lord Lever, chairman of one of the contesting companies, saw Lady Plowden confidentially to discuss it before the IBA had made up its mind to advertise it. The story has already been told many times. It deserves a chapter to itself.

5

Breakfast Time

B<small>Y THE TIME</small> the 'Breakfast-Time' contract was advertised,
there were people inside and outside 70 Brompton Road
who thought of it as the new jewel in the IBA's crown. Yet the
offer made by the IBA on 24 January 1980 was cautious, even if,
unlike any other offer made then or earlier in the Authority's
twenty-five-year-old history, it covered a national, not a regional, contract. *Broadcast*, with a side glance at Channel 4 and with
more than a touch of irony, listed some of the public percep-
tions of the new contract, described in the application of one
contender, Morning Television, as 'one of the last real broadcasting challenges in the United Kingdom'. The phrase that
still lingers is that 'Breakfast Time' was 'one of the last tracts of
virgin territory in TV, the last refuge for the frontier spirit'.
Broadcast's own verdict, however, was that 'Breakfast Time'
was 'the only remotely innovative idea in an otherwise highly
conservative list of proposals.'

There were some Members of the Authority who shared this
sense but the majority thought of 'Breakfast Time' somewhat
less imaginatively simply as a 'fresh' thing in a varied list of
offerings, and its officers knew that there was nothing fresh
about the idea. Individuals and groups had been lobbying at
least since 1978 for a new use of early-morning hours which
were unexploited, by the existing companies or the BBC –
unexploited that is, except on BBC 2 by the Open University
which had been driven into them. And six years had already
passed since television transmission hours had ceased to be
controlled by the Government. It was caution, through infec-
tion, perhaps, which on 24 January led the Authority to

describe the breakfast-time contract modestly as only the third of five 'new features of the franchises', ranking after the addition of two more dual ITV contracts and the transmitter and relay changes.

The language of the 'The Particulars of Independent Television Contract: National Breakfast Time', published by the IBA along with the other contract particulars, was somewhat ponderous as well as cautious, scarcely suggesting that the Authority had devoted much time to discussion of how an idea which was not its own could be effectively or speedily translated into practice. There was a contrast from the start, therefore, between the bright language of expectation and the muted language of Authority. 'The Authority,' the four-point Foreword to its Particulars began, 'is prepared to consider applications from those wishing to provide a breakfast-time service, consisting primarily, but not exclusively, of news, information and current affairs, on a nationwide basis. . . .' The penultimate sentence in the fourth paragraph was even more tentative: 'But it gives no undertaking at this stage that a breakfast-time contract will be awarded or that, if awarded, it would necessarily run from the beginning of 1982.' And so to the punch line: 'The actual starting date (which would not be before 1st January 1982) would be a matter for discussion with any successful applicant.' In this respect the successful contractor would be in a different position from all other contract holders, although it was 'likely' that, like them, he would be informed of the Authority's decision (as also would the losers) by the end of the year.

In examining the applications, the Authority spelt out, particular attention would be paid to the proposed programme content, the soundness of revenue and cost estimates and, vaguest of phrases, 'the implications which particular proposals may have for the Authority's other broadcast services.' The applications could be inspected by the public, who could also obtain copies of the précis, and would be presented to two of the IBA's final public meetings. No special conditions were allowed to breakfast-time advertising, the likely volume of which was crucial to the success of the venture. Applicants were merely referred to the current edition of the IBA's *Code of Advertising Standards and Practice* for details of the amount, distribution and acceptable selection and presentation of commercials.

Although applications would be considered, the Authority stated, either from 'new groups' or 'from applicants (including existing contractors)' who were 'applying for' or were 'associated with an application for another ITV programme contract', the Authority knew that existing contractors were still showing relatively little interest either individually or collectively in the exploitation of the hours between 6 a.m. and 9.15 a.m. Yorkshire TV and Tyne Tees TV had tried out an experimental weekday programme 'Good Morning Television' for nine weeks in April and May 1977, but resources had been limited, there had been no national news base and only modest promotion. There had been no real model there, therefore, nor had it been intended that there should be. The Authority itself limited the promotion of its own proposal when it left open in the first paragraph of its Foreword the possibility of pre-empting the national 'Breakfast Time' service on special occasions and making 'special arrangements, failing agreement among all contractors, where the area contractors could be engaged in a continuous broadcasting activity spanning the 6.00 a.m. to 9.15 a.m. period (for example, after polling at a general election).'

There might be exciting occasions, therefore, when a breakfast company might not operate. There was a further limitation. Whenever it did operate, news and current affairs, of course, were to be its main staple. It was not to go the way of some American commercial companies.

There was remarkable openness, nonetheless, in the third paragraph of the Particulars where the Authority asked applicants to state how they would relate their operations, if at all, to those of existing contractors:

Although the service is seen as being provided by a single programme contractor, the Authority is asking applicants to say whether they have in mind the introduction in due course of regionally originated elements, and, if so, whether some cooperation with regional ITV programme contractors is envisaged.

There was one existing interest within the independent television broadcasting system which was bound to be affected by what would happen after a breakfast-time contract was

111

issued. The Foreword to the Particulars, produced by the Authority, was compelled to make reference to the special position of ITN, the news organization which already operated within the Authority's own framework and which in an IBA statement of November 1979 had explicitly been granted 'news provision' for Channel 4. In the case of 'Breakfast Time', however, it was equally explicitly stated by contrast, that 'the Authority is making no stipulation that the news content should be provided by ITN.' Applicants would be asked, however, 'to say what kind of association or cooperation (if any) they would contemplate with ITN.' In fact, of course, ITN was to submit its own application: its executives believed that they already had all the necessary facilities at their disposal.

It was also a fact that much of the pressure for a separate breakfast-time service had come from journalists associated with the press and television, some of them inclined to regard ITN not merely as an interest, but as a vested interest. They were professionals looking for new roles and keen to experiment with new formats and techniques, and often by instinct as well as by experience they were critical not only of rivals but of 'administrators' and 'managers'. They wanted to run their own show. Among the groups which had lobbied the IBA in 1978 and 1979 and which were to submit applications for the new contract, two were led by journalists; and although interest in 'Breakfast Time' was shown too, even at that time, by financial interests, the professionals were looking for finance rather than the financiers for professionals. In general, indeed, as far as both professionals and financiers were concerned, the search for quick profits was less important as an incentive in 1980 than the knowledge that in the case of this particular contract there was no incumbent to dislodge. The field, apart from the presence of ITN, was clear. And detailed plans about the other new venture, Channel 4, which was also to attract professional talent, had not yet been published.

As far as profit expectations were concerned, it was considered that, while profits might take time to accrue, it would be possible to make an operational start with only modest initial capital and, because of newer and cheaper technologies, with minimal risks. Estimates of likely audience size and likely advertising revenues – and these were made chiefly by consultants – could vary considerably, of course, as the detailed applications were being prepared. Moreover, so also could suggestions about the necessary initial inputs of capital. For the most part, 'economy' was never a main consideration. Low costs might be an incentive, but so too could the thought of glamour to come.

The IBA seems to have devoted little attention as a body to basic economics. When the 'Breakfast Time' idea was first canvassed there were IBA officials at Brompton Road, nevertheless, who saw the financial issues in different terms from the applicants. A separate national contract for 'Breakfast Time' seemed to them unnecessary: at best, it would divert capital from the other parts of a system which already required substantial new investment. What, they asked, would be the effects of a breakfast-time contract on the future financing of Channel 4 and of new independent local radio stations to which the Authority was committed? Once established, they went on, would the winner of a new breakfast-time contract earn enough revenue to maintain the viability of the programming arrangements it had set out in its application?

In deciding to go ahead the Authority doubtless assumed that breakfast television would not divert investment from other parts of the system and that it would introduce to independent broadcasting a new audience without at the same time involving deleterious consequences for existing contractors through significantly reduced takings from advertisers. In any case, as far as the Authority was concerned, the risk would be passed on for, as a crucial sentence in the Foreword to the Particulars put it, 'A national breakfast-time service would need to be self-financing and pay the Authority a realistic rental (initially not less than £500,000 per annum, to be subject to later increases in the light of the results of the service).' Whoever else lost, the Authority would gain.

This sentence, more definite than most of the others, obviously did not chill would-be applicants. Some of them at least had made sophisticated surveys and forecasts before the closing date for applications, 9 May 1980, the same date as that for applicants for the other contracts. One detailed survey by Harold Lind, commissioned for a group chaired by Lord Lever, shrewdest of all financiers, reckoned that advertising revenue would depend not on any distinctive features of breakfast-time as sales time, but on the same factors as other advertising revenue: it might amount, it was estimated, to around £12 million by the mid-1980s (only 1 per cent of all advertising revenue). ITV as a whole would not suffer seriously, therefore, nor would Channel 4. Meanwhile, two independent local radio managing directors, who joined competing applicant 'Breakfast Time' companies, argued that television and sound radio at breakfast-time could complement each other to the profit of both; and one of them invited all the other ITV companies to associate themselves with the consortium he had joined. Possible BBC competition was usually left completely out of the picture.

The detailed questionnaire for applicants, requiring information – and, indeed, commitments – under nine subject headings, included two subparagraphs containing two leading questions concerning future finance. First, on what assumptions of audience size and nature had the estimates of revenue been reached? Second, what would the applicant do if his estimates of revenue were not realized? (The Authority might also have posed the question to itself 'What would *it* do?') Such leading questions were even more basic than a further question asking what particular arrangements were planned for the sale of advertising time. There were no direct questions on management, however, the answers to which were to become very pertinent at a later stage, before and after the contract had been awarded, although applicants were asked to state what would be the relationship between their top executives and the board. Questions on the intended composition and structure of staffing duplicated those in the regional contracts questionnaires.

The eleven programme questions ranged from the general to the specific. What were the applicant's main programme intentions? How would he organize the supply of material for what was a new enterprise? What programme constituents would he propose and what would be the editorial pattern? Would there be a difference between weekday and weekend programmes? During what hours would he broadcast? Would the applicant seek to reach different sections of the audience at different times within that broadcasting period? What would be the place of regional elements within the programme mix? On what date would the applicant wish to begin operations, if not on 1 January 1982?

The content and order of the questionnaire reflected first thoughts on the part of the Authority, which demonstrated that it too felt the need to learn. Indeed, although this was not explicitly stated, the Authority knew that it would only be possible for it to judge the financial prospects of 'Breakfast Time' after it had collated all the possible evidence from different applicants. It was stated, therefore, that there would be discussion with applicants at a later stage and that the Authority would 'wish to approve' the constitution, list of directors and financial structure of the groups it was seriously considering. 'Any information about a company's business activities or about persons connected with the group which is confidential and which cannot be revealed publicly at this time may be communicated to the Authority at the interview stage,' although such information was to be kept back only when 'strictly necessary' (i.e. in the applicant's judgement).

In March and April 1980 the Authority had second and third thoughts about the publication of financial information, as it had also in the case of the regional contracts; and on 21 April it explicitly released applicants from public exposure of any of their financial plans. 'In view of price-sensitivity and other public considerations,' any applicant who asked to give his forecasts privately to the Authority would be allowed to do so. It would be up to each applicant to make the case that he, in particular, should be allowed to go ahead, proving in the eloquent words of *Broadcast* that he would be neither a lame duck nor a cuckoo in the nest.

At this decisive moment, as in 1955 when the first commercial companies won their contracts, American experience was deemed irrelevant to this country. There no commercial company depended on a breakfast-time service alone. The three networks gave sizable budgets to their early-morning programmes, but only 15 per cent of their viewers saw them and only 10 per cent of their profits were derived from them. In 1980 viewers in the United States were watching television for an average of forty hours a week as against twenty-one hours in the United Kingdom, and whereas in the United States there was a

115

large majority of homes with two television sets, in the United Kingdom there was only between 15 and 30 per cent. Within its social and cultural context 'Breakfast Time' was as British an idea as the traditional British breakfast of bacon and eggs, which, it should be added, was itself under threat – and had been for some years – in 1980.

Not everyone thought, however, that 'Breakfast Time' was as good an idea as bacon and eggs. Some people, indeed, challenged the claim of the IBA in its 1979–80 Annual Report that, by offering it, it was meeting a public need. For Alexander Chancellor, for example, writing in the *Spectator* in November 1980, the claim was humbug. And Chancellor was writing six months after no fewer than eight applications for the contract had been received and were being carefully considered at Brompton Road. 'The public need for breakfast television,' he argued, 'is no more evident than is the public need for any other inessential consumer product. The need will be created by marketing men. Breakfast television will fill two needs: the need of a certain number of people to make a lot of money and the need of any organization – in this case the IBA – to feel that it is expanding and increasing its power.'

The Authority published the names of the eight applicants on 10 May. They had each contrived to find a different name, but in two cases only just – AM Television (AMT), AMTV, Daybreak TV, Daytime TV, Good Morning TV, Morning TV and TV-AM (subsequently renamed TV-am). ITN, which only hours after submitting its application was involved in an awkward industrial dispute about ENG, electronic news gathering, submitted the application in its own name.

Whatever the attitudes of the first seven contenders towards each other, they were united in thinking that the contract should not go to ITN. They believed that there should be a plurality of news sources for television as there was for the press; and although there were groups among them that were willing to rely on ITN for some or even most of their projected news facilities, there were others which wanted to go it alone. The eight had to be united also, of course, in stressing by order if not by choice, as the IBA required, that they would provide a substantial diet of news and information at breakfast-time. Entertainment was to come second. The menu had to be presented, of course, they all recognized (with varying degrees of experience to sustain them), in such a way that it would suit the viewers' early-morning mood. There were to be other recurring items in everybody's diet also, like weather forecasts, but in suggesting how they would serve it up there were significant differences in the balance and in the designation of minor ingredients.

From the time that ITN submitted its own application it could take no part in discussion with any of the seven other applicants on their plans for presenting news; they themselves, therefore, had to deal separately with the IBA's questions about 'implications', not knowing whether they would be acceptable to ITN. The fact that ITN had been in dispute with members of its own workforce about the staffing implications of ENG at the time of making its application was a warning, however, to other contenders also, when they produced plans involving the use of new technology. It was unlikely that it would prove as 'cheap' as some of them had believed. There was no question that interested the unions more.

Since ITN was owned entirely by the existing fifteen commercial television companies, it was bidding within the system. Its chairman in 1980 was John Freeman of LWT and it claimed that it was 'uniquely equipped to produce a better service more economically than any other organization' and that 'its involvement in providing the broad range of breakfast-time television would powerfully reinforce its other worldwide operations.' Some of its staff had suggested that if it won the contract it should hive off its breakfast-time activities to a subsidiary company, but its board had decided against this. It would make full use, it stated, of its existing studios, its ENG units, its film facilities and the resources of its international newsfilm agency partner, UPITN.

In its specific programme proposals it offered fixed pattern segments, with a twenty-four-hour day-to-day computerized news and information service, presenting news items on a regular and strict schedule as its central activity. 'What's On' and sports programmes would be added on Saturdays, and children's interests and leisure interests would be covered on Sundays, when programmes would start not at 7 a.m., as on weekdays, but an hour later. 'Children Make the News' would be a Sunday feature. Weather forecasts would fit into both weekday and weekend timetables, and there would be a man–woman duo at the helm every morning. The country would be divided on a duo-basis also into two zones, with split feeds of commercials from London. There would be no need for any new facilities except a third studio, which was already being planned at Wells Street, and four extra ENG units.

Another applicant, Daybreak Television, with a share capital of £5 million, also began from established premises and was already connected with an extensive ITV operation. Among its principal shareholders were ACC (with 15 per cent), the holding company of ATV Network chaired by Lord Grade (which was also applying, with a new company, ATV Midlands, for the East–West Midlands franchise), and Express Newspapers, which had leapt to ATV's defence against its rivals. Great Universal Stores and Morgan Grenfell were also named as members of the consortium. The chairman, Sir Leo Pliatzky, sat on the ACC board, and the managing director, Francis Essex, sat on the ATV Network board. Daybreak proposed to base its operations on the Elstree television studios, owned by ACC, where under Essex as director of production the major network programmes of ATV were being produced in three large colour studios. A new Daybreak executive programme committee included Essex and Charles Wintour, who was also on the main board, Alan Whicker, William Davis, Professor Tessa Blackstone, Mike Brearley and Drusilla Beyfus; and 'Good Morning' programme plans (the title was the name of a rival contender) included music and news from 6.30 a.m. to 7 a.m. at the start of the day, a large number of short items in between with quick changes of subject, and short programmes for mothers and preschool children between 9 a.m. and 9.15 a.m., when breakfast was over. There would be adult education time at weekends before 8 a.m.

With Wintour's Fleet Street experience, Daybreak intended to organize its own news gathering while maintaining good relations with ITN. It would have six ENG units and, when established, small studios in the regions; there would be input points in Scotland, Wales and Northern Ireland. In dealing with industrial relations, a field that could not be ignored by any of the applicants, it would seek to avoid confrontational

118

approaches in its programmes, since 'few industrial disputes are solved between 7.00 a.m. and 9.00 a.m.'

As if to reinforce the point, it claimed that access to Elstree's varied activities – and staff – would carry with it a sharing of the burden of unsocial working. This was not the last time that talk of Elstree, already raised in the ATV application, figured prominently on the agenda.

A third applicant company, Good Morning Ltd, included on its board two well-known figures from the broadcasting world, Ned Sherrin and Julian Pettifer, and had among its consultants Phillip Whitehead MP, one of the most knowledgeable parliamentarians associated with that world, Sir Joseph Lockwood, with a long experience of EMI, and Miriam Stoppard. Also on the board was Tim Rice, writer of musicals, and Sir Peter Thornton, businessman and ex-civil servant, was chairman. The major shareholders were the music company, Chrysalis, Arbuthnot Latham, and very appropriately, given the named personnel in the application, the talent agency, MAM. The total number of staff would be kept low, it was stated, around forty-five, since the company had the AIR record studios for conversion and would contract with the facilities house TVI to provide facilities management and outside-broadcast and ENG equipment; 'hard news', including regional items, would be provided by ITN and ITV contractors. The company would have its own reporting teams and ENG units, but wanted ITN to employ special breakfast-time reporters in addition to its existing staff.

Among the programmes projected were a Saturday show taped before an audience 'by an exuberant character emphasizing the richness of life' and a Sunday children's phone-in programme called 'Have You Done Your Homework?' The weekday programmes would begin with a teleprinter news at 6 a.m. and with 'pure entertainment' from 9 a.m. to 9.30 a.m. A note of cheerful optimism, evident throughout the application, extended to the estimates of growth of gross advertising revenue. For the first year's operations these were set at £5 million, but they would quadruple, it was projected, in Year 3.

Morning Television, in this case unpreceded in its name by the adjective 'Good', proposed, nonetheless, a 'Good Morning Programme' from 6 a.m. to 9.15 a.m. with a 'recognizable and

119

reliable pattern'. Its share capital was set at £4·8 million, rather less than that of Daybreak, and 25 per cent of it would be on offer to the general public. Forty per cent of the voting rights would be vested in the founders. The board included Stefan Sargent of Molinare, the Soho sound and video facilities company which would provide studios, Michael Townson, editor of Thames's 'TV Eye' (non-executive), Graham Dowson, ex-managing director of Rank and ex-director of Southern Television, and a worker director to be named later.

Emphasis was placed in the application on independent news gathering and presentation. 'MTV believes that news gathering and reporting is the essential part of the responsibility for running a breakfast-time TV programme, and does not therefore propose to invite ITN to undertake any of these functions.' Five independent regional studios would be opened from the start, and there would be a small interview studio in London with two ENG cameras, shared by ENG units. A staff of eighty technicians, almost half of a total staff of 200, would be recruited and a new Molinare training school would be created.

Daytime Television Ltd, which had a planned capital expenditure of £2·75 million and a forecast net advertising revenue in its first year of £2·75 million, had a different history from the other contenders. It could be traced back to 1978, when thirty individuals who were 'dedicated to developing innovatory methods in television management, programming and the use of technology' met weekly to plan the future. The group's first objective was 'a better use' of day-time television hours in London (hence its title) than had been made, in its opinion, by ITV programme companies. It was interested also, however, in cassette recordings and video-tape services long before the challenge of the new communications technology hit newspaper headlines. DTV's first approach to the IBA was to suggest a three-way division of the London contract. The group would provide, alongside the existing contractors, a 'balanced output' of programmes between 8 a.m. and 6 p.m. on weekdays and 8 a.m. to 12 o'clock at weekends. It offered also to set up a trust which would play a part in programme planning and which would include staff representatives and an independent producer.

Such an approach was bound to fail. It broke against the rock

120

of the IBA's dependence on the network system. Neither of the existing London companies would have found it possible to work with a third group, no matter how talented. When the new contracts were announced, however, Daytime Television Ltd was re-formed to apply for the breakfast-time contract, with the Baroness Trumpington, Sir Arthur Sugden, chief executive of the Cooperative Wholesale Society, and Jerry Kuehl, ex-Thames and then head of studios of the National Film School, among its twelve non-executive directors. Four other members were to represent the interests of shareholders and employees – and the public interest.

DTV staff, it was promised, would reflect the composition of the UK audience and its 'interwoven minorities'. The company was committed to staff access to information, to extensive staff training, to a system of internal promotion and to regular consultation between staff and viewers about programme content. There were to be no shareholders with any stake in existing companies, and all shareholders had to have a reason, related to the company's purposes, for participating in the business. They included Philips Industries, Fitch and Company design consultants, British Printing Corporation Ltd, the Industrial Commerce and Finance Corporation Ltd (ICFC), Exchange Telegraph and, from contentious Merseyside, Liverpool Daily Post and Echo Ltd. Yet, for all the Merseyside connection, the regional offices, linked to a new London studio, were to be in Manchester and Glasgow.

The group, true to its origins, called for 'different corporate structures and a different style of management from anything so far attempted by British TV.' Transmission from 7 a.m. to 9.15 a.m. was to take the form of an informal rolling magazine programme, intended to brief viewers for the day ahead, but there would be an earlier slot for caption news, schools programmes to be recorded 'off-air', and for special broadcasts for the deaf. The main news stream – with ITN cooperation – would be planned so that there would be no talking down to the audience. Nor would the company seek consensus. Viewers would be expected to reach their own conclusions on the important issues. Minority issues (and presenters) were a part of the pattern. The studio set was to resemble a living room. Weekend programmes would be for the whole family, with imaginative use of visual effects. No parallel application – for any of the IBA contracts – was quite so 'socially purposive'.

Three other contenders with very similar names – AM Television (AMT), AMTV Ltd, and TV-am – all had nationally well-known names on their lists of board members, executive staff and consultants. All of them too had what seemed to be strong financial backing, and with famous names of institutions prominent among the backers. AMT had as chairman Christopher Chataway, four-minute miler and former Minister in charge of broadcasting, and as lead share-holder (with 20 per cent) Pearson Longman Ltd, one of Britain's best-known publishing houses. Directors included John Fairley from YTV (also involved in Mercia Television's application for the East and West Midlands contract), and Jimmy Gordon from Radio Clyde, and the group looked for its news service not to ITN but to the *Financial Times* and to the United States broadcasting network, CBS.

AMTV had Lord Lever, Minister in the last Labour Government, as its chairman and the *Guardian*, the *Observer*, the *Economist*, Mills and Allen International plc, Capital Radio (heading a group of independent local radio companies) and Radio-Télé-Luxembourg among the formidable array of its shareholders. Directors included Sir Claus Moser of the *Economist*, Covent Garden and Rothschilds, Sara Morrison, who had sat on the Annan Committee, Herbert Hardy, a director of LWT, Professor Alan Thompson, formerly BBC national governor for Scotland, and John Whitney, managing director of Capital, who was to succeed Sir Brian Young as Director General of the Authority.

TV-am, a brainchild of one of the best-known television personalities, David Frost, and of Michael Rosenberg, deputy chairman of Frost's production company, David Paradine Productions Ltd, had Peter Jay, former British Ambassador to the United States, as chairman and Sir Richard Marsh, former Minister in a Labour Government and now chairman of the Newspaper Publishers Association, as his deputy. Its directors included Paul Hamlyn, chairman of the Octopus publishing group and a director of News International plc, and Jonathan and Timothy Aitken, the former a Conservative MP and chairman of a new investment company, the latter cited as director of Investment Intelligence Ltd; both were descendants of the press tycoon, Lord Beaverbrook, who had been no lover of television. Other people associated with the venture were well-known inside and outside the industry – Michael Parkinson, Michael Deakin, Nick Elliott and Robert Kee.

Each of these three groups had money as well as names at its disposal. AMTV and TV-am, for instance, each had £8 million of capital available. AMT contemplated two possible future scenarios. Television advertising revenue was envisaged as rising in the 'low' scenario from £8·2 million in 1982 to £14·3 million in 1984 and as rising in the 'high' scenario from £9·4 million to £18 million. In the light of what was to happen after 1982 – as described briefly below in chapter 8 – it is fascinating to look back at these projections.

The programme plans of the three companies were ambitious too, with TV-am stressing the 'paramount' importance of 'flexibility of daily response' and of its 'mission to explain', a brilliant phrase of Peter Jay. Unlike AMT, AMTV wished for cooperation with ITN from which it would take regional materials; like AMT, it would have no regional offices of its own, it stated, but would employ its own news-gathering teams and arrange for additional backing from Visnews and the US Cable News Network. TV-am said that it would like short bulletins and other coverage from ITN, but added that, like other contenders, it had not been able to discuss possible cooperation with ITN to sort out details. It planned regional studios in Glasgow, Manchester and Cardiff to inject or to opt-out news and other items – with Birmingham and Belfast to be added at a later stage – and if ITN's services were not available, it added, it would provide a full alternative service of its own.

While AMT stated that it would lease studio facilities in Central London, AMTV was proposing a purpose-built studio near Sadlers Wells which would incorporate a computerized newsroom. TV-am said that it would base itself at the studio of the former fashion designer, Keith Ewart, in Wandsworth, South London.

There were differences also in programming plans. AMT offered a varied magazine programme with special segments, including the arts (with book reviews and criticisms of first-night performances of plays), education (with a 'School Report'

123

at weekends in which pupils would be invited to submit reports on their schools) and 'humour' (with AMT 'humour columnists'). AMTV talked of three regular presenters of news, starting with a 'First Edition' at 7 a.m., and of a gossip columnist and a guest cartoonist. It would set up a formidable editorial committee from the *Guardian*, the *Observer* and the *Economist*, it promised, and would present the television equivalent of a weekly periodical at weekends.

TV-am, which remarked genially that successful morning programmes would be regarded by their viewers 'with special attention and affection at the outset of their working day', stated that it would plan 'reality programming' to meet its 'proper entertainment function' alongside its 'serious social function'. It would offer four programmes – the 'Early Show' on weekdays from 6.15 a.m. to 7 a.m., perhaps extended in time from 6 a.m.; the 'Breakfast Show' on weekdays from 7 a.m. to 9.15 a.m.; the 'Saturday Show' from 6.45 a.m. to 9.15 a.m. on Saturdays; and the 'Sunday Show' from 7.15 a.m. to 9.15 a.m. on Sundays. Each 'show' would be geared to its time and its day and to the needs of its audience, with whom the company would seek to open up a 'dialogue'. The first programme would have a team of young presenters with a 'free-wheeling approach' to news. The second programme would be a magazine, 'popular intelligent journalism in all aspects', with contributions from five well-known presenters, three of whom were named in the initial applications – Frost, Parkinson and Kee; each would appear exclusively for twenty-six weeks in a year for the initial two years. (At that time Esther Rantzen and Angela Rippon, who had agreed to join the company, would not allow their names to be divulged, and Anna Ford did not join until October 1980.) The third and fourth programmes would incorporate documentary features, and special units would be set up to prepare them during the course of the week. There would be 121 TV-am staff in London and twenty-two in each regional centre.

No chief executive had been appointed when the application was made after a hectic weekend of joint production. Peter Jay, as chairman, was responsible for the form that it took and for its style. He had no hesitation in affirming that he was exceptionally qualified to oversee the translation of TV-am's ideas and ideals into a 'practical and successful service to the public'. The projected names of the first director of programmes and the first director of features (Nicholas Elliott and Michael Deakin) were not then announced, and Elliott was to drop out later. Although the application was something of an individual *tour de force*, the main emphasis in it was on collective effort. 'TV-am feel that the spirit of a cooperative of highly experienced and responsible broadcasting professionals, both in front of and behind the camera, is the proper inspiration for British television in launching this new development.'

Faced with such a striking array of names and ideas, not just in this application but in many of the others, the IBA must have been surprised and dazzled on 9 May 1980; and the public, whatever its previous interest in the breakfast-time venture, must have been equally dazzled when the details were published a day later. Nonetheless, there was an element of concern too at Brompton Road. Was not the breakfast contract drawing off professional talent as well as financial investment, talent which otherwise would have been employed in the general system? Press concern on a very different point had already been expressed in the *Sunday Times* on 13 April. Would not the breakfast-time contract (and Channel 4) provide the IBA with a smokescreen behind which the Authority could 'hand back the current franchises unscathed'?

The dazzle survived both concerns, neither of which was to linger. By December 1980 the Authority was justifying its decision to initiate the new service by pointing to the number of applicants for the contract; and, long before then, sections of the press had come to recognize that there was no smokescreen and that there might well be dramatic changes in other contracts also. Meanwhile the public meetings went ahead with far less publicity than might have been expected given press headlines like 'News with the Cornflakes' or 'Breakfast with Anna'. On 24 September a promised public meeting at Croydon to discuss the breakfast-time contract took the form of a personality parade, but the general public was less conspicuous, and it was less conspicuous still at Darlington where representatives of the eight applicants and of the press seem to have outnumbered the local audience. Where else at one meeting, however, could any audience have heard in turn (according to the alphabetical order of the names of their groups) Christopher Chataway, Lord Lever, Francis Essex, Baroness Trumpington, Julian Pettifer, David Nicholas, Robin Scott and Peter Jay?

Towards the end of October Ladbrokes had opened a book on the IBA breakfast-time award. The odds then were:

ITN	5 to 2
AMTV	3 to 1
Morning TV	3 to 1
Daybreak TV	16 to 1
TV-am	7 to 2
AMT	6 to 1
Good Morning TV	14 to 1
Daytime TV	20 to 1

It was not until 11 December, late in the interviewing process, that the eight applicants, each of which had survived bouts of publicity and of indifference, were summoned to Brompton Road; and by then the Authority itself had doubtless learned more of the problems and opportunities of the venture than it had known in January 1980. It had also received the views of applicants for ITV contracts on the merits and likely consequences of breakfast television. 'ATV wishes well to the possibility of the establishment of a separate breakfast-time service consisting primarily of news and information' was the message from the sitting company in Birmingham. 'We do not at this stage plan to contribute to such a service, although we would not preclude the possibility in the future.' 'In time it might well become a showpiece of British television,' LWT suggested. Yet it seemed improbable, LWT went on, that during the early 1980s at least adequate advertisement revenue would be obtained 'to fund both the fourth channel and breakfast-time television in addition to the existing ITV service,' stressing also that thus even 'a successful separate breakfast-time service' would be 'likely to be particularly damaging to the London Weekend company.' YTV felt that Channel 4 should come first. Thames, welcoming the initiative of the Authority in opening up the possibility of a breakfast-time service, opted firmly and unequivocally for handing it over to ITN: 'we believe it to represent a lively and realistic guarantee of journalistic excellence.' Among new applicants TSW supported ITN also, while TVS replied to the Authority that it was 'not convinced of the need for a completely separate breakfast-time service either on programme or on financial grounds.'

There were as many varieties of response from the eight applicants for the breakfast-time service as there were from the existing companies which had been asked their views about it, and the lessons were by no means clear. The range of estimates for capital expenditure, for example, was wide – from around £3 million to £10 million (including loan on call). Estimates of advertising revenue were even wider. Thus TV-am, which reserved its estimates for the Authority, contemplated £20 million in the first year, while Good Morning drew on a more modest forecast commissioned from MORI. In Year 1 there would be £5 million, in Year 2 £8 million and only in Year 3 £20 million. Two leading agencies prepared diametrically different forecasts of ratings. Studio plans were equally diverse, as were estimates of size of staffs.

It is impossible to tell how searching were the interviews of the eight applicants on Wednesday and Thursday, 10 and 11 December, but there was certainly little time to probe. Three companies were seen in the afternoon of the 10th and five between 9.30 a.m. and 5.10 p.m. on the 11th (with a short working lunch of an hour for members of the Authority). One remarkable comment of Anna Ford has survived from the TV-am interviews. 'If you give us the franchise and we do not succeed, our reputations are at stake.'

ITN was still being quoted by Ladbrokes at 3 to 1 in the second week of December, when there had been some shifting in the odds. They now read:

ITN	3 to 1
AMTV	4 to 1
Morning TV	3 to 1
Daybreak TV	9 to 2
TV-am	9 to 2
AMT	6 to 1
Good Morning TV	8 to 1
Daytime TV	20 to 1

And there were still two weeks to go.

6

The Ordeal

AFTER SUBMITTING THEIR applications, each of the various contenders for the sixteen franchises, including 'Breakfast Time', had to face an ordeal which inevitably lasted for several months and which went through several different phases. The crucial stage doubtless seemed to be the contract interviews held in private at IBA headquarters, and these were scheduled – after revision – from 10 a.m. on Wednesday, 22 October – that for Northern Ireland TV, a newcomer, and at 11.20 a.m. on the same day that for Ulster TV, the sitting incumbent – until 3.50 p.m. on Thursday, 11 December – that for Daybreak, one of the 'Breakfast Time' consortia.

The contenders knew, of course, that all this time the IBA would or might be discussing them behind the scenes. They knew also that although their formal contacts with the Authority would be limited and that there would be no private talk or social contact on the side, they would be expected to answer supplementary questions on their applications and on their replies to them at unscheduled dates between September and November; every conceivable 'fact' might be required at that date. They knew further that regional public meetings had been arranged by the IBA in the name of 'public accountability' at which they would listen to questions and, in no more than seven minutes each, present their case. The meetings would be chaired by the IBA members who would be involved in the final decisions. Not surprisingly some of the contenders took the advice of consultants, including old officials of the IBA, as to how best to stand up to this ordeal. They were used to the idea of 'dry runs' and they decided to try them now. Only one contender, Tellecom (Broadcast) Television Ltd, fell out before the ordeal was through.

The companies in possession were, for all their experience, at something of a disadvantage in the protracted franchise process. For one thing, they still had to go on providing the daily fare of television while thinking about what would happen after January 1982. Like the IBA itself, they had routine business to transact, and at least one programme controller felt that the franchise affair took up too much time. He and his colleagues were concerned inevitably about the possibility of falling advertising revenue, of new wage demands and of industrial disputes, and of the likely impact of Channel 4 on their fortunes; and, given the procrastination of the Government, even had there been no franchise process they would still have felt some apprehension about the future. The 'pre-election period' had been too long and there had been too many shifts of mood within it. The fact that it was not until 13 November 1980 that the Broadcasting Act was passed was bound to worry them more than it worried the new contenders.

There was a third kind of ordeal all contenders had to face. The local press watched their moves, following its own timetable, collecting readers' letters and making its own editorial judgements, usually concentrating, as was almost inevitable, on the shortcomings of the company at present holding the contract. News and views could easily be fused. Moreover, some issues and some names inevitably attracted national attention. What happened in the West, where it was impossible to keep Peter Cadbury out of the headlines, was given more attention nationally than what happened in London, for it had many of the ingredients of a drama on the television screen. And there was a wide range of contrasting characters in the cast, capable of as many surprises as Cadbury. In July 1980, for example, Bill Cheevers, managing director of Westward until he was ousted by Cadbury after a defeated boardroom coup of 1970, made news of his own when he penned his signature to an affidavit pledging his support to Cadbury who was himself ousted as chairman by Lord Harris of Greenwich. And Harris himself made news in September 1980 when he turned to the IBA in an effort to seek its support should an extraordinary general meeting of shareholders result in Cadbury being reinstated. This was widely felt to be a desperate resort. And there was more news to come before Cadbury finally cut all his financial links with Westward in November. Cadbury himself, accompanied by his solicitor, had met Lady Plowden, Lord Thomson, Sir Brian Young and Anthony Pragnell on 14 October at Brompton Road three days before the extraordinary general meeting was due to be called. In the light of that meeting, which was vividly reported in sections of the press, the extraordinary general meeting of Westward shareholders was adjourned *sine die*, but even that was not the end of the affair, for a requisition order was served on the Westward board by dissident shareholders in December three weeks before the contract for the South-West was announced.

There were other areas besides the South-West which received particular attention in the national as well as in the local press, among them the Midlands and Yorkshire. ATV was an 'alien face' in the Midlands, a Birmingham councillor was reported as complaining on 16 October 1980: 'They have more in common with bloody downtown San Francisco.' 'TV Men plead, protect us from our Bosses' ran a *Sunday Times* headline about Yorkshire on 11 November. Yet such remarks did not go unchallenged. The *Daily Telegraph* in a leader 'Brum on the Box' rightly pointed out that 'a diet of town hall news is not as universally appealing as councillors understandably think it should be', while the *Daily Express* in more militant mood boldly asserted that the pity was that Lord Grade of ATV was not 'running Birmingham' in place of the local councillors. The fact that Sir Harold Wilson was made chairman of the contending Yorkshire consortium, Television Yorkshire, would once have been greater national news than it was, but both he and Jonathan Aitken, who was to make greater television news in the future, had their share of it. The possibility of 'Ilkla Moor baht Trident' was the headline of a *Daily Telegraph* article in November 1980.

Other areas figured in the national press only from time to time, but they too could occasionally be treated in depth. Thus, the *Daily Telegraph*, which had more to say about the franchise affair than any other national newspaper, featured the South and South-East on 15 September – in the wake of a public meeting at Canterbury – and the role of Trident not in

Yorkshire but in the North-East on 3 November. No contender in that area could have been greatly pleased with a comprehensive comment in the *New Statesman* (7 November) that 'what is beyond dispute is that whoever wins, the Tyneside viewers will lose.' It was a specialized publication, *TV Home and Video*, however, which went further when it scathingly dismissed London Independent Television on the basis of one programme – 'one wonders whether the IBA can seriously consider a bidder whose spokesman was responsible for one of the worst programmes ever to be screened on ITV, "Double Your Money".'

The public meetings had become a necessary element in the process of franchise allotment – and they figured both in the IBA's plans and in the Government's own proposals for the future when at last details of them were announced – but they were strongly criticized at the time both locally and nationally. The most pungent critic was the *Spectator*, another invaluable press source, which claimed that the people attending them were so unrepresentative of viewers as a whole that they could not have been better chosen had that been the object: the IBA 'travelled the land, listening to the opinions of twenty thousand of the unlikeliest people ever to pose as the general public.' 'They will begin a series of public meetings,' Patrick Sergeant wrote in the *Daily Mail* before the first meeting was held, 'which on form will be attended mainly by members of Gay Lib, the Festival of Light, and those with the hope of catching an off-duty glimpse of Melvyn Bragg.' This was a mockery of the idea of 'taking the public's mind', it was suggested, which did not go as far as the 'Ascertainment Surveys' of the American Federal Communications Commission which were explicitly directed to 'community leaders . . . who can logically speak for others within the community and within their areas of interest and expertise.'

A correspondent of the *Financial Weekly* who attended the Canterbury meeting in September came to the conclusion that out of the 350 people present there was only the 'occasional average viewer'. The rest were 'consortium people', their local supporters, mobilized with varying degrees of efficiency, although the power to muster was hardly a fair test of the likely efficiency of the contenders as programme providers; observers from other franchise areas; and 'a dozen or so local councillors and local authority officials' whose 'sole purpose appeared to be to persuade whichever applicant was eventually successful that their boroughs had ideal sites for new studios.' 'What happened at Canterbury,' the report concluded, 'may, as the IBA claims, be taken into account when decisions are made, but it is hard to believe that the proceedings, for all their lucid exposition and impassioned polemic, can carry more than token weight in the Authority's deliberations.'

Broadcast, which chose as its headline for its report on the same meeting 'IBA's Canterbury Tales', described it as 'a strictly middle-class, middle-aged, middle-of-the-road affair': 'of those 300 people at the meeting only a handful were *bona fide* disinterested, genuine 22 carat viewers. . . . So few were they – and so many were the vested interests,' it went on, 'that it was the independent members of the public that felt it necessary to situate themselves, claiming no interest whatsoever other than the one interest which the IBA had come down to listen to: the quality of programme output.'

Such reports in *Broadcast* were acute and well written and focused on issues as well as on personalities. The financial issues were well taken up too in the financial press and in the business columns of the national newspapers, particularly in April 1980 at the time of publication of a Vickers da Costa report on ITV revenue and profits. Yet the emphasis could be quite different there from the emphasis in the columns devoted to broadcasting. It was left to *Marketing Week*, however, to suggest (11 April 1980) that, while the views of investors were being watched carefully, the IBA had made no efforts to consult 'the putative funders of the next round of successful ITV contractors – the advertisers. . . . One wonders what the Authority in charge of all this . . . is up to?' *Campaign* maintained firmly from inside the advertising world (16 May 1980) that 'what would not be sensible, or merited, would be for any of the present television contractors to be ousted altogether in favour of some totally new company.'

Within less than a month of this statement the first of the IBA's final public meetings was held at St Helier in Jersey on 3 June. All in all, there were twenty of them, the last in Aberdeen on 30 October. They followed in the wake, of course, of the

IBA's preliminary round of meetings in 1979 and the first three months of 1980. They were advertised publicly in the press and on the air, and were sometimes chaired not by a Member but by the Chairman or the Vice-Chairman of the Authority. They were taken seriously enough by other Authority Members to be present at times, along with at least four members of the IBA staff, among them the Director General, the Director of Television, and the Chief Engineer; although, as *Broadcast* also put it, what they could have learned from them 'remains a mystery'. There were certainly more grumbles than opinions, and since the IBA's functions were often misunderstood by the public, there had, of course, to be some outlining of these – not always complete and not always to the satisfaction of the audience. Not even Lady Plowden could compel the Welsh audience to accept her ruling that the Cardiff meeting was not being called together to discuss how Welsh Television should be organized.

Attendances varied. Some were low – there were only 150 at Manchester and Liverpool – but there were 800 people present in the Queen's Hotel in Leeds and 600 people present at Queen's University in Belfast; and there were audiences of 500 people at the London franchise meetings at Caxton Hall chaired by Lady Plowden. The Liverpool meeting, like earlier meetings in Liverpool, was dominated by the pressure groups for a separate franchise for Merseyside. According to the *Liverpool Echo* (7 July, 1980), which detected in consequence signs of a greater attention to Liverpool on the part of Granada even before the IBA decision was reached, 'irate councillors and frustrated businessmen' were using the meeting only to bombard 'IBA officials for an independent TV service for Merseyside'.

Stacy Marking of Daytime Television, who attended Cardiff and Bristol meetings to discuss 'the West', was struck by the fact that at Bristol as well as at Cardiff opposition to the dual contract for Wales and the West was the main feature. She felt that Anthony Pragnell, Deputy Director of the IBA, was confronted with a very difficult task in trying to explain that the decision taken in 1979, to retain a dual region, had been based on financial considerations. 'We are the customers,' a Portishead councillor told him at the Bristol meeting, 'you are providing a service, and we feel that the service is wrong.'

Attempts by the IBA Chairman, Vice-Chairman or Members to prod the local audiences into talking about general issues like breakfast television or competition with the BBC were for the most part unsuccessful. Regional or more narrowly local issues always predominated. At Nottingham, for example, where there was little criticism of ATV's programme record, there was no enthusiasm for the IBA's splitting up the Midlands region. Indeed, the IBA was criticized more than ATV. At Leeds a former Lord Mayor of Sheffield won laughter and applause when he insisted that 'the centre of the universe is not Leeds, it is Sheffield.' There was an extra element of drama at Leeds, however, when a former ACTT shop steward attacked the claims of the new contender, Television Yorkshire, to be offering the prospect of a new and more responsive management. 'I would not trust this lot as far as I could throw them,' he declared.

Viewing conditions, the responsibility of the IBA rather than of the contractors, were very widely raised – at the Norwich meeting, for example, and at Canterbury. Yet at the latter meeting Anglia, criticized at the first, was held up by one speaker as an example of what a regional station should be. At the final London meeting in Caxton Hall, presided over by Lady Plowden, it seemed for a time that there would be no questions at all. An attempt by the Chairman to start off with financial issues met with no response. Individual programmes were barely discussed, although as the meeting went on lobbies took over. An attempt to raise the question of the strike then in progress at Capital Radio was firmly put down by the Chairman. 'This meeting is about television,' she explained.

The short 'sales pitch' speeches made by representatives of the contenders at the end of the meetings did not always suggest that the spokesmen making them were very knowledgeable about salesmanship or, indeed, were in the communications business at all. Some of the audience walked out while they were being made; others shuffled in their seats. There were many contrasts of style, however, from the brash to the softly persuasive, and a few of the speakers, not necessarily those whose companies were to win the contracts, were said to be excellent. At least a majority of speakers were carefully prepared. From verbatim transcripts of the meetings, always a difficult source for the historian, many of the rest of the speeches delivered at the meetings look verbose and rambling, though there were occasional flashes of wit. Some of the sitting companies made what was perhaps the most effective use of the meetings by inviting members of the audience to write to them or to take up with them some of the subjects which had been discussed. Most of their representatives, however, would probably have agreed with Lord Windlesham that 'the incumbent' usually received more criticism than the other contenders, often, of course, *from* the other contenders.

The most informed meeting appears to have been that at Glasgow where, according to Doreen Taylor who reported for *Broadcast*, more questioners than usual had taken the trouble to read and digest the full version of all the applicants' proposals. Yet even there, she concluded, 'what emerged most strongly was the misunderstanding of the functions and role of the IBA itself, its various advisory committees and how the public could ask it to respond.'

It is highly doubtful whether the public meetings contributed anything substantial to the internal discussions of the Authority, its judgement of the contenders or its decisions on the structure of the system from 1982, although in supplementary questions to the franchise applicants in October 1980 it asked them if they wished to say more about questions asked or points made at the meetings. The border area problems, which had been raised more frequently than any others and which would have involved transfers of relay stations from one company to another, were already well known to the IBA's engineers and to the regional officers before the 1980 meetings took place; indeed, the engineers already knew the limited range of options and had settled in the published contract offers on the ones they preferred. At most, the speeches made by the contending spokesmen at the end of the meetings served as an introductory prelude to the franchise interviews in the autumn for those Members of the Authority or of its staff who were present.

The Chairman of the Authority, recollecting in relative tranquillity in February 1981, felt that the meetings provided 'as good public participation as you can get'. Yet a serious attempt to test opinion on the applications would have had to take a different form from a public meeting at which a 'platform party' confronted an unrepresentative audience sitting below it. In at least one area a local newspaper challenged the chosen method of testing opinion. The *Exeter Express and Echo*, which conducted a readers' poll on local attitudes towards the programme performance of Westward, sent a copy of the conclusions to the Home Secretary.

In Yorkshire, where the company challenging YTV held meetings of its own, one of them was attended by around 600 Yorkshire Television employees. 'I've never seen such a movement of staff together, not even during a strike,' reported Stella Richman, and there were complaints that on this occasion there was no IBA presence. Subsequently, in November 1980, following a less well-attended meeting in Leeds Trade Hall, a 'unique' poll of staff showed 492 in favour of the proposed TVY, 184 against, but there were 1100 YTV staff in all and it was possible, therefore, for a trade unionist to challenge the result at the IBA's public meeting. In the Midlands, one of the most important trade unions, the ACTT, placed its weight behind the existing contractor as did many trade unionists representing workers in the industry in other areas. It urged, as its journal *Film and Television Technician* put it, that workers should be given 'basic job protection' on any reallocation of a contract; and at the end of the day its general secretary was to claim in the same journal that the Authority had acted 'like hooligans'.

Another fierce critic, writing in the *New Music News* in May 1980 before the sequence of public meetings began, complained that 'despite an avalanche of publicity, the decision-making process . . . will not be subject to any *effective* public scrutiny. . . . It is disgraceful that the IBA will be allowed to mount the debate in public and then retreat to smoke-filled rooms to make its decision.' And an added point was made in the same month by Allen Wright in a report in the *Scotsman* with the headline 'Secrecy obscures the Franchise Battle'.

In fact, the second stage of the ordeal faced by the contenders – the interviews by the Authority – was a secret stage, and even now some of the people who were interviewed are unsure, first, why the interview took the form that it did and, second, how important it was in the Authority's own decision-making process. So much seemed to have been predetermined, not always as a result of detailed study of all their relevant materials. The interviews themselves, which were attended by the IBA's top executive staff, were crammed into eleven Wednesdays and Thursdays; and one further day, Thursday, 17 December, was devoted entirely to members' private discussion, for which the staff provided supporting analytical papers setting out options. There was no dialogue at all, of course, at this point, and when on 18 December the 'normal Authority meeting' was held there were 'no lunch guests'.

The programme for each interviewing day allowed half an hour's preliminary discussion at 9.30 a.m. to precede two interviews which were held before a one-hour working lunch (except on the two Thursdays when 'normal' IBA meetings took up the morning); after discussion over lunch of the morning's interviews, two or three further interviews followed. Discussion of these was usually expected to start after 5 p.m. and on two occasions at 6 p.m. The scheduled length of every interview was one hour and twenty minutes, although some overran to one and a half hours and in one case (the ATV interview on the first day) to two. The whole of one Wednesday and the morning of a Thursday were devoted to the six contenders for the South and South-East dual region contract, and one Wednesday for the two Yorkshire and Tyne Tees contracts in each of which Trident was involved. Verbatim reports of the interviews were made by the IBA, destined only for the eyes of the participants on each side of the table. It is clear that the interviewers on the Authority's side were carefully preprogrammed, with specific questions – and roles – assigned to individual Members, and that the Chairman, Lady Plowden, present on all occasions, kept a firm hand on the proceedings.

A point of particular interest in many of the interviews was the financial structure of the company. The Authority had obviously decided to test the views of existing contract holders on the possibility of redistributing shares, giving a bias to people living in the area, and this topic was raised doggedly and apparently naively even to the exclusion of other financial issues, some of which were of special importance to the contenders. Where other financial topics were raised, there seems to have been considerable miscommunication so that what happened in further talk after the interview, even after the contract awards, was more crucial than what happened at the meeting itself. The bigger network companies, like LWT and Granada, on which the future of the system depended, seem to have been able through forceful presentation to raise their own questions about escalating programme costs and the failure of the IBA to pay enough attention to their implications.

The final outcome of all the IBA's contract awarding process, described below in chapter 7, was, of course, 'a package', and the form that the package took reflected not only separate decisions on the fate of the contenders in particular areas but the attempts by the Chairman and the members to secure what they could present to the public as a 'balanced settlement' for the system as a whole. In dealing, therefore, with ATV or with the two Trident companies, however much the Authority focused on the local situation in Birmingham, Leeds or New-castle, it had to weigh very carefully the consequences of undermining the financial basis of the system. Indeed, its Members knew that if they could make only limited changes in key places, the only radical changes that they could make were in a limited number of regions. In such circumstances they were bound to look at the interviews from very different vantage points from those of the individual contenders.

Whatever their experience, the contenders must have found it difficult, as in an academic examination, to assess the importance of written work and oral presentation. A few, among them the two new companies which were to be successful – TVS and TSW – perhaps because of their success, look back with actual enjoyment to the oral test. A few, among them Southern, which was to lose its contract, look back with amazement, feeling that it was extraordinary that in a bland interview there were few, if any, intimations of the possible fate in store, and that major questions relating both to finance and to programming were never put at all. Other interviews, among them interviews of companies whose contracts were renewed, appear to have been more robust, with hard hitting and good humour on both sides. Yet there were contenders also who saw the Authority's questions as ill-informed and combative, and one contender complained that a request to add an explanatory statement was denied.

One of the most interesting recollections of an interview has been recorded by Kevin Goldstein-Jackson of Television South-West, which was to win the contract for the South-West. 'The interview was quite extraordinary,' he told a *TV World* reporter in February 1984.

First, they asked where Jonathan Harvey was. I told them he wasn't a director. They asked why the co-founder of TSW wasn't a director, and I told them he was an artist. Before I could explain further they interrupted, 'You need say no more, we understand.' In fact Jonathan never wanted to be a director of TSW. I couldn't understand that we weren't grilled. There wasn't a question we couldn't answer, but nothing gave us the least worry. I suppose we got the contract because we *were* different and because I was able to say we had the million pounds not in promises but signed up.

Individual and company reactions to the interviews varied in part – although certainly not exclusively for this reason – according to experience. All the existing contractors, or the individuals representing them at the interviews, had been through the awards process before on one or more occasions. They were known corporately and individually to the IBA members and staff – some, indeed, were ex-employees of the IBA – through working relationships and, in most cases, through social contact. There may have been an element of advantage here for the experienced over the newcomers to compensate for the relative advantages newcomers had at the public hearings. Yet in the case of Southern, at least, there was no sense of advantage. Indeed, among most of the existing contractors there was some doubt, fanned perhaps by press speculation, as to the status of the interview, 'the supreme moment of the IBA's power', within the contract-allotting process. While it was the climax of the whole process, was it as significant an evaluating instrument as it might have been? Had the Chairman, if not the Members, already made up her mind? Just what was predetermined? How much was façade? Given the obvious imperfections of public meetings as evaluating instruments, such questions were of considerable importance.

There was special importance too, therefore, in any supplementary questions which the Authority was disposed to ask after the interview was over. It does not seem to have made much use of these in relation to the companies which were to lose their contracts or the companies which were to replace them. It had put supplementary questions to the companies, however, before interviews were held, in the case of YTV at least, giving some kind of indication as to what form the interview would take; and the officials of the IBA attached great importance to them in the whole process. A letter from the Secretary to the applicants, posted in early October, stated that the anwers to supplementary questions would be taken into account 'when your Board meets the Authority for interview'.

The supplementary questions put to particular companies dealt with special features of the local situation – the position of Trident, for example, in Yorkshire and the North-East, and the future of ATV programme-making in relation to the dual region in the Midlands (would schedules in both centres be the responsibility of one director of programmes?). Several of the supplementary questions put to newcomers suggested that the information presented in their applications had been inadequate or ambiguous; they included, for example, 'The company plans some ten hours a week of purely local programming. Can it give an indication of how these programmes might be accommodated in their programme schedules?' and 'What assurances have the group been given that if they were awarded the contract for this area the studio centre would be completed and equipped before the start of the new contract period?' There is evidence from some of the supplementary questions that were put before the interviews that the Members of the IBA were seeking to clarify their own minds on general policy before reaching specific decisions. 'What areas of production offer opportunities for economies without seriously affecting audience appeal?' was one such question. Another was 'What weight was given to audience research and to whom does the person responsible for audience research report?' Quite different considerations must have influenced the framing of the question 'What policies is the company following in relation to the employment and advancement of women?'

Further use might have been made of supplementary questions after the interview and of second interviews, but obviously the stringent timetable, settled long before the event, was held responsible for the failure to pursue such a line. The most frequent point pursued after the interview was finance; and correspondence and discussion of contract conditions, described below in chapter 8, were to continue with the successful companies after the awards had been made. Gossip on financial points before the awards were made suggested that the Authority was contemplating a series of shotgun marriages between existing contractors and rival groups. There were to be few signs of such thinking, however, in the final announcements. It was after January 1981 that the Authority was forced to think afresh. It had proceeded with too few assurances for the future and with far too little direct contact with the contenders.

It is not completely clear what happened between the final meetings of the Authority to consider the awards on 17 and 18 December and the announcements to the winners and losers on 28 December. There was one supplementary meeting – with ATV on company structure – and Christmas, of course, intervened. Given the protracted and complex nature of the early stages of the contract-allocation process, it seems absurd that there were only a few days left after the interviews – the sole occasions in the process for direct dialogue – for the Authority to take its final decisions on the basis of all the evidence it had collected. Silence and security were complete during these few days: the ordeal had culminated with an anticlimax before the drama of the announcement of the awards began. There was some limited speculation, however, on the odds on the different contenders for the regional contracts as well as for the breakfast-time contract. 'Forecasts are risky,' wrote Philip Purser in the *Sunday Telegraph* on the morning of 28 December before the 'charade' began, but 'if you think of today's dispensation as some giant game of Monopoly, I'd be happy to hold Anglia, Border, Channel, Grampian, HTV, London Weekend, Thames and Ulster. If I held ATV, Southern, Tyne Tees or Yorkshire, I would be open to offers. If I held Scottish I think I would be resigned to offers. If I held Westward, I'd be prepared to go to Jail, not collecting £200 on the way.'

7

The Outcomes

WHEN THE BREAKFAST-TIME contract was offered to Peter Jay's star-studded consortium, his reaction was spontaneous – 'I am thrilled to bits. It was an eight-horse race, and I didn't expect to win.' Not everyone involved in the protracted franchise affair resorted to games metaphors on this occasion, however. Nor did the press when it commented on the IBA's decisions. 'Shell shock!' and 'Shake-up!' were among the headlines. 'No one had expected the scale of change', wrote Peter Fiddick, whose 'franchise game' imagery had been displayed on the television screen from the luckless Westward earlier in the year. There had been talk of only minor adjustments. Instead, 'IBA demanded the restructuring of two of the Big Five companies and demolished two others.' For once, even the breakfast-time contract did not steal all the headlines. 'ITV's Wheel of Fortune?' was the headline on 11 January, 1982, in *Broadcast*, which chose a question mark rather than an exclamation mark: 'Will the Plowden gamble pay off?' The *Financial Times* referred to a 'flutter', the *Times* to 'Britain's closest equivalent to a national sweepstake'.

There had been seventeen days between the last of the interviews and the announcement of the names of the successful applicants for the fifteen regional contracts and for the breakfast-time contract on Sunday, 28 December. What happened behind the scenes during those days is still as obscure as what happened behind them between 9 May and 11 December. The secrecy, even the security, had been absolute. And the touch of absurdity which characterized the security arrangements on 28 December – sealed envelopes, separate summonses, dispatch riders carrying the news from Brompton Road to Whitehall, to be picked up by an official at the Home Office; messages sent to the Stock Exchange, which was, of course, closed for the day; the press conference recorded by ITN – had never been entirely absent earlier. During the summer and autumn of 1980, for example, Lady Plowden and Sir Brian Young had declined an invitation from Southern Television to Glyndebourne; only the Northern Ireland member of the Authority had attended the twenty-first birthday anniversary dinner of Ulster TV; and there had been no IBA representative from London at all at the twenty-first birthday celebrations of Anglia.

Yet such security had magnified rumour rather than disposed of it, while the continuing insistence on secrecy after the event could never dispose of charges of arbitrary use of power before it. 'Each contender has a different theory over the outcome,' *Broadcast* wrote, pointing again to the 'gamble' element. 'Perhaps in decades to come the IBA's official historian will tell all.' For once, however, even the official as well as the non-official historian was to be placed in a difficult position. Lady Plowden's successor as Chairman of the IBA, Lord Thomson, speaking long after the event at a dinner in November 1982 in honour of Sir Brian Young, who had retired from the Director Generalship of the Authority in the same month, remarked somewhat forbiddingly that 'nobody not present at the Authority's deliberations can accurately gauge what went on, or appraise the process.'

Even at that late date the bitterness had still not disappeared. It had been well expressed in a letter written to Lord Thomson in January 1981 by David Wilson, chairman of Southern Television, which lost its contract. 'The Authority,' he claimed, 'had performed an act of arbitrary power based on a secret process of assessment, exercised without opportunity for defence, questioning or appeal, and we believe it had already decided that there had to be at least one supreme sacrifice regardless of whom the replacement was to be. . . . This can be no way to conduct affairs of this importance; it surely defies every concept of natural justice.' The only reply Lord Thomson could make was to echo Lord Hill in 1967 and point out that 'the Authority has a duty laid upon it by

Parliament and has to discharge this duty in the public interest, however painful particular decisions may be to particular companies and people.' Nonetheless, Lord Thomson himself was to use strong words in May 1981 when he described the franchise-allotting procedures which had been followed as 'a very clumsy tool and a very brutal one'. In January 1981 he had said quite categorically, 'We must not do it like this again' (*Bristol Evening Post*, 2 January 1981).

Whatever the difficulties and however inadequate the available evidence, it is essential to try to appraise the franchise-allotting process in the light of its outcome. Indeed, the Authority itself, for all its secretiveness, provided a number of clues for 'enlightened guesses' even at the time. It described the process then as 'elaborate and complex', implying throughout that it was concerned not just with the merits of individual contenders for sixteen unrelated individual contracts but with the operations – and balance – of the system as a whole: in its final statement of 28 December it talked of 'mutual dependence'. Its object, it had stated on 24 January 1980, was 'to ensure that the system would continue to be in the best possible shape so that in the 1980s it can sustain a public service of television on two channels.' It had never had a *carte blanche* for, in Lady Plowden's words, it was 'unrealistic' to take the whole system to bits and start again. If it wanted to make changes – and it did, if only in order to show its power – those changes would be limited. It 'had to take account,' in its own words, 'of the effect of change in one area upon all the others.'

The word 'shape' stands out in its statement of January 1980. The complete phrase 'in the best possible shape' was taken, of course, not from the language of the media but from the language of doctors and their patients; and it was echoed in a further IBA statement that ITV's 'framework' had to be 'sufficiently robust' to provide 'a true alternative service to the BBC' and to stand up to the rigours of the 'harsher economic climate' in the 1980s. In the light of this natural preoccupation with the health of the system, it was obviously unfortunate for the Authority when Lord Thomson himself, using the same vocabulary, had to admit in September 1981 that the process itself had involved 'bruising', 'dislocation' and 'suffering'. The people 'bruised', 'dislocated' and 'suffering' – and they included some new contenders – would have chosen a stronger adjective than unfortunate. Indeed, it was central to their complaint that they had not been given the opportunity to question the Authority before the awards were made or to challenge the relevance of the questions the Authority had earlier put to them. Some outside commentators used the same language, talking even as late as 1983 of wounds so recent and so deep that most were trying to seek post-operative anaesthesia.

Others, less attracted by such images, discerned further weaknesses in the Authority's approach. What had all the stress on 'public involvement' amounted to? Just how much attention had the Authority paid to public judgement in reaching its cluster of individual decisions? Would it have reached the same conclusions had there been no open face to the process at all? 'What is this Authority,' asked the *Daily Telegraph* on 24 December 1980, 'that can make or break companies? . . . The IBA, as yesterday's antics showed, is . . . using criteria which are purely subjective.' More seriously, they were criteria which were expressed publicly in only the most general terms. For the *Sunday Telegraph* the 'purge' was a 'characteristic mélange of vacillation and savage decisiveness'. For the *Sunday Times* this was 'the nanny state brought to life. . . . Last Sunday's proceedings caught the reality of state control over broadcasting. They showed it to be not so much sinister as fussy.'   '

Lady Plowden certainly did not believe that she represented 'state control'. She was a strong Chairman of the Authority in her own right, and she had strong views of her own, strongly expressed. She also had her own contacts, as did other Members of the Authority, all of them scattered part-timers from different walks of life, whether or not they deliberately chose to restrict their social contacts in 1980 itself. (In Peter Fiddick's game one IBA card read 'You meet Lady Plowden at a party and don't recognize her – miss a turn'.) And leaving on one side the difficulties of being completely 'objective' in such circumstances, there were other aspects of the process which were bound to focus attention on the meaning of the word 'authority' with a small 'a'. IBA Members did not like to feel that there were prominent people in the 'television industry' who did not much care for their authority or who could treat it without 'due deference'. They were in the last resort conscious of their power; and when they were confronted in 1980 with a wealth of names new to independent television – this was perhaps the most healthy element in the process – it was tempting in such circumstances, when change was possible, as it usually was not, to turn to new names rather than old ones in order to demonstrate that they were not 'playing safe'. It was less 'cronies', perhaps, than 'rookies' who provided the greatest temptation when new decisions were possible, a point missed by *Private Eye* which felt wrongly that all existing companies were cronies.

After the event Lady Plowden maintained that she had 'deep sympathy' for the companies and managements whose loss of contracts had 'caused deep distress', but it is by no means clear that for all the IBA's monitoring system she appreciated fully how the structures and attitudes of the existing contracting companies had changed, with or without pressure, over the last few years. She was not privy to their own internal discussions, nor did she show much interest in them. Indeed, she was content in the event to reiterate in the firmest possible manner that 'we had a job to do and we did it to the best of our ability'. Lord Hill had led the way when after announcing the HTV award in 1967 he had stated simply that 'programme contracts have a finite term. The Authority can never be in the position where once an appointment has been made, the company has more or less automatic right to reappointment.' There were to be no freeholds.

At least one prominent personality in the world of independent television, Lord Bernstein, believed strongly with Lady Plowden and with Lord Hill that it had to be stressed that there was 'no automatic right of renewal'. 'There is no divine right involved, just merit,' he stated firmly in an interview on the occasion of the twenty-fifth anniversary of Granada in May 1981. And Sir Brian Young made the same point in different language when he suggested in the light of his own experience that it would never be possible for the IBA to eliminate from the franchise-allotting process 'those elements that had given, and would again give, a great deal of pain. . . . If the franchise process was a reality and not a charade,' he went on, 'there had to be a genuine search for the best available company in each area. . . . The commonest complaint is one which treats the franchise process as though it were a review of fitness, rather than a fresh selection of candidates for a job, with the previous job holder as one of those who are standing.'

Yet it was known in 1980 and 1981 that there were several of the franchises, including those of the Big Five, which were of such a kind that it was quite impossible for the Authority to look at them in this selective way. The London franchises, in particular, were in a class of their own. The smooth working of the system – and its finance – depended upon them. Moreover, even in relation to the other regional franchises, the number of applicants and the value of the franchises varied so much that in each case selection involved different tests of what Lord Bernstein called 'merit'. In fact, no incumbent company facing only one contestant lost its contract in 1980, and few new requirements were attached to the London contracts. Thames was commended for its 'considerable all-round strength and the ability to sustain good programming in the future.' LWT was said to have developed 'diverse good qualities . . . over recent years' and to have made a strong application.

Such reports did not add much to the elucidation of what the IBA itself meant by 'merit'; the successful contracts could be referred to in the press as 'Lady Plowden's Prizes', but no one knew just why they had been awarded. One of the few relevant comments came from a disappointed contender for the Central Scotland contract, Lowland Broadcasting, which said of the successful incumbent that 'they picked up on all the areas that we thought needed strengthening, and that were in our application, but decided to make STV adjust to them, and that's fine for the viewers.' Few losers seem to have been so generous, although a successful chairman is said to have written to an unsuccessful one: 'It could just as easily have been us.' It was one of the successful chairmen, Lord Townshend of Anglia, who pointed most sharply to the weaknesses of the IBA's general approach. 'Whatever political arguments there may be for such an application process,' he remarked in March 1981, 'one has to say with due respect that it does no good to the fabric of the industry and is unlikely to bring any benefits to the viewers.'

From the Midlands, where the Authority had required a major reconstruction of ATV Midland, Lord Windlesham remained highly critical. In a lecture 'Broadcasting and Public Policy at the Crossroads' delivered in 1982, in the presence of both the Home Secretary and the IBA Chairman, as part of a Home Office bicentenary series, he pointed not only to the 'arbitrariness' of the 1980 process but what seemed to be 'capriciousness'. 'If one or two of the troops are to be taken out of the ranks and shot, and others are to be disciplined as an example to the rest, how are they to be selected?' Justification had to be produced after the event in lieu of criteria before it. Nor could the process be defended because of 'good intentions'. Consequences mattered more than intentions. 'Like *The Quiet American* of whom it was said that no man ever had better motives for all the trouble he caused, that only made it the harder to bear.'

From the trade-union side, Alan Sapper, general secretary of ACTT, was less polite: he accused the IBA in far stronger language of acting like 'industrial hooligans in the way it created mayhem among the franchise holders and their employees with no apparent advantage to either the public or the television industry.' The mayhem was to continue particularly in the aftermath of the Authority's decisions concerning Lord Windlesham's company, ATV Midlands, and it was aggravated – as was the problem of raising new finance – by a business recession which brought with it unprecedented unemployment and large numbers of industrial failures, particularly prominent in the Midlands and the North-East of England, where the Authority had demanded radical restructuring.

Not surprisingly, faced with the 'Plowden inheritance', Lord Thomson had to spend much of his time 'binding the wounds and mitigating the harshness', a task for which he was well suited. Nor was his the only consoling voice from Brompton Road. Colin Shaw, the IBA's Director of Television, who had moved to Brompton Road from Broadcasting House and was within a short time to move to ITCA, remarked early in 1982 at the start of the new contract period, when another test was beginning, that 'no one who has lived through that experience would deny that the process is a deeply destructive one . . . confidence is inevitably lost – the confidence of programme-makers uncertain of their futures, the confidence of management unwilling to make long-term investments, the confidence of investors, doubtful of a proper return on their stakes.'

It was the staff of the IBA, not, of course, the Members, who prepared drafts of the letters to successful and unsuccessful candidates for the press conference of 28 December; and the Director General and the Deputy Director General were present on that day at the fifteen-minute interviews with representatives of existing companies, successful and unsuccessful, and with successful new applicants. Indeed, it was the Director General and the Deputy Director General who by themselves received new applicants who had not won contracts, presenting most of them with a formal letter which said little except that they had not been successful.

The arrangements for the great day were meticulous. Special care was taken, for example, to ensure that chairmen of rival consortia did not meet each other. They were conducted to an anteroom by one route and left the conference room after the interview, described by *Broadcast* as 'courtroom-cum-tribunal', by another. There were journalists' cameras, including the ENG cameras of ITN, at the entrance and the exit, but journalists were not allowed entry to the building until 2.30 p.m., when they were regaled with hot soup after a cold morning on the doorstep. By a neat, if ironic, timing the eight applicants for the breakfast-time contract were summoned together in the afternoon at 2 p.m. – with Peter Jay singled out on the list prepared by the staff to meet the Chairman at 2.10 p.m.

Lord Thomson was to insist months later that there had been no conflict between the staff at Brompton Road and the Members about the pattern of the settlement, although it was undoubtedly the close security which had made possible any rumours – and there were many – concerning this particular point. Certainly the carefully composed paragraphs of the public statement which presented details of the regional contracts, including specific new requirements or conditions of offer, were testimony to the labours of the IBA staff. The fate of the breakfast-time contract was a particular topic for rumour. It did not help that Lord Lever, chairman of one of the unsuccessful consortia, had been told that he must go to Brompton Road on Sunday, 28 December, rather than have the news telephoned to his home.

149

Copies of the introductory part of the public statement were distributed to the press at a meeting held at 4.30 p.m. It was presided over by Lady Plowden, who was joined by Lord Thomson, Sir Brian Young and Anthony Pragnell. The statement revealed that, although the Authority had for eighteen months resisted all proposals that the companies concerned and the public had a right to know the reasons which had led it to reach its conclusions, it was nonetheless anxious to suggest, at what then seemed to be the end of the day, that justice had been done. The meticulous detail of specific new requirements or specific conditions of offer, contract by contract, was, it implied, a testimony to the procedure which the Authority had followed. Yet not everyone was impressed by the testimony that the Authority had 'gone through every comma'. 'Psychopathic bureaucracy' was one comment which sticks.

The settlement of December 1980 did not merely provide one totally new national franchise and remove two existing regional franchise holders – Southern and Westward. Although there were no 'shotgun marriages' in other regions, major structural changes were required in three other incumbent concerns. In particular, the fortunes of ATV and YTV, two of the major network-providing companies, were transformed, and the settlement was thought of explicitly as a 'restructuring'. In March 1980 the *Economist* had observed that 'veteran franchise-watchers say the IBA probably will not touch the five major companies,' and had added to its account a few weeks later that 'if ITV2 is approved, a costly second commercial channel, so heavily dependent on the first, is not compatible with an army of rookie contractors learning how to make programmes and profits. So most, if not all, of the old brigade are likely to keep their contracts.' It had been proved wrong. Quite deliberately the IBA had conceived of future 'shape' in different terms. For it, the 'rookies', including, perhaps particularly, the winners of the breakfast-time contract, were not really rookies at all. For it, they were 'all the talents' groups with a strong professional experience, and in its view they would bring new ideas into the system, including the system of local programming required of all contract holders. In an interview after the event Lady Plowden, referring to the removal of the Southern contract, talked of a new team 'giving the kind of look that we wanted for television in the South and South-East in the next decade.' 'You have to look at the top boards of companies,' she said, 'because it's the top board who lays down the philosophy, who hires and fires, who get the right people to make the programmes you want.' It all sounded good, but as Chris Dunkley, the regular television columnist of the *Financial Times*, put it, for all the programme talk, 'the drama and the shake-ups' of 28 December were concerned 'almost entirely with directors and shares. . . . The matter of programmes and programme standards came a very poor second.'

He was writing in the right place. The *Financial Times* would have preferred the application of 'free-market principles', rejected in the early 1950s, to the 'paternalism of a quango'. And there had been more than a touch of 'paternalism' in the Authority's insistence that access to profits should be more widely open, particularly at the local level. In consequence, the future financial 'shape' proposed involved at least seven new offers of television shares to the public. How attractive the shares would be would vary from one contract area to another, but it seemed obvious enough that there would be difficulties in selling some of them, just as there would be in getting new corporate backers. The IBA worked through accountants in reaching its decisions, not through merchant bankers or stock-brokers. For all the financial difficulties of the previous few months television remained all in all a business in which institutions would be more concerned than individuals. There had been an element of naivety in the Authority's talk of attracting and maintaining a high proportion of local share-holders for each company, and it was merchant bankers rather than solid local citizens (or local authorities) who were to profit most from financial deals which were to take months to finalize. Indeed, by September 1981 Lord Thomson was reported as saying that 'the importance of regional shareholders should not be exaggerated.'

The final 'shape' was to look very different from that which the Authority had seemed to envisage, and even in the immediate short run there were surprises. Thus, after the news that Westward, following its boardroom squabbles, had lost its contract, Westward shares gained 3½p to reach 25p. The assumption, of course, was that the new contractor would seek to acquire Westward's property and equipment. Before long the IBA itself was to be looking for institutional investors which it would have criticized or spurned in 1980, including distant investors, like D.C. Thomson Company Ltd in Scotland, whose stakes in Southern had been a matter of controversy but who were rallied to the new Central by the Authority itself. There were no public Southern shares, of course, to register Stock-Exchange movements on 29 December.

A few companies among the contenders posed no problems for the Authority. The Borders, which came first in the alphabetical list of contract awards, was one. (The choice of alphabetical order for the announcements meant that the two most crucial decisions came last.) There had been no rival to the incumbent Border TV, and the company itself had only recently stated that television finance was so difficult that if the Borders area had not been extended it might not have put in an application at all. Yet the IBA felt that it must say something and its rather schoolmasterly style of reporting on companies was apparent from the outset in the judgement on Border TV. 'The Authority commends the Company's performance.' The company was told, however, to watch local interests, including those of the Isle of Man, and when a new chairman was appointed to consult the Authority closely about the succession so that the continuation of 'a strong regional control should be ensured.' Grampian too won praise, but was likewise told to allow for a wider representation of the area on its board and when cash was available to supply a better service to outlying parts of the region following consultations with the local communities concerned.

The second and third contracts announced – for Central Scotland and for Channel Television – also involved no change. In the former area Scottish TV Ltd was deemed to be the 'most impressive and substantial' of the three contestants, 'both at interview and in its proposals', and in the latter area there was felt to be obvious 'loyalty' to the company in control. In Scotland, however, development of programmes for children and minorities would be discussed, it was said, with the company, and proposals were required from it for the training and recruitment of middle management. Meanwhile, the Authority 'will be exploring with the company new ways in which

152

the public can make known its views on programme policy, especially as it reflects the national and regional culture.' In the Channel Islands proposals for an increase in hours of broadcasting were expected from the company, so that viewers would have access to 'some of the output of mainland companies' not then seen there.

Granada won the contract against a contender who went unmentioned in the decision. In one of only two references in the IBA awards statement to the application interviews it was noted that Granada 'gave a good account of themselves at interview, with elements of self-criticism as well as of pride.' Its record of network production was 'distinguished', but it needed to improve its 'balance of regional programming'. From 1982 onwards it would be expected to pay close attention to the different parts of the region, watching not only the balance between Merseyside and Greater Manchester but that between other districts – it was in fact already doing this – and to find ways of sounding public views on its programmes. (It would be 'pushed' to see that it did, said Lady Plowden in an interview in February 1981.) The Authority also wished to see an expansion in Granada's board 'to take account both of the geographical extent of the region and of the Authority's belief that there should be a representation, a greater independent element among the directors.' It also wished to pursue the possibility of enabling the public to invest in the company.

The two applicants for Northern Ireland both 'impressed the Authority', and it required a 'very full discussion', the IBA statement read, to reach the decision to offer the contract to Ulster Television, with its 'record in a difficult area' and its 'effective rapport' with its audience as 'considerable factors' in reaching the decision. The Authority would discuss with the company UTV's top management structure for the new contract period and the successor in 1982 to its present chairman. It would also pay attention to the company's development of its programmes to reflect 'the wide range of interests' in the whole region and especially in drama, children's and religious programmes. The suggestion that there would be future monitoring to ensure that the Authority's recommendations were carried out was common to many of the reports. It is not clear, however, why such a process depended on the kind of franchise-

153

allotting process which had been followed.

HTV Ltd with its 'solid record of achievement' in the dual Wales and West of England region and its 'realistic and forward-looking approach to the even more complex questions of the 1980s' gained the franchise against its one opponent. It was required, however, to look for Welsh representation on its main board and for executive directors with experience of Wales and the Welsh language. This implied a different scale of commitment. The Authority, it was added, might require HTV to increase its facilities to meet the needs of both channels in both languages.

Yorkshire Television Ltd, 'whose programme record and programme plans both for the region and the network command respect,' was offered a renewal of contract subject to structural changes by which Trident would no longer control the company. This change (indicated in the IBA's invitations to apply) would have to guarantee financial autonomy and separate identity, the Authority insisted, to the two contractors for Yorkshire and North-East England. YTV was required to arrange, therefore, after consultation with the IBA, for its managing director to be supported by a joint managing director who, among other duties, would have special responsibility for industrial relations, and the new chairman and the new joint managing director would be required to live in the franchise area. In its note on the new independent structures of the two companies, the Authority added that it was prepared to consider 'common working arrangements (including the selling of advertising)' if suggested by them. It expected to have firm proposals for the restructuring of shareholdings in YTV and Tyne Tees TV in two months' time, not later than the end of February, and failing that it would 'consider afresh the offer of the two contracts'. In this way Trident, which had come into being with the Authority's blessing, was, it seemed, no longer to be left with a major stake in commercial television. The intractable problem of the overlapping audiences of YTV and Tyne Tees which had provided the original rationale for the Trident 'umbrella' now seemed to receive little attention. At best, Trident would have to relinquish majority control of YTV and Tyne Tees. Parent companies in general – northern or southern – were warned in the announcements of the allocations that

154

they would have to guarantee that, whatever their interest in new communications technology (video, cable, etc.) or in the leisure industry, such interests should not conflict, in the words of the IBA, 'with those of a television company and the audience which it is serving.' It was a warning which would prove difficult to maintain even for television contracting companies which were not part of bigger clusters of interests.

There was more of a shotgun element in the YTV and Tyne Tees awards than in any other contract award, although in this case the Authority was proposing a shotgun divorce rather than a shotgun marriage. It was asking also, as in other areas, for opportunities to be provided for 'shareholdings for people living in the two areas, including those who had come forward to support the rival consortia in the applications which had been invited earlier in 1980.' Tyne Tees, however, like YTV, kept its contract as a separate company in face of its two contenders. There was no 'merit award' in the IBA's announcement of this franchise. The only relevant statement read that 'the Authority decided that the best' of the three applications was that of Tyne Tees Television.

In the Midlands also the decision on the new dual East and West Midlands contract went, against two rivals, to ATV Midlands Ltd, described as having 'a good record in a number of fields' (although the company applying for the contract was, in fact, a newly formed one, which ATV Network Ltd had taken pains to differentiate from itself). The chief news editor of the *Birmingham Evening Mail* had predicted on the eve of the awards that ATV would survive with a major restructuring, and so it did. No fewer, however, than six conditions for 'renewal' were spelt out in some detail. They did not satisfy ATV's local critics – 'axe-grinders' the *Daily Express* called them – who described them as 'cosmetic', but they were nonetheless far-ranging enough to influence the working of the whole system. The control of ACC, total owner of ATV Network Ltd, was to be reduced to 51 per cent, divided into voting and non-voting shares in proportions as agreed with the Authority. Preference in the allocation of the remaining 49 per cent shareholding was to go to local people and companies, with special consideration being given, in a vague and controversial phrase, to 'those who had interested themselves in the other groups bidding for this franchise.' ACC retained control of a company which in the previous year had contributed £3·9 million of the group's £14·1 million profits. Yet half the non-executive directors of the new contractor – which was to have a new name – were to be nominated by other shareholders and the positions of chairman and managing director had to be held separately, with an ACC nominee being allowed to hold only one of them.

The distinctive nature of the two parts of the franchise, East and West, was to be emphasized by the creation of separate area boards, each with its own chairman and general manager, with ACC nominees taking over one of these positions only in each area. Finally, the company was to find a new name to indicate that it was a 'substantially new company for the dual region'. The Authority required proposals to meet its six conditions by the end of January, a totally unrealistic request even though there had been previous talk on the subject. In the event of ATV's failure to meet it, the Authority stated that it would consider afresh the offer of the contract. It is not surprising that Lord Windlesham, representing ATV, should have been closeted longer with Lady Plowden on 28 December than any representative of other companies.

For the South-West franchise, the Authority, in its own words, had 'a particularly difficult choice'. Westward, the IBA stated, 'had earned praise' and had 'tackled management problems' in 1980 with a determination for which 'the Authority had regard', as it had for the staff who had maintained the output throughout 'disagreeable months'. Yet there had been two strong contenders, both 'offering a professional and interesting service', and while boardroom disputes had had nothing to do with the decision, the prize had gone to TSW for the 'particular promise for the ITV system' offered by its plans, the calibre of its chairman and board, and the ideas of its 'fairly young' (an understatement) team. The Authority, however, would need to approve the management, finance and share-structure (new for an ITV company) proposals of TSW, which was asked to discuss with an extremely disappointed Westward the means for a smooth transition by January 1982.

The South and South-East England franchise, for the second new dual area, had attracted three times as many contestants as any other, presenting 'an impressive array of programme talent and financial experience' and 'fresh proposals for tackling the new task'. Southern's 'good record' in a number of fields, including opera and children's television, and its local news magazine, 'in some ways a pioneer in the past' (the historic tense sticks out), were recognized. The Authority had debated long, it said, as to which of the companies would best fulfil the responsibilities of the franchise in the 1980s: 'which would have the right enthusiasm and talent to serve the area well', now a dual region area, and also offer the network and Channel 4 programmes 'of high quality'. The eventual decision had been to take away the contract from Southern despite its record and despite the fact, as the *Economist* put it, that there had been 'no loud discontent among viewers'. Instead, the lucrative contract – that was its chief draw – was given to TVS (South and South-East Communications). Its 'board and programme makers' suggested 'particular promise', an explanation which indicated that the Authority felt greater confidence in the programme abilities of the new group than in the continued performance of the existing company.

The reaction of Southern to this decision was the strongest of any of the defeated contenders. The *Daily Telegraph*, for example, reported that the staff were 'stunned'. The feeling of the board, however – and it was a more alert and enterprising board than Lady Plowden implied in her February interview – was one of righteous anger. The blandness of the December interview and the failure of the Authority to ask any leading questions either about programmes or finance had misled both board and management. No effort had been made to probe or to argue. The capital reconstruction and profit-sharing proposals which could have benefited the universities in the South and the arts generally in the region, and in the long run influenced both company policy and management, appear to have attracted no attention. Southern had a far better press than the Authority in December 1980 and January 1981. Nor were any 'justifications' offered by the Authority particularly convincing. Like Westward, which had a sound management and production staff capable of maintaining continuity in difficult times, it was a sacrificial victim.

The Authority's decision on the breakfast-time service – and

157

here there were glittering prizes, it seemed, rather than dire penalties – was given in a page made up of two long paragraphs of which only the last six lines announced the winner.

There had been speculation in the press that a decision on the breakfast-time contract would be deferred and that in the meantime two or possibly three of the applicants would be invited to submit a joint proposal. In the event the contract was awarded to one contender, TV-am, with only 'a delayed start to enable better preparations to be made.' 'Have we won it outright or do we share it with anyone?' was David Frost's first question to Peter Jay when he telephoned the news from Brompton Road. The launching of the new service was set not for January 1982 but for some time in 1983, at least a year after the other contracts and after Channel 4 had gone on the air. The expansion of independent local radio was also mentioned as a factor influencing this delay, but there was no further spelling-out of the point. In fact, a total of sixty-seven independent local radio stations was being planned at that time, with an average of six or seven new stations in each year. A factor not mentioned was BBC competition: the Corporation announced its intentions to introduce its own breakfast programme, however, the day after TV-am won its contract, promising that they would begin in the spring of 1983. This was real competition of the kind that always mattered most.

The IBA statement on 'Breakfast Time' repeated the story of the IBA's hesitation over introducing the service, the arguments which had led it to invite applications without commitment to an award, the character of the specification for the contract, and the decision arrived at finally 'in principle' to offer it, having special regard to the high quality of the eight applicants. By then 'the question had been reduced to one of timing.' This was past history: TV-am was 'future-orientated'. Yet Keith Ewart, the use of whose studio figured in TV-am's future plans, looked back to the past in a message to David Frost, quoted in Michael Leapman's *Treachery? The Power Struggle at TV-am* (1984): 'I am glad the best men won. In the good old days (come back Lord Reith) the BBC was an example to the world. I honestly believe that it is now *your* turn.'

The six lines which were devoted to the franchise decision in the IBA statement did not entirely explain why *it* thought that the best men had won. Among 'the strong consortia which came forward . . . there were elements new to the ITV system,' the statement read. One other applicant (and not a 'new element') and the winner were the only companies mentioned; there was no side glance at Lord Lever, Christopher Chataway or Sir Joseph Lockwood. 'Despite the unquestioned strength of ITN,' the award went to TV-am which 'offered the highest promise'. On these four words the case rested. Never could 'merit' have been appraised so swiftly or apparently so decisively.

Peter Jay, chairman and chief executive of TV-am Ltd when the company came into being, did not hesitate to give his explanation of why its application had been successful. It fell under four heads. First, its philosophy, a very articulate philosophy, had appealed to the Authority: his concept of the service as that of offering the public a popular daily newspaper in all its aspects 'from the front pages to the back' had struck the right note. So, too, had his phrases, one of them to be picked up by Lady Plowden, 'the mission to explain'. The approach had not been too heavy, however: he had made it a part of the philosophy that it was his intention and his colleagues' intention that television was 'to be fun'. Second, he considered that the Authority had been impressed by the sense of commitment on the part of talented and successful senior people, prepared to put their careers at risk to back this philosophy 'without any significant extra financial reward'; the commitment had helped to convince the IBA that the philosophy was 'not to be thrown away as soon as we won the contract.' Third, the 'mega-stars' (*Campaign*'s term) were founders and shareholders, 'fully participating members of the family, not merely very skilled and attractive and successful with the audience but also people who have the intellectual depth and experience and skills to carry the situation,' a point which was reinforced at the first glittering TV-am press conference at David Frost's home, when the names of Nick Elliott and Michael Deakin were announced for the first time. Fourth, 'the quality of the technical parts of the application and . . . the impressive nature of the financial backing, both the amount and calibre of investors,' had been bound to impress. The four arguments all led to the one conclusion, but they did not all point in the same direction. TV-am more than any other of the successful contenders was to suffer most in the aftermath.

If much press comment focused for once on other decisions of the IBA, it was still the breakfast-time contract which was mentioned first in the headlines of the *Times*, the *Financial Times* and the *Daily Telegraph*. There was more general comment on what the *Financial Times* called 'opening the floodgates to a new wave of broadcasters', but Channel 4 and Jeremy Isaacs, rather than the new companies and their leadership, were picked out in that paper for special attention. The Authority itself added a note on Channel 4 to its public statement. 'It has been important in offering contracts,' it said, 'to obtain satisfactory assurances from the applicants of a full commitment to the establishment of the fourth channel; those who have been offered franchises have given such undertakings. The Authority will also be taking steps through its control of scheduling to ensure that its two television services have a proper basis of complementarity.' *Campaign* from the inside of the advertising world was more cynical. It quoted an advertising executive who had said, 'Nothing will change – except different people will be making money out of it.'

In general the advertising industry – both advertising companies and advertising agencies – welcomed the IBA decisions, particularly the launching of 'Breakfast Time' and the split of YTV and Tyne Tees. A second advertising executive affirmed that 'the IBA has gained in stature as a result of this. It has shown a purpose which is very heartening.' But yet a third executive was quoted who objected to the emphasis which had been placed by the IBA on more regional programmes, while a fourth seemed to be challenging the whole basis of IBA intervention when he claimed that it was a temptation 'to offer people what you think they want rather than what they actually do want. The main commercial channel should continue to aim for being popular.' That particular philosophical point was not settled in December 1980. What is surprising, in retrospect, is that there was much else of a more practical kind that was not settled either.

8

The Aftermath

'THE AUTHORITY IS grateful to all those who have maintained the service of programmes during such a testing
time,' Lady Plowden declared in her public statement of 28
December 1980 on the contract awards, four days before she
ceased to be its Chairman. 'A new kind of test is now beginning.' There was still a year's delay, however, before the new
contractors were put to the test of providing regular programmes for the public, the only real test; and during that time the
'routines of television' were expected to go on as usual with the
old contractors. Some of the new contractors were having to
think harder about finance and industrial relations than programmes, and there was even a fear of blackouts on the screen.
Meanwhile, behind the scenes – and during this period there
was no pretence of publicity – many of the most crucial
decisions were being taken about the future of individual
elements in the system.

There were protracted and often difficult talks between the
IBA and the contractors behind closed doors, mainly about
regrouping, with awkward financial issues to settle, many of
them settled ultimately – after more than one deadline had
been passed – in a way that made a mockery of the financial
priorities laid down in Brompton Road during the months
before the awards; and there were equally complex, but frequently more speedily resolved, discussions, also behind closed
doors, between old and new contractors about staff and studios.
Sir Brian Young talked of 'six months of brinkmanship' once
the drama or melodrama of 28 December was over. 'Telling
companies to shut up shop, open new studio complexes, sell

161

shares and reorganize boards is one thing,' wrote the *Financial Times*. 'Getting everything done in the year that is left before the new franchises start is another.' It was not until the end of March 1981 that the *Investors' Chronicle* could report that 'ITV's network shows signs of unravelling.'

Already by then the two new contractors for the South and South-East and the South-West had held their first board meetings, happy in the knowledge, Max Hastings reported, that 'good television' mattered more to them than 'the prospect of making large sums of money.' It would be several months before they would actually take over. 'Shall we not all discover in two or three years' time,' Hastings asked, 'that today's whizz kids are producing pretty much the same kind of television as yesterday's rejects?'

There were more immediate perspectives than that, and not all of them were happy ones. Television South-West had still not begun work on a new site; Television South had failed to acquire the old Southern Television studios and was faced with the prospect of converting rented warehouse premises in East-leigh as well as building a new complex in Maidstone; Trident's subsidiary YTV still had not given the IBA full details of a plan to reduce Trident's stake by 20 per cent (the first deadline date, 28 February, had already passed and it now had until 7 April to do so); and ATV had not yet been able to release to its non-voting shareholders details of its enforced broadening of ownership.

In many ways the ATV position was the most complicated of all to unravel, since the IBA had ordered the company to be 're-formed' with a new name. It had been laid down, in the form of a ukase, not only that there had to be eight new directors on the two regional boards who had had no previous connection with ATV, but also that there had to be two such persons on the main board of what was to become Central. The creation of 'some form of educational and arts trust' – an idea imaginatively developed elsewhere in the application by South-ern Television, which lost its contract despite this – was to be 'considered positively', although the word 'positively' sounded odd in this prescription, given the declared purpose – that of serving as 'a means of providing machinery for the election of certain non-executive directors.' Either the chairman of the

162

main board or the company's managing director could have a connection with ACC, but not both; and either the chairmen of the regional boards or the general managers. In addition, no fewer than seven new senior programme posts were to be filled. The biggest change of all, however, was the requirement that in the offer to the public of 49 per cent of the shares in the restructured company 'preference was to be given to East and West Midlands investors, with special consideration [not defined] to those who had supported the other consortia which had bidden for the franchise.' Mercia, a defeated rival, was said to want the lot. Was that permissible, let alone desirable?

The Authority had always been forced to recognize that questions of finance were of equal importance with questions of programming, and the television industry as a whole – along with the IBA itself, which dreamed of attracting new cash without strings – was confronted with general as well as with specific difficulties after the new contracts had been offered on the Authority's terms. Total advertising revenues for the industry were down in January and February 1981 – by 7·7 per cent and 4·3 per cent, compared with 1980 – and companies knew that, in a year's time, in addition to their rentals and levy they would have to pay monthly subscriptions to Channel 4 as well as to produce programme offerings for it. (ACC shares fell by 30p to 48p in the week before the awards were announced on the basis of a declared half dividend.) Clearly new cash would not descend like manna from heaven. Critics of the IBA complained that its reorganization would entail 'a patchy and penurious service', and Peter Fiddick in the *Guardian* quoted a bitter executive in one of the companies who had exclaimed 'Bridget Plowden laid an egg and everybody else is having to unscramble it.'

Paradoxically some of the companies which had failed to secure contracts were more sanguine than those which had secured them. They were turning optimistically not only to the possibility of making programmes for Channel 4 on a profit basis but to exploiting video, cable and satellite. For the *Economist* such a 'regional beauty contest' as had been held in 1980 'need never happen this way again.' 'By the time these franchises expire, the new technologies of satellites and cable television will have penetrated Britain, making nonsense of the regional jigsaw into which Britain's commercial television has been divided.' The same point was made by Lord Windlesham in his Home Office lecture. In May 1981 the Home Office had published a 'seminal study' of direct broadcasting by satellite (DBS): with extra channels from DBS and from cable there would not only be new opportunities for programme makers and for the public but new policy questions for governments. The finance of the new development posed problems of its own, but no longer need policy rest on the assumption that television transmissions must be limited by the shortage of frequencies in the radio spectrum to convey them. For this reason one unsuccessful contender for a 1982 franchise, Michael Rice of Eastern England Television, described the IBA's allocations as not only 'ill-advised' but 'not very mature'. The latter comment might have been made about the Annan Committee, which had had next to nothing to say of technology and its implications.

The particular difficulties of YTV and ATV in 1981 have to be considered within this general context.

While YTV was looking for new backers, Trident's second company, Tyne Tees Television, found its investors more readily. It had no network obligations and, with the Authority's requirement for the ending of the two companies' joint advertisement sales arrangement and fixed percentage revenue split, would gain viewers from the separate set count in each area. Trident had its difficulties in dealing with the Authority. It had to protect the interests of Trident shareholders and it had also to put forward proposals for the refinancing of the two companies which would be viable and would also be acceptable to Brompton Road. The letter which it had received from the Authority on 28 December had told Trident what to do without telling it how to do it; lawyers as well as accountants (and merchant bankers) had to be brought into complex negotiations, described by both the *Times* and the *Guardian* as 'unscrambling an omelette'.

After rejecting a first proposal relating to Tyne Tees, the Authority on 19 March accepted a second as a 'substantial basis for further discussions', but stated that it was still 'continuing seeking the best way of assuring that' in Yorkshire 'a soundly based company of network status services the region.' It added that it would 'now engage in immediate discussions

164

both with Trident and with those who last year expressed interest in funding new television companies' and 'whose interest is still active'. In other words, it would bring back into the reckoning the old contenders from Yorkshire and contenders from other parts of the country. Whatever the deal, there would have to be 'new capital to be found by flotation or placement'. A substantially modified arrangement for YTV proposed by Trident was not accepted by the Authority until 9 April, and even then, as Lord Thomson put it, the verdict was 'an extremely close-run thing, the outcome of which was in doubt right up to the end of a day-long meeting.' What was in no doubt was the IBA's expressed anxiety to secure that Paul Fox remained with the company.

To win the contract, YTV had, unlike Tyne Tees, to convince the Authority that its proposals, unpublished, were better than the counter-proposals. These were submitted in sealed envelopes from Midlands TV, contender against ATV for the East and West Midlands contract, and the Charterhouse Group, unsuccessful in the South and South-East.

The new company, YTV Holdings, was to have share capital of £12·6 million and was to be owned and controlled by five major shareholders, with holdings varying from 5 to 25 per cent; their names were not announced until May. Trident, which had suggested a 20 per cent holding, was to receive instead 15 per cent; an unexpected investor, Bass Ltd, which was diversifying its brewery interests, took 25 per cent, Pearson Longman 25 per cent, the *Yorkshire Post*, an existing Trident shareholder, 10 per cent and Bishopsgate Nominees 5 per cent. N.M. Rothschild, the merchant banker, was left to hold 15 per cent unplaced shares beneficially for Trident, to be made available later, it was said, to 'local interests'. (When in July 1984 Trident, with the IBA's approval, sold its residual holding in YTV to W.H. Smith and Sons (Holdings) it still had 29·86 per cent to dispose of.) The new YTV was to pay over £8 million to Trident for an eight-year use of its studios, with an option to buy for £11 million up to January 1985, and would for five years rent Trident's technical assets at a charge of over £6 million.

The Tyne Tees arrangement gave 20 per cent of the stock of the new company and two seats on the board to Vaux

Breweries, a major shareholder in the Norseman group which had unsuccessfully contended for the franchise. Trident retained 20 per cent and a further 5 per cent was held for disposal by Kleinwort Benson. The Industrial Commercial and Finance Corporation Ltd (ICFC), a new investor, was given 15 per cent, and two existing shareholders – Telefusion Ltd and United Newspaper Publications Ltd – each took 7·4 per cent. The share offer in April was oversubscribed, so that by the time an extraordinary general meeting of Trident was held in July this particular arrangement was watertight. The new Tyne Tees Ltd would buy the existing studios from Trident by the end of 1981 for £3 million and for eight years would pay rent to it of £3·25 million for new studios, with an option to buy, along with a charge of £2·5 million for five years for technical equipment.

The new YTV company, pronounced acceptable by Trident at the meeting in July, was brought into existence in December 1981 and, along with the other successful regional contractors, signed its agreement for appointment with the IBA on 31 December. The new YTV chairman was Derek Palmar, chairman and chief executive of Bass.

As a result of this restructuring, Trident's balance sheet, the *Financial Times* calculated (29 April 1981), had received an injection of £10½ million for its predominant shares in YTV and Tyne Tees, while still holding a share in each; and it stood also to receive £11 million over eight years from the rental of its studios and £8 million over five years for the use of technical equipment. It also retained exploitation rights outside the United Kingdom of all YTV and Tyne Tees programmes in production up to 31 December 1981.

If the Authority had suggested any such elaborate reorganization in the South and South-East rather than taking away Southern Television's franchise, it would doubtless have been possible for Southern Television to have survived likewise, as part of a new IBA-imposed consortium. As it was, however, the new company had to find new capital on its own, in the knowledge, familiar enough to potential investors, that the forward advertisement bookings of Southern Television already guaranteed it a handsome immediate revenue in an area which was relatively prosperous, quite different in character and prospects from Yorkshire and the North-East. TVS had none of the financial worries of YTV, which the IBA insisted would be more profitable than Trident predicted and more, indeed, than was to be the case. But TVS did not find forecasting entirely easy either. The capital to be provided for the new production centre in Kent was only part of the financial picture in the southeastern area of the dual contract. There were revenue questions too. If, with half a million potential new viewers there, TVS was to be financially successful in the eastern part of its dual contract, it would have to entice viewers in homes where aerials were tuned to the Crystal Palace station for Thames and London Weekend. There would be a 'very competitive battle' in 'real front-line territory' in the most prosperous part of the country, Martin Jackson, TVS's public affairs director, told *Campaign* in August 1981. And there would be only a very short period, twelve months in all, to prepare for it.

In its application to the Authority TVS had promised that it would give 'first consideration' to Southern staff in relation to continued employment, promotion opportunities and the chance to transfer to the new South-East centre, for which it would need a significant increase of personnel. But when David Wilson, the chairman of Southern Television, and Frank Copplestone, his managing director, arranged a staff gathering in the Southampton studio in February 1981 – with vision and sound links to staff in Dover and London – to hear and to question the senior figures in TVS on the company's plans and on their own future, there were as many mixed reactions as there had been in leaders in the local newspapers when Southern's loss of contract was first announced. *Broadcast* reported contrasting accounts of the occasion ranging from 'glacial' and 'stiffly courteous' to 'amicable'. At this date no decision had been taken on the future of the Southampton studio, and TVS could say no more on the problem of pension rights than that the subject was a major concern in its dealings with the sitting company. Faced with staff suspicion and union demands, it could only repeat its previous assurances that there would be security for staff below management level. Its departmental heads needed urgently to hold meetings with the staff with whom they would soon have to deal: a speedy 'solution' was

167

essential. By April 1981 TVS had a completely new team in command at the top, the team spotlighted by Lady Plowden, some of its members recruited from other companies, some directly from the BBC.

It was in that month, on 27 April, that a joint statement by TVS and Southern Television announced the signing of an agreement whereby the former took over Southern's shares and assets, including its studios at Northam, Southampton, but excluding Southern Pictures and Southern TV Ltd's programme catalogue. The price, not revealed, was said to be £11 million. For the new South-East centre, Southern sold to TVS (it was said at a profit) the site it had acquired before the loss of the contract at Vinters Park on the edge of Maidstone, and work could start on the two-studio centre there, one studio to be as large as that at Northam.

The new centre was intended to provide half TVS's output, was to become operational by summer 1982, and would cost £16 million. As with many other new ITV studio projects, equipment was to be leased, with the option to buy after five years, thus leaving open the choice of new technology. Until the new premises were open TVS was to start its new programmes for the South-East in January 1982 from Southern's small Dover studio, to which in April 1982 it would add a converted cinema at Gillingham.

The agreement of 27 April covered 620 out of 640 staff and ensured the transfer of pension rights. During the second half of 1981, therefore, TVS was able gradually to arrange for enough production facilities to be available and for some production staff to be seconded to it to make a start on stockpiling programmes for January 1982. The losers among Southern's staff were some twenty members of middle management who were of an age when finding new employment was uncertain. Some forty staff had already made moves during the previous months of negotiation, among them key figures in new companies, or had chosen not to accept the new company's offers.

In August 1981 TVS announced programme plans requiring the appointment of 200 extra staff, some at Southampton, more at Maidstone. Its news and current affairs department would be equally divided between the South and South-East centres, and the total editorial staff would be almost trebled. 'Access' programmes were to be mounted in different parts of the dual region, with mobile cameras reaching towns or villages each week. There would now be three outside-broadcast units to produce a weekly sports magazine. TVS was doing its best to implement its application. It would specialize, it said again, in programmes for children and young people (as Southern Television had done), with an hour's programme on weekdays and programmes on Saturday mornings and Sunday afternoons, and it would also supply the science and technology magazine that ITV lacked, developing a specialized unit for scientific and industrial journalism. Most of its resources would be put into programmes made for the South and South-East; TVS considered that the terms of the Live Network Agreement with the Big Five did not allow for a good return on programme outlay. Its programme-making skills would be employed, it added, to fight the competitive battle with the London contractors and other overlapping ITV services through the attractiveness of its own programmes and the offer to its viewers of an alternative to the network schedule.

The IBA's Annual Report for 1981–82 was to commend the new contractor's output from January to March 1982, particularly the new hour-long news magazine 'Coast to Coast' which provided for the two South and South-East areas over half an hour of their own separate news and information, with a common central section incorporating ITN News at 5.45 p.m. It mentioned the many new programmes transmitted during TVS's opening weeks, notably its weekly science programme 'The Real World' presented by Michael Rodd (formerly with BBC's 'Tomorrow's World'). At the end of TVS's first year the IBA's *Guide to Independent Broadcasting* noted some thirty new programme titles and formats and 600 hours of originated programming.

By April 1981 the TVS group of companies had formed itself into Television South plc, the parent company, South and South-East Communications Ltd, the contract applicant company, and TVS Television Ltd, the new main subsidiary company set up to buy Southern Television's assets, including its Southampton studio complex. Other subsidiaries included Blackrod, an independent production company set up in 1980 by Michael Blakstad and Michael Rodd for programmes on

169

science and industry, TVS Music for music publishing and TVS International for overseas sales. The main investors in the group and holders of voting shares by that time were European Ferries Ltd and London Trust Company and Associates with 20 per cent each, British Car Auctions with 15 per cent, the Television South Charitable Trust, an interesting venture formed to fund local arts and sciences, recreation and community projects, also with 15 per cent, and a number of individual directors, one of them, James Gatward, holding 10 per cent and two, Michael Blakstad and Tony Brook, 7 per cent each. The proportion of issued share capital represented by voting shares was then at an all-time ITV low at 0.02 per cent; and when in November 1981 a quarter of the non-voting shares were offered on the Unlisted Security Market, packaged with £1·884 million of unsecured loan stock, the issue was fully subscribed by lunchtime.

TVS's accounts for its first six months of operation, published in September 1982, met the initial profit target of its November 1981 prospectus, although costs had been higher than had been forecast; and when British Car Auctions sold its interest in July 1982 it had made a capital gain of over 40 per cent in just over a year. The first TVS Annual Report covering the year 1 November 1982 to 31 October 1983 showed an almost 60 per cent increase in turnover, an increase of 23 per cent in advertising revenue, 5 percentage points ahead of the national average, and a pretax profit of £4·46 million. But TVS's subscription for Channel 4 became a matter of argument with the IBA, an argument which was won by the latter. There was a consequent cutting-back of staff at Vinters Park and a reduction in the regional programming on which so much emphasis had been placed.

In the South-West, where the IBA had discerned 'particular promise' in the Television South-West team, there had been a promise by the new company since early 1980 both to increase staff numbers and to take over all Westward staff below management level who were union members. The old Westward studio building was less easy to take over, however: it was in need of updating and re-equipping. The two studios shared an out-of-date single master control and soundproofing was inadequate. TSW's application had concluded, therefore, that

170

a new studio complex would serve the company's purposes better than Derry's Cross with the substantial alterations and additions it would require. Even the staff problem became more complicated than had seemed likely, concerned as it was with the safeguarding of pension rights and the transfer of pension funds from Westward to TSW.

The most obvious solution was a TSW takeover of Westward, although this would have meant the abandonment of plans for a new production centre. In fact, necessary negotiations were delayed by both boards and staff morale fell. The danger grew that Westward would run down the company and that TSW would not inherit a going concern.

Finally, in April, arrangements were concluded to make possible the transfer of the Westward staff pension fund to TSW, and Rothschilds were brought in to negotiate a takeover. The TSW bid was £2·3 million and was described as not negotiable. In addition TSW said that it was prepared to spend £3 to £4 million on Westward's studio centre at Derry's Cross and wished to take control as soon as possible, even before the end of Westward's 1980–81 financial year on 31 July. Westward's board began by disputing the terms of the bid, but in July TSW was able to close its offers to Westward's shareholders, having acquired all the voting shares in the company and obtained a 90 per cent response to its offer. It was thus in a position to keep the Stock Exchange quotation for shares in the regional company without re-registration of it.

Meanwhile, TSW had been discussing with the IBA an innovation in independent television company structure – its proposal, set out in its application, that all the company's ordinary shares should confer equal voting rights. ('Disqualified persons' under the Broadcasting Act would be unable to register shares with the company under its Memorandum and Articles of Association.) The agreement eventually reached with the IBA on the company's capital structure, recorded in due course in the Authority's Annual Report and Accounts for 1981–82, was, however, that there would be separation of share ownership from the exercise of voting power. The initial list of shareholders having been approved by the Authority, the shares would be freely transferable in any amounts without prior reference, but TSW's Articles would provide that no

171

initial shareholder could without the IBA's permission exercise more than 5 per cent voting power if his holding were less than 5 per cent, or more than his approved percentage if he held more. Without the IBA's permission no new shareholder could exercise more than 5 per cent of the total vote.

Westward's board held its last meeting on 7 August 1981, and on 12 August TSW moved in. With less than five months left of its run-up year, it had immediately to set in train its £4·5 million programme of work to enlarge the studios, to build a new control room and to instal new equipment, including its five projected lightweight camera units for local centres, in Bridport, Truro, Taunton, Bideford and Plymouth. Until the end of 1981 it retained the Westward programme pattern while making plans for its promised schedule of local programmes to meet the 'tastes and interests' of the region, as revealed by its audience surveys early in 1980 and as suggested by its advisory boards.

TSW's opening show on 1 January 1982 at 6.30 p.m. was a disaster, described by *Broadcast* as 'more of a lurch than a launch'. Yet very quickly the new management, supported by a hand-picked board, established the distinctive identity of the company, represented in its news magazine 'Today South West' and the weekly documentary series 'Scene South West', of which one edition won the Royal Television Society's 1982 award for the best regional programme. The company made its mark also not by its own programmes but by what it did with other people's programmes, when the programme controller, Kevin Goldstein-Jackson, who became sole chief executive in July 1982, startled the independent system by transferring 'Crossroads' from its network placing at 6.30 p.m. in answer to a local poll: '37 per cent hated "Crossroads", while 32 per cent liked it but wanted it placed earlier.' He went on to criticize the ITV networking system as a whole and its effects, claiming that it blocked regional contractors' flexibility to schedule their programmes to suit the tastes of their audiences and thereby to maximize audience size and company revenue. In particular he criticized the system under which the content of network programmes was unknown in advance to regional contractors (and obtained the introduction of advance distribution of network schedules before the quarterly Network Programme

172

Committee's meeting).

Obviously the IBA had chosen a contractor for the South-West who took nothing for granted, including the Live Network Agreement. A further TSW criticism related to network practice in the matter of film purchases: among a film package left by Westward Goldstein-Jackson found thirty-nine foreign films never transmitted which he planned to show on Friday nights. At the end of 1982 TSW's programme schedule, reflecting such criticisms, dropped a number of network scheduled programmes over Christmas week and on New Year's Eve, replacing them by its own substitutes. Criticized in return during the first months of 1982 for its bottom-of-the-table rating in the ITV audience share record, TSW rose to third place in July 1982. But it fell again by September and was close to the bottom for the month of December.

Financial results for its first year of operation down to 31 July 1982 (five months of it in 1981 transmitting Westward's programmes) were 'healthy', with a first half-year profit before tax of £705,000 rising in the second half to £988,000. Over the whole year turnover was up by 20 per cent, profit after tax by almost 14 per cent and advertising revenue by 19 per cent. The Annual Report, published in November 1982, reported changes in shareholdings, with the major shareholder Phicom plc having disposed of its 15·1 per cent interest, and ICFC Ltd having increased its holding to 11·32 per cent; new investors were Citystep Ltd, with 10·03 per cent, and the London and Manchester Assurance Group and Prudential Nominees each with 5 per cent. By then the company had begun to look ahead at cable and satellite projects and had made its first overseas sales.

TSW's region with its 1¾ million viewers ranked eleventh in size in the IBA's empire, above Ulster and the three smallest regions, Grampian, Border and Channel. By contrast, the Midlands, now divided into two subregions, West Midlands and East Midlands, was one of the largest, and before the reallotment of contracts ATV had served as a major network provider since the beginning of independent television. In 1980 the contest in the Midlands for the contract had been tough, yet in some respects the story was only just beginning.

Finding that the loss of 49 per cent of ACC shareholding was not open to negotiation, Lord Grade, who perhaps more than any other person had helped shape the policies of the network, obtained Lord Thomson's consent, as the new IBA Chairman, to hold back on disposal of the surplus shares. Proposals were duly put to the IBA on 4 February, but it had already become clear that Lord Windlesham, the most experienced managing director in the independent television system, was not willing to become managing director of a restructured company as the IBA had been ready to accept.

During exchanges on this subject the Authority expressed a policy view, then a relatively novel one which had never been applied systematically, that the managing director of a contracting company was the key figure in its control and that the chairman should be thought of as a non-executive figure from outside; and the subsequent choice in April 1981 of Sir Gordon Hobday, the retiring chairman of Boots and Chancellor of Nottingham University, as chairman of the new company, to be called Central Independent Television, fitted into this pattern. Ironically enough as it turned out, ATV's search for a managing director for the new company took until October and ended with the choice of thirty-five-year-old Robert Phillis, managing director of Independent Television Publications Ltd, who had presided over a new look for *TV Times*. Phillis, who had begun his career as a printer, had no television background. More important in this context, he had no connection with ACC or ATV (except in so far as the latter was one of the fourteen ITV companies jointly owning ITP Ltd). His appointment, said Lord Windlesham, completed 'a top executive team of high calibre'; another key figure was Charles Denton, director of programmes. He had been appointed by Lord Grade, but he was the first director of programmes not to be working directly to him.

The restructured Midlands company was registered in July 1981 as Central Independent Television Ltd, and at last in late November S.G. Warburg was in a position to offer ACC's 49 per cent shareholding for sale. The prospectus gave Central's capital structure as £25 million, with £1 million voting and £24 million non-voting shares, ACC holding 51 per cent in each class. The company said that it would give preference, as the IBA required, to Midlands residents and to financial supporters of its unsuccessful competitors. The prospectus was not well received. The current rating of ACC shares was low and there was City hostility to ACC majority control. As a result efforts to complete the capital investment (in which Anthony Pragnell, Deputy Director General of the IBA, was active and 'most helpful') ended only days before the closing date of 15 December with the appearance among the investors, described as 'fortuitous', of D.C. Thomson Co. Ltd 'which had some money to invest'. All the applications for shares were submitted to the IBA, since voting and non-voting shares were packaged together in the units offered for sale. The result was hardly what the Authority would have chosen. Indeed, it might not have been acceptable if the situation had not been so urgent. There were only two weeks before the new contract opening date.

D.C. Thomson, the Scottish magazine publishing company which had held 25 per cent of the shares of Southern, rejected for the 1982 South and South-East region contract, some said because of their distance, thus switched to a 15 per cent shareholding of a distant Central. Ladbroke Group Ltd, the leisure chain, took 10 per cent, and Pergamon Press/British Printing Corporation 9·2 per cent voting and 7·9 per cent non-voting shares. As *Broadcast* put it, while it might be argued that, with 10 per cent and 15 per cent stakes and a seat each on the board, Ladbrokes and Thomson could not exercise any substantial control over a fourteen-strong board, 'that argument hardly consorts with the IBA's normally punctilious concern with every single voting shareholder.'

Moreover, after all these transactions, ailing ACC's position vis-à-vis the new contractor for the Midlands was still dominant. It remained Central's parent company, with a 51 per cent holding and two directors on its main board. It was Central's landlord in Birmingham and its lessor until 1983 of the Elstree television studios, during the long period before the East Midlands production centre could be built. It also held foreign distribution rights for Central's programme catalogue and, as a result of the settlement, cash in hand.

But the story of Central's financial structure did not end here. Nor did that of ACC. ACC's annual general meeting on 10 September 1981 had been attended by Robert Holmes à Court, the Australian entrepreneur of the Bell Group and TVW Enterprises, who by this date had acquired a 28 per cent

175

holding in ACC. By January 1982, when Central came on the air, this holding had risen to 51 per cent, and in April 1982 TVW Enterprises owned over 95 per cent of non-voting and almost all voting shares, giving it control of the ACC group.

TVW, incorporated in Australia, was barred by the Broadcasting Act from ownership of a majority holding in a British ITV company; consequently ACC's 51 per cent holding in Central was frozen and placed in trust (ACC receiving the interest) from January 1982 for over a year. Finally, in January 1983 Holmes à Court decided to dispose of his shares, and in May the IBA approved of new dispositions for Central which had been arranged by Warburgs. The new shareholder, Sears Holdings, the Selfridges and British Shoe Corporation Group, with a Midlands base, took 20 per cent, D.C. Thomson and the Ladbroke Group increased their holdings to 20 per cent each, British Printing and Communications Corporation/Pergamon Press increased its interest to 13·8 per cent voting and 12·5 per cent non-voting shares, and the Prudential Assurance Co. kept its 5 per cent. Out of some 840 institutional and private shareholders who took up the rest, including 3·2 per cent of the voting shares, about half were resident in the contract area. Their disposal, Central claimed, was 'consciously done to spread them as widely as possible.'

If ACC's total elimination from the Midlands contract, a delayed outcome, went beyond what the Authority had thought of in December 1980, there was a further change of outcome. The Authority had insisted on strong Midlands investment but Midlands investors had not chosen to respond. Nevertheless, Lord Thomson welcomed the settlement: 'it would enable Central and its staff', he said, 'to go forward on a settled and known basis about its future composition and control.' The Authority had insisted, however, on the completion of the new major East Midlands production centre which required £21 million capital at a time when ACC was short of funds and which had led to protracted staff and union problems which the Authority does not seem to have appreciated. They dragged on, indeed, until September 1983, costing £8.25 million in staff relocation and redundancy payments in 1983, Central's second year of life. The 'real-life drama' of Central always involved, as *Broadcast* put it, 'business megastars' on

176

the one side and 'a shopfloor cast of thousands' on the other.

ATV's bid for the dual contract had included a handsome design for a £20 million studio centre on a 15-acre site near Nottingham, to come into operation by the end of 1983, and in March 1981 a 17-acre leasehold site had been bought at Lenton Lane, near Nottingham University; it was designed to produce half Central's studio output and to employ 650 people.

The ATV bid had envisaged the setting-up of a new ACC subsidiary company to exploit the facilities of Elstree, developed by ACC after 1968, but this company was not formed, and in July 1981 Elstree staff were told that the studios there would close when the new East Midlands centre opened. Comparable jobs were guaranteed at the two Midlands centres, but sections of the Elstree staff, some of whom had worked at Elstree since 1954, were unwilling to move. Nor were they satisfied with what the company considered to be generous redundancy payments in lieu of making the move. Consequential union difficulties blocked the opening of a temporary studio in Nottingham and, when the date of 31 July 1983 was fixed for the final move from Elstree, the unions refused to tell Central, until the severance payments were increased, how many staff would move and how many would accept redundancy. The Central Arbitration Committee's ruling still did not finally settle the severance issue, and the new Lenton Lane complex was not opened until 4 March 1984; by then the *Financial Times* could observe that it might well be 'one of the last major studio complexes to be built in the United Kingdom.'

At the end of the day 360 out of 900 Elstree staff had moved to the Midlands to take up new jobs with Central, 200 had left through natural wastage, and 340 had accepted redundancy terms. Some of the transferred staff were employed at the completely refurbished Birmingham centre opened by the Home Secretary in January 1983; £1 million had been spent on it. The Duke of Edinburgh was to open Lenton Lane.

During two years of upheaval Central, the second biggest ITV company, had taken up its networking role in the ITV system. Indeed, the IBA Annual Report for 1981–82 noted that ATV and Central (in the last three months of that financial year) had together produced the highest network programme hours of any programme company, 885, up by six on ATV's total in 1980–81. There were other successes for Central too: in April 1982 it won the Golden Rose at the Montreux International Television Festival with 'Dizzy Feet' which had been selected by the British commercial companies for the national ITV entry. By January 1983 the old ACC London connection had been completely broken. In the opinion of Robert Phillis, Central's managing director, the shake-up had tautened the company's operations and given it invaluable experience for 'the greater competition which ITV companies would have to face in the future. . . . We are certainly very different from ATV,' he concluded, 'a much more independent company now that it is no longer a subsidiary of a large conglomerate.' Ironically the 'large conglomerate' referred to, ACC, had become one only on the foundation of one of the first ITV franchises granted in 1954.

There was no large conglomerate behind TV-am, which was to provide the most dramatic of all the episodes of the franchise aftermath. In January 1981 Anthony Howard wrote in the Langham Diary in the *Listener* that he couldn't 'help hoping that we've heard the last of breakfast TV for a bit. With luck the ITV star-spangled version is still well over two years away.' This hope, at least, was never to be realized.

Since TV-am had a longer period of waiting ahead of it in January 1981 than any other company there were bound to be changes in the aftermath of the award. A speedier start would have concentrated the effort. Nevertheless, in retrospect even the first phase of the pre-launch story before December 1981 carried portents for the future. In this case, at least, problems began at the top, with Peter Jay who carried an impossible dual responsibility as chairman and chief executive. The point was picked up in the IBA interview, it is said by both Lady Plowden and Lord Thomson: who was going to run TV-am? Brilliant although he was, Jay had experience of neither task, and only if he had been backed by an experienced, vital and loyal board would it have been possible for him to develop from an exceptionally gifted initiator and a superb improviser into an efficient and acceptable manager. There were other problems at the top also. Nick Elliott, Jay's choice as controller of programmes, decided not to leave LWT, and Michael Deakin, with whom Elliott's managerial relations would have been ambiguous, was not close enough to Jay for them to work harmoniously together to realize the programme philosophy which had won TV-am the contract. And Jay himself was much occupied with the business of working out the new form of agreement with the IBA required for the new national breakfast-time contract. Meanwhile, the financial position became less and less satisfactory even before the first 'Daybreak' broadcast went on the air at 6 a.m. on 1 February 1983, almost two weeks after the first broadcast of the BBC's own 'Breakfast Time' show. 'My money goes on the "Jay All Stars" ' was the *Daily Mail*'s verdict, but on the very first morning the BBC outscored TV-am by a margin of 56 to 44 in the London area and 72 to 28 in a second sample area, Lancashire. There had been more than a touch of rhetoric, therefore, in an eve-of-start letter to TV-am staff from Jay and Frost on 31 January which described TV-am as 'the most valuable addition to the British way of life since Yorkshire pudding'.

Serious financial trouble followed immediately on the opening in February 1983: dismal figures for audience and revenue in the first weeks required an injection of £5 million of new capital. 'We never expected an overnight success' was the Barclays Merchant Bank comment. The second crisis followed Peter Jay's resignation in the middle of March 'for the sake of the future cohesion of the company'. According to Timothy Aitken, the new chief executive, appointed on 14 April, TV-am remained 'very strong financially' and there was 'no possibility of running out of money', but in April another £2.5 million of capital had to be obtained from a cluster of institutional investors. In May, when outlay was drastically cut, the question was whether those of the first programme ideas which still remained would be cut too. Even then there was a third financial crisis in June, with a new programme schedule being described defensively as 'as close to IBA guidelines as commercially possible'. A fourth crisis which began in October saw TV-am in Aitken's words as 'within three hours of bankruptcy'. Restructuring, very different from anything anticipated by the IBA in December 1980, was not complete until 22 November, a month when there was an equally unexpected sharp decline in revenue. This led to a fifth crisis in February 1984, when the company was forced to seek further savings of £1·5 million. 'Disaster loomed', in the words of the *Sunday Telegraph*, until a union deal for cuts was made on 17 February. Once again, however, it was not averted. A further £4 million re-financing in May brought in new investors for 52 per cent of the company. There were further cuts and in July falling revenue and union demands led TV-am to drop its Olympic Games coverage, close some regional offices and disband its children's programmes department. And in the 1983–84 accounts TV-am still owed the IBA £901,000 in rental, deferred by the Authority since the first crisis of February 1983.

There are more anecdotes – and cartoons – about TV-am than about any other company and, since personalities played such a prominent part both in the pre-launch and in the post-launch story, structural factors influencing the aftermath received little public or press attention. TV-am's board, strong as its membership appeared on paper, seems not to have intervened enough to require managerial and financial controls. Within TV-am itself there was too much reliance on personalities, far too little on procedures. There was too much spending and too little budgeting. And the board for long, far too long, proved as willing to improvise as Jay. Lord Marsh himself, holding responsibility first as deputy chairman and then as chairman, could reveal when he resigned in May 1984 that there had been 'a tendency not to see TV-am as a purely normal business which has to have financial controls, manage-ment information, cash-flow forecasts.' He added that it was a very small business, although it was a small business which quickly accumulated large debts. The IBA itself, however, cannot escape responsibility. It settled for 'Breakfast Time' when there was no perceptible public demand for it. It chose TV-am among all the contenders for the contract after far too little scrutiny.

Meanwhile ITCA had taken up a hostile stance against TV-am's full membership in the television companies' trade association, and until membership was granted in November 1983 TV-am's external relations suffered in consequence. By then the composition of the TV-am board had itself changed out of recognition – as much, indeed, as the team of presenters, 'the Famous Five', who through their enthusiasm had done so much to win the contract. Angela Rippon and Anna Ford were sacked on 20 April 1983, Robert Kee was withdrawn from presenting in June 1983, and the last appearance of Michael Parkinson was on 6 February 1984, although he remained a shareholder. In August of that year Michael Deakin resigned as director of programmes.

There were financial changes too with broader implications. The refinancing of May 1984 approved by the IBA had brought in Australian interests: Consolidated Press owned, by Kerry Packer, with a 22 per cent holding, and Bruce Gyngell (who had been deputy managing director of ATV from 1972 to 1975 and a former chairman of the Australian Broadcasting Tribunal) as chief executive.

Faced with changes in personalities and finance, the Authority warned TV-am in April 1984 that it must seek approval for major changes of programme policy or of staffing levels (*Financial Times*, 25 April 1984) and served notice that it required the information content of programmes to be strengthened. It went on to note in its Annual Report for 1983–84, published in September, that some progress had been made during the summer, and that major attention had been paid, 'rightly', during the school holidays to the increased number of children in the audience (when Roland Rat made his appearance). But for the Authority there was 'much [that] remains to be done', and Lord Thomson emphasized in an address to the Royal Television Society on 10 October that in dealing with the company 'we continue to concentrate on areas of programming, particularly in the news and information field, where there is real need for improvement.'

TV-am's initiatives included an approach that month by Timothy Aitken, now its chairman, to ITN, with a reported offer of a 15 to 20 per cent shareholding, which came to nothing, and the recruitment (which proved short-lived) as programme controller of Michael Hollingsworth, the first senior producer of BBC's 'Breakfast Time' and subsequently of its early-evening news, to reconstruct TV-am's journalistic strength. In January 1985 TV-am announced that David Frost had renewed for a year his contract to present the Sunday morning current affairs hour for twenty-six weeks, and that Jonathan Dimbleby, a front name in the pressure for a breakfast-time contract and in TV-am's competitor AMTV, had accepted a contract for the Sunday programme for the other weeks and as roving reporter of major events, both home and abroad.

By the end of 1984 TV-am's ratings had overtaken BBC 'Breakfast Time', claiming 66 per cent of the weekday audience in December; but the 1984 financial year results showed losses and write-off since February 1983 of £20 million, and it was forecast that it would take to the end of the company's contract in 1991 to clear the deficit. That was as long-term a perspective as anyone had ever envisaged. However, 1985 began with an improvement and a new advertising drive, and in March the IBA was reported to expect the company 'to start paying some rental shortly' (*Media Week*, 8 March). In April TV-am's advertising revenue forecasts were buoyant, looking to a small profit in 1985, a substantial one in 1986 and an Unlisted Securities Market flotation that year. The *Financial Times* (1 June 1985) remained cautious, foreseeing a small loss in 1985, with a profit margin in 1986 but reporting a 1986 flotation as still 'speculative'.

The story of change – and survival, with the will to survive accounting for most of the change – had led the *Economist* to generalize as early as 9 April 1983 about the whole role of the IBA both in contract allocations and in monitoring. 'The prospect that in order to survive a franchise holder may have to abandon the promises by which it defeated its rivals,' it argued, 'expresses the IBA's weakness. It is not impotent, but its sanctions are too powerful to be credible deterrents – enforced liquidation or the withdrawal of a franchise before the end of its life.' And in Parliament both the chairman of the Conservative Back-Bench Media Committee, Tim Brinton, and the Opposition spokesman for broadcasting, Shirley Summerskill, agreed. 'They awarded the contract to TV-am,' the latter said in the Commons on 21 April, 'in competition against other people who could well have succeeded where TV-am have failed: but now they are just sitting inert and not doing anything about it.'

The IBA defended itself through John Whitney, its then Director General, a man who had been in a very different place in December 1980. Yet clearly then and earlier the IBA found 'the mission to explain' as difficult as TV-am had done. And in its case it had to defend not only its decisions, including what Richard Last, television critic of the *Daily Telegraph*, called 'its mission to make TV-am get things right soon', but the concept of authority which lay behind them. The last chapter of this book turns back to the central question of authority in the changing context of 1980 and of the years since.

9

Judgements

THE STORY IS told. What then of judgements on it? 'There must be a better way' was a common, if not general, cry in 1981 itself. Indeed, Lord Thomson noted in the IBA's Annual Report for 1980–81, published in the summer of 1981, how the franchise process had involved a distraction and diversion of energy from programme-making to corporate survival. In consequence, therefore, 'overall performance' had been less assured than in a number of years during the mid-1970s. 'Competitive edge' had been lost, and by that Lord Thomson meant competitive edge vis-à-vis the BBC, the competition that mattered most. There is truth in this verdict, although some new programming ideas and personalities were injected into the system after the franchise redistribution.

In September 1981 Thomson looked at the whole process in perspective when he told an interviewer, Christopher Griffin-Beale, that at the time of his arrival at Brompton Road as Deputy Chairman 'the major points of the franchise strategy had already been decided upon at the IBA's Egham conference.' He might have added 'even before'. 'Though I participated fully in the franchise decisions, it was, of course,' he went on, 'essentially Lady Plowden's great achievement. The last eight months I have been carrying on with the consequences of these decisions.' He knew how tangled the consequences were and how protracted, particularly in so far as they involved finance.

In the same month Lord Thomson was present at the biennial Convention of the Royal Television Society at Cambridge when the main topic on the agenda was the franchise process. Much old ground was covered again and little attention was paid to the new ground – and to the space above it – which would be bound to influence future franchise processes. It is significant that at this important meeting technology and its implications for future franchising scarcely figured at all in the discussion, just as it had scarcely figured at all in the Annan Committee Report of 1977 which maintained confidently that 'broadcasting will not be revolutionalized before 1991.' It may well have been right, even if by fluke, for the timetable of technological change is almost impossible to predict, and, for all the rhetoric, it seems even more difficult to predict now than when Annan reported.

The relationship between new technologies and decision-making for regional television is certainly still not clear, and if only for this reason there remains as much mystery in the franchise affair as there was at the beginning of the story. Nor has the role of the Authority, no longer the sole 'Authority' in the field of communications, been settled as a result of its display of power in 1981. On the one side there are critics since 1981 who have urged it to 'use its full powers' while 'the world changes around it'. On the other side the *Financial Times* had maintained in the spring of 1984, the Orwellian year, that then was the right year to establish 'a free market in broadcasting'. As for the Government, which through Parliament is the ulti-mate arbiter, it too has not yet made up its mind. It seems uneasy about the broadcasting system as it exists, but it is waiting for guidance before deciding what should supplement or replace it. We still seem far from the world foreseen by Peter Jay, casualty of TV-am, at the Edinburgh International Tele-vision Festival in 1983, in which 'the whole inverted pyramid of regulation and control' would be dismantled, broadcasting regulations would become unnecessary and no 'general laws' would be required other than those which already govern broad-casting. The so-called 'publishing model' is not being followed.

In 1981 itself there had been less dramatic intimations of new shapes of things to come in technology. *TV Today* (26 January) pointed out that 'television is an international business now in a way that it has never been before' and that the old national boundary lines would not hold, while the *Economist* (3 January) in an article significantly headed 'Last Hurrah for Regional Television' warned the British TV industry that 'by the time these franchises expire, the new technologies of satellites and cable television will have penetrated Britain to make nonsense of the regional jigsaw into which Britain's commercial television has been divided.'

In the autumn of that year the *Economist* and the International Institute of Communications held a conference in Vienna on 'Satellite Broadcasting: The Next Television Opportunity?', while *Europe 20* in February 1980 chose as the main headline on its cover the question 'Une nouvelle guerre des étoiles?'. An issue of the International Institute of Communications periodical *InterMedia* had been devoted to the subject in July. It traced the history of the European Space Agency (ESA), set up in 1973, examined the evolution of national policies relating to satellite development, and noted that a private consortium, Satellite Television Ltd, had been set up in Britain in 1980 by Brian Haynes – ex-Thames TV – with financial support from Barclays Bank and Guinness Mahon. 'What are Europeans doing about this almost unlimited source of electronic power from space?' Haynes asked in the same number. 'Broadcasting organizations are proceeding through a series of boxes in their minds' was his reply. 'Just as one circumstance seems to be understood, and one box left behind, then further questions and opportunities dawn.'

Nonetheless, the fact that when criticisms were made of the franchise-allotting process in 1981 they came out of an old box of issues does not mean that they have lost their relevance. They are still a significant part of any judgement. Indeed, given that the full implications of technological change are not likely to be operative by 1990, the old box of criticisms is still firmly in place. There were seven interrelated criticisms, and most of them retain their validity whatever the course of new technology may be.

Lord Thomson's critique of the diversion and 'the loss of competitive edge' attendant on the franchise-allotting process, the first of the criticisms, was heard more often in the regions in 1981 than at Brompton Road; and there was a feeling in the companies, which still persists, that despite Lord Thomson's statement in the Annual Report the effects of the process on programme-making had not been fully appreciated. Indeed, Southern Television, still operating in 1981 although it had lost its future franchise, was struck by the fact that, while it had had a particularly successful year as far as programming was concerned, its programmes were only barely touched upon in the 1980–81 Annual Report. History had been made to stop. Nonetheless, the report did express gratitude to all the companies in general for avoiding a 'steep decline in standards', adding that it 'would not have been surprising' if this had happened 'in view of the uncertainties about the post-1982 contracts'. There was, in fact, no decline. Indeed, some new programmes were introduced on the eve of the decisions. In general the old pattern persisted. There was more continuity than change.

A second familiar criticism in 1981, well expressed in the pages of *TV Today*, also focused on programme output. No matter how mediocre the assessed performance of a company might have been before 1980, *TV Today* observed, it could have remained in existence in 1981 simply 'because of lack of opposition or indifferent opposition' in the franchise process. Three companies had faced none. Likewise – and it was the other side of the same coin – a company faced with a large number of competitors had been placed in a position where it was vulnerable on all sides; and although its track record on programming might have been as good as or better than that of successful companies in other areas, it could nevertheless have lost its franchise. There seemed to be something inherently unjust about a system where there was no evening out of bids, particularly since, during the franchise-allotting process, 'weaknesses' of incumbent companies which were challenged might have been exposed by contenders in whom the Authority itself was soon to show no confidence. It was as a result of this criticism that ideas were soon to be put forward for spreading out in time the franchise-allotting process. Less attention was paid to the possibility of diverting applicants to areas different from those for which they had applied. Of course, such diversion would have militated against what has been called 'the myth of regionalism': it would have made redundant much that was written in applications for franchises.

A third criticism, like the second, also centred on 'injustice'. The IBA had been forced to think in terms of a 'package' – the economics and politics of its final settlement as a whole – and by deciding to retain a particular interest in one place, largely on financial grounds, in order to sustain 'the system' it might have been persuaded for this reason alone to sacrifice an interest elsewhere – one, perhaps, which was thought by it to be less 'strategic'. There was no agreement among the critics, however, about the answer to this 'problem', or whether the Authority was justified in seeking to show its muscles in such circumstances.

With the passage of time, of course, arguments about 'injustice' were bound to recede into the background, for the successful companies, old or new, became part of a status quo. Individual fortunes had been made; individual and corporate losses were forgotten. Nonetheless, it was inevitable that unless procedures were to be changed such arguments would recur at the next round. Indeed, the newly successful companies, if they remained as applicants, would be placed in the same position at the next round as the companies which they had displaced.

As far as the sense of a 'settlement as a whole' was concerned, there was no unanimity among observers and critics. Some critics thought that the IBA system consisted of too many pieces; others thought that the pieces were too few and that the closer that companies were to their own 'local' audiences, the more likely they would be to produce the most desirable programme output. The Authority, tied to regionalism, set regional programme targets – found too high by some companies – but there was little public support for regional television as such and little public knowledge of the networking system and how it operated. The Authority had decided against large-scale changes of boundaries. Its introduction of new dual franchises was a reasonable one, conceived in the interests of viewer areas which were distinct but not large enough to support a separate regional contract, but it did not go far enough to satisfy opinion in all parts of the country.

The fourth criticism, and a more substantial one, was that the IBA itself was suspect as an Authority, now a very vulnerable title. Its own conception of a 'settlement' seemed badly thought out, particularly in its financial aspects. There was less financial horse sense at Brompton Road than there had been in the earlier years of independent television, and however concerned the Authority might be about programmes – and some critics claimed that its knowledge was inadequate or incomplete in this field also – it did not relate programming to finance clearly enough when it considered either the individual companies or the system. It was over-preoccupied with securing regional finance for regional contracts. This was put as a criterion to which it was inclined to pay more attention than to programming. Lord Thomson wrote the *Economist* in January 1981, 'takes over an Authority which is dependent on amateurs, but determined to be increasingly interventionist. It will need to become more professional if it is to keep up with, and have a bearing upon, the changes now hitting television.'

The *Times* too spoke of the Authority as a 'lay body' allowed 'to choose the companies permitted to operate an absolute monopoly in a field which has in the past made fortunes for some of those who won the IBA's approval.' The professionalism of independent television largely lay in the companies, not at Brompton Road. And certainly the profits, which could be windfall, and the losses, which could be traumatic, as in the case of TV-am, the Authority's favourite child, were a company matter with ramifications at every level of their organizations. There is reason to doubt that the Authority fully recognized the implications of the patronage and the penalties it imposed. There were long-term as well as short-term implications which were not pointed to in the *Times*. If there were to be another round of franchise applications on the same lines would some of the contracts look sufficiently attractive to applicants of quality?

It was the law rather than the composition or practices of the IBA which was responsible for the fifth criticism. As the Pilkington Committee had put it, the relationship between the Authority's monitoring function and its allocating function had been (deliberately?) left far too vague in legislation. For one critic, a former managing director in ITV, the IBA, indeed, should never have been granting contracts at regular intervals. 'When it is responsible for that *and* for policing them, there is bound to be a conflict of interest.'

In fact, although the IBA had issued letters of guidance to companies in the years of uncertainty before franchises were advertised and these set out limited (though often vague)

189

recommendations, they gave little by way of warnings about the future. In 1974, for example, the Chairman of the Authority had written to the chairman of Southern Television stating that 'the Authority has a high regard both for the company's performance (including the high technical quality of its operation) and for the part it plays in the collective affairs of the industry.' What had happened between 1974 and 1979 to change this verdict? If something had happened, Southern itself was not informed. Nor was it told at the interview, which Members of the Authority were said to have found 'bland'. Qualified opinion in Southampton was that in both respects the position had actually improved since 1974. There was substantial support for this opinion from outside.

Evidence from other regions suggests that the IBA, for whatever reason, did not choose to use its monitoring process to the full – and that would have been the most effective way of showing its muscles – before the franchise-allotting process began. Nor was it to use it after the process had been completed. In the case of TV-am many of the initial programme ideas which had appealed to the Authority were abandoned, but the Authority, drawn into concession after concession, felt bound to continue to support TV-am simply on financial grounds. 'It seems you have to make a number of programme proposals to the IBA in order to get a franchise,' *Broadcast* was to observe in September 1984, 'but once it is in your pocket and a little time has passed you can do exactly what you like with it.' Lord Thomson was referring a month later (speech of 10 October 1984) to 'the financial albatrosses' that 'hung around the neck of TV-am before it went on air'. It was the Authority, however, that sent the albatrosses on their flight.

A sixth criticism was that some of the criteria according to which the Authority had made its judgements in 1979 were either not obvious or had never been properly debated in public (despite the emphasis placed by the Authority itself on public debate). In particular, the public had had little chance to comment on the attitudes of the Authority towards ownership, towards holding companies, particularly diversified holding companies, and towards regional shareholding, a very dubious concept even in a public relations context. Public meetings seldom touched on such matters, and a different way of

190

consulting opinion had to be found. Points might have been raised by way of comment which would have helped the Authority. For example, even if regional shareholding could have been strengthened, how could its perpetuation have been guaranteed through the operations of the share market? More seriously, would it really have been possible for the Authority to keep more or less the same kind of mix of financial interests in the companies throughout a whole contract period? Any merchant banker would have said no. Despite the amount of time taken up during the early months of 1981 in complex renegotiating with companies which were asked to reconstruct, the finances of successful new companies do not seem to have been considered as carefully as the finances of existing companies. Were they given the benefit of the doubt?

The Authority seems to have approached financial issues naively, with set answers in mind and with too little outside advice. 'It is now evident,' Peter Fiddick wrote in March 1981, 'that the IBA had anticipated neither the problems its edicts would create nor the force of the trauma on an already demoralized system'; by the end of the year the financial outcomes in particular cases – and the mix of financial interests within companies – were often completely different from those which the IBA had considered desirable, even necessary, before the event.

Another divergence between intention and outcome was due not to the search for new investment, described in chapter 8, but to a financial deal with the contractors, reached in November 1981, only after months of protracted discussions with an ITCA working party, which felt that the Authority was seeking to tighten the screws on the companies, even to ask for 'discretion' amounting to an 'open cheque'. In particular there had been continuing argument until October about the clause in the draft Agreements for the Appointment of Television Programme Contractors which determined how the level of Channel 4 contributions was to be fixed. The rental payments raised questions also. Were there to be 'unconscionable' increases? Finally the levy, always an awkward arrangement, complicated – and still complicates – debate. After a government review of it had been completed in July 1981, the decision was reached to postpone for 'one or two years' consideration of any major change in its basis – with the possibility of a return to a levy on revenue – until after the new contracting companies, including TV-am and Channel 4, had begun to operate. In April 1982, however, in consideration of ITV contributions to Channel 4, the threshold of levy payments was raised from 66·7 per cent above £250,000 of profits, or 2 per cent of advertising revenue, whichever was the greater, to 66·7 per cent of profits above £650,000 or 2·8 per cent of revenue. A further official review which began in 1984, the results of which are not yet known, took place in circumstances which the Government does not seem to have anticipated in 1981.

There was to be a serious decline in ITV revenues in 1984 and early 1985, coinciding with the prospect of higher subscriptions for Channel 4 in 1986 and disputed higher rental payments to the Authority. A sense that the age of high profits was over was bound to influence all discussions between ITCA and the IBA, including discussions of the franchise-allocation process. The Government was also bound to be attracted by suggestions that the BBC might be financed, at least in part, by advertising, suggestions seldom mooted officially in 1980. The Peacock Committee, set up in April 1985, had the possibility of BBC advertising as its remit, and Professor Peacock himself stated in an interview (*Financial Times*, 29 March 1985) that changes in one sector of broadcasting 'would inevitably affect the rest.'

The seventh charge against the franchise process in 1980, when the mood was different, related to procedures, although more than procedures were involved. There had been no early-warning system for companies under threat of losing their franchise. Nor had the interview itself allowed for any fight back. Moreover, while one competitor, ATV, had been called to a second interview before the award to give further information, and while YTV and Tyne Tees TV, after gaining their awards, had been drawn into continuing discussions in 1981 on the conditions for retaining contracts, others among the unsuccessful who had not been called back might have been able to deal adequately with particular points raised by the IBA, including financial points, had they been given the chance to do so. Programming plans – their feasibility and their possible place in the network – had not figured prominently in all the

192

interviews, and some applicants would have welcomed the opportunity of fuller discussion of these. There was no dialogue, and the sense of grievance was strongest perhaps on this point. If the Authority thought, for example, that Southern Television, a non-network company, did not make an adequate contribution to the network, it did not say so.

It did not help when Lady Plowden told Alastair Hetherington in an interview on Radio 3 in June 1981 that 'it would be destructive to have hearings in public because you can ask in private questions you can't ask in public.' This presupposed that such questions had been asked in private. They frequently had not been. Nor did it help when Lady Plowden, in the same interview but in different vein, admitted that, while she knew that companies felt that they had taken part in a lottery, she did not know the right answer and that it needed 'looking at in real depth before the next eight years come around.' Did the detailed IBA staffwork from 1977 or earlier and the elaborate IBA procedure from 1979 to December 1980 fail to achieve 'real depth'? If so, why?

Lord Thomson himself recognized the validity of the seventh criticisms when he described the procedure followed in 1979–80 as 'a very clumsy tool and a very brutal one'. He also acknowledged the importance of the second and fifth criticisms when in April 1981 he spoke of either 'staggering the franchise awards' – with perhaps three franchises being reviewed every year over a five-year period – or alternatively of introducing a 'rolling-on system' under which a company's performance would be monitored every two years and its franchise automatically renewed if its programmes were thought to be satisfactory.

The first alternative, whatever difficulties it would have encountered, particularly within the network system, would have allowed some of the groups which had put in unsuccessful bids in 1980 to have been offered an earlier chance in the future of securing a contract for that area or elsewhere: 'people who had been disappointed in one area could have a go somewhere else.' The second, however, if automatic, would have been open to the charges that it was reinforcing monopoly and that by allowing people 'to carry on simply because they are not doing too badly' it was excluding 'others who would like to have a go'. Even if not automatic, it would have been open to the charge that it would inhibit what a former Chairman of the Authority, Lord Aylestone, had called 'cross-fertilization'.

For *Broadcast* (4 May 1981) the IBA had been 'flying a few kites', and in September 1981, at the time of the Royal Television Society's Cambridge Convention, it described Lord Thomson as despondent. It was 'inconceivable', he had said then, that 'Parliament would agree to what in effect would be virtually permanent tenure of IBA franchises,' local monopolies in economic terms. Sir Brian Young, still in the saddle, sounded resigned. In the same month, after listening to all the criticism, he concluded that 'if the franchises are still desired and there are more contenders than there can be contract holders, then a process something like the 1980 franchise awards will have to happen again.'

There were few people in Britain – although there were some – who argued then that franchises were simply licences and that they should go to the highest bidder in money terms. The argument is easy to set out but difficult to sustain. There is a quality element in a television contract, clearly recognized not only by the politicians but by the economists of communications when they ask themselves the question 'Why regulate utilities?', and although whatever regulations deemed necessary by Parliament could be imposed through monitoring processes, this would not necessarily guarantee quality. Nor, however, of course, does competition. To account for quality within the British broadcasting system historians rightly point to a strong tradition of public-service broadcasting, subject to parliamentary approval, to which the IBA belongs as well as the BBC. Lady Plowden herself had once been vice-chairman of the BBC; Lord Hill had been chairman of both, and scriptwriters, producers, performers, engineers and administrators have moved without difficulty from one 'sector' to the 'other'. There has been as much complementarity as competition.

Given the drawbacks of the alternatives to regular franchise reviews, there was a return to the discussion of procedures. Indeed, by June 1981, when Lady Plowden in her interview with Alastair Hetherington recognized the need for a look in 'real depth' at the franchise-allotting procedures, the Authority had already been engaged in such discussion. In particular it had considered the possibility of fuller contract specifications

194

from the Authority at the start of the process; a revision of the regional map; a lengthening of the allotment process, with more IBA meetings and more interviews with applicants (seen by many members, however, as prolonging an uncertainty which was already bound to be debilitating); an extension of public debate (which some members felt had 'increased bitterness' in 1980 and introduced 'elements more theoretical than practical'); the 'drafting' of contenders by the IBA into 'areas most in need of strength' (very difficult to do); the addition of follow-up interviews; and the adoption of other means of indicating 'how the Authority's mind was moving'. Meanwhile, Sir Brian Young, while continuing to express doubts as to whether there were 'any easy and obvious improvements' to make in their procedures, was arguing, completely in character, in November 1981 that efforts must be continued to make the process 'more just and open and considerate' and to 'resolve as many points of conflict' as humanly possible.

When Lord Windlesham, one of the *dramatis personae* in earlier chapters of the story, delivered a Home Office bicentenary lecture in April 1982, there was a new factor to take into the reckoning in relation to reviews of what had happened – the experience of the new dispensation in practice. Windlesham concluded that 'the undeniable fact remains that the impact of this great upheaval in terms of the programmes screened on ITV, especially the network programmes, is already showing itself to be minimal'; and although there had been a few genuine innovations, the fruits of new talent, his judgement was basically correct. By then, however, new technology was coming more and more into the picture, and Windlesham was looking 'to the variety and diversity of channels' which in the lifetime of the present ITV franchises would become available for broadcast *and* cable use, and to the right decisions on the most appropriate shape and form of regulation for them, to 'prevent a recurrence of the unhappy events of 1980.' So also was John Whitney, then Director General Designate of the IBA. Speaking on 8 November 1982 to the Broadcasting Press Guild, he foresaw that 'the degree and pattern of broadcasting control would be very different from today in ten years' time,' and said that he could not see a repetition of 'the process of franchise reshuffling' taking place then.

195

By November 1982 the IBA itself had changed and was still changing. There were seven changes in the membership in 1981 and four in 1982 and there were to be two in 1983. Even more important, by the end of 1984 all the top IBA officials were new – the Director General from November 1982; the Director of Administration replacing the Deputy Director General, Anthony Pragnell, in April 1983 (the post of Deputy Director General was abolished); and the Director of Television from October 1983. With changes in composition, particularly at the top, came changes in style. There was now a different relationship between Brompton Road and the companies – more willingness, perhaps, to share confidences, to make 'deals'. Long before then Members and officials had already been forced to take serious account not only of the mixed fortunes of the franchise winners, particularly those of TV-am, which lurched from one financial crisis to another, and of their shifts of personnel, but of the implications of technological change and of the relative roles in any new communications development of itself and the BBC. This meant taking account also of the intentions of the Government, which was directly involved in broadcasting and new technology both through the Home Office, which was responsible for broadcasting policy and legislation, and through the Department of Industry. There seemed to be new marketing possibilities if Britain could establish a lead, and a Minister of State, Kenneth Baker, was appointed in 1980 with special responsibility for information technology, including satellites, and an Information Technology Advisory Panel was set up.

At first the BBC forced the pace in relation to the new technologies, informing the Home Office that it wished to control two satellite channels, one showing a mix of BBC 1 and BBC 2, and the other a special pay-TV service. At that time neither the IBA nor the companies were so clear or so determined in their thinking, and after the publication by the Home Office of *Direct Broadcasting by Satellite* in May 1981 the IBA's view was that 'expanded ITV' and Channel 4 should be given priority over any new development. It was not until January 1982 that it produced a further paper restating its view that while 'the heartland of broadcasting', as it was to call it, was its main concern, it would be willing, in 'a process of evolution (involving public debate)', to play a role 'in any proposal to establish satellite services designed to be self-financing.'

Questions of finance were to matter more than reports, White Papers and even legislation in relation to the formulation and the implementation of both satellite and cable proposals. And there was never much public debate. The most significant developments took place behind the scenes, with cable and satellite issues impossible completely to separate from each other even when different interests were involved and with, as yet, no clear outcome. When legislation finally reached the statute book in the summer of 1984, it covered both, and it was through the development of both that the viewer was promised both 'abundance' and 'choice'. Yet the uncertainties continued even after the legislation came into effect, and they affected both the IBA and the BBC. The Government, unlike those of some other European countries, was unwilling to provide public finance in an attempt to give Britain a lead, yet while it favoured 'market philosophies' it was inevitably drawn into difficult negotiations of a kind which would paradoxically have been greatly simplified had it been willing to provide funds. This was in no sense a period of *laissez faire*. Indeed, it had something in common with the years 1920–22 when the future of sound broadcasting, then in its infancy, was being discussed. Then, however, business concerns had been brought together because of scarcity of wavelengths. Now they were being brought together in the cause of communications plenty. Throughout, the Government was sensitive to business pressures, but it in turn applied pressures on business. It seems to have been unimpressed too by broadcasting institutions. Long before the Peacock Committee was appointed, John Naughton writing in the *Listener* at the time of the BBC's sixtieth birthday detected 'a whiff of institutional mortality in the air'.

To a historian of the future Josephine Tey's book *The Daughter of Time* (1951) about Richard III, which retells the story of the Princes in the Tower, may be more relevant reading than *The Franchise Affair*.

The full significance of what has happened during the three years from 1982 to 1985 can be properly judged only from a vantage point in time further away than the present. It is already obvious, nonetheless, that while all 'general laws' will not be swept aside, things can never be quite the same again. Any future franchise distribution, the theme of this book, will be carried through within a new context. When as Home Secretary Leon Brittan opened a *Financial Times* cable and television conference in February 1984, he recalled (with more than a touch of exaggeration) that as recently as four years before, when he had been helping as Minister of State to pilot a Broadcasting Bill through Parliament, 'cable and DBS [direct broadcasting by satellite] were barely on the agenda.' Now, by contrast, he was grappling with new legislation which centred on them as did all the formative discussions behind the scenes. The Broadcasting Act of 1980 to which he was referring and the consolidating Broadcasting Act of 1981 had strengthened (through significant rewording and reordering) the weight of the IBA's position vis-à-vis the companies, and in this respect they were like all previous Acts since 1954. The new Cable and Broadcasting Act 1984 suggested not an end but a beginning.

The Peacock Committee, appointed in the following year, was expected to report in fifteen months. There had been an earlier, even shorter and sharper, report on communications matters in 1982, prepared by a three-man committee under the chairmanship of Lord Hunt of Tanworth, a former Secretary of the Cabinet. Hitherto, public inquiries into the future of broadcasting had been protracted and responsible, under the aegis of committees representative of different shades of opinion, and the ensuing reports lengthy and weighty. In 1982, however, the Hunt Committee had been given only six months to look into the most advantageous way to 'secure the benefits of cable', and it had produced a report in October 1982 of only fifty-four pages in reply to this very specific request. It was the kind of inquiry – and report – that Mrs Thatcher's Government liked. It followed naturally after the Information Technology Advisory Panel had recommended earlier in 1982 (in *Cable Systems*) that the Government should commit itself to the cabling of Britain at the earliest opportunity.

There were shades of the past, however, also in a second part of the Hunt Committee's remit. It was called upon to suggest how 'the benefits of cable' could be obtained 'in a way consistent with the wider public interest, in particular the safeguarding of public-service broadcasting.' The IBA felt that it had the

198

answer, but significantly that answer was not accepted either by the Hunt Committee or by the Government. In its evidence to the Committee the IBA had argued simply that in the light of its 'relevant experience and expertise' it should be the 'regulator' for new cable services, not only on the grounds that 'this would undoubtedly be the quickest, most practical means of creating the necessary supervisory structure,' but because 'adequate regulation' remained necessary for 'a social influence as powerful and as persuasive as broadcasting'. 'A good regulatory system,' it claimed, 'is part of the total broadcasting culture'. The argument was rejected both by Hunt and by the Home Secretary, the latter telling the Commons decisively in December 1982 that cable television is 'not another form of public-service broadcasting.'

In the future, whatever happens to cable in Britain, this statement may stand out as a landmark. Douglas Hurd, then Minister at the Home Office, went even further when he explained to a Consumers' Association workshop that if one cable operator failed to provide what was wanted another could come in. 'Consumer choice, not the guidance of an authority, would decide.' This was to be the message too of the Government White Paper, *The Development of Cable Systems and Services* (Cmnd 8866), in April 1983.

There was, notwithstanding, to be a new 'Authority' to deal with cable, with a Chairman, six other part-time Members and 'a small but well qualified staff'; and while it was emphasized that this was 'not a Broadcasting Authority' in the same sense as the IBA – it would neither be 'large' nor 'bureaucratic', nor, in the words of the Home Secretary, would it have the same 'style' – its four main functions would be strictly comparable. It would promote the development of cable systems and services; award franchises; regulate (within what were admittedly new limits) programme content and advertising; and monitor the performance of the operators. And the Home Secretary was to appoint its members. This was an answer which was no more calculated to appeal to believers in a full-blooded market philosophy than the Conservative Government's Television Act of 1954. It did not point the way to Peter Jay's future pattern of completely free publishing.

It was not until October 1984 that the new Authority was

formally set up following the passage in July of the Cable and Broadcasting Act, of which the first text, subsequently to be modified substantially, was published in November 1983. Long before that, however, the IBA, faced with something not too unlike a mirror picture of itself, had abandoned its doubts, and thereafter, in the words of its Annual Report for 1983–84, it 'looked forward to working closely with the [new] Cable Authority.' It had already recognized that it was that Authority, an Authority with far fewer 'teeth' than the IBA had asked for, and not itself, which would be left to ensure that the participants in existing media should not have a stake in cable such as to produce a concentration of power in their field – press, TV or radio – which would be 'contrary to the public interest'. It continued to argue, however, that there should be public consultation in the first round of cable franchise awards as in the case of its own awards. 'Unless it is proposed to try to keep the applications totally secret (and this seems unlikely to be acceptable) it seems inevitable that there will be public comment upon them.'

In its contracts for appointment with the companies in December 1981, after the franchises had been allotted – and they were still not called franchises – the IBA had identified cable television as a 'prescribed activity', along with pay-TV in cinemas, subscription TV, satellite broadcasting, video discs, tapes or cassette manufacture and other diversified activities, which required the IBA's prior written consent; and in its evidence to the Hunt Committee it had referred to possible dangerous influences within an extended communications system 'on the fundamental features of British public service broadcasting, balanced standards and national coverage.' Now in January 1983, in its comments on the proposed White Paper (Cmnd 8866, paragraph 2(x)), it had told the Home Office that, subject to safeguards, ITV companies should be allowed to acquire controlling interests in cable operations, and when the White Paper was issued, its first reaction was that 'cable, in the words of the White Paper, should increase the possibilities for genuine and healthy competition in the provision of programme services'. It had 'gone a long way in meeting the concerns of good broadcasting – that competition should be fair and that the choice, range and quality of programmes available

200

should be not undermined, but enhanced.'

The contracting companies themselves were told that 'a company's conduct of its cable services would be taken into account as a factor in any future franchise application'; and that they would not be discouraged from becoming involved with cable as long as the Authority was satisfied that 'the extent of diversification was not likely to result in the switch of undue resources and effort.' Although there were few takers, the companies reached agreement with entertainment unions for the sale overseas of ITV programmes to cable in April 1983.

There was a further dimension to cable. It was known that from mid-1983 it would be possible to distribute cable television entertainment in Europe by low-power satellite and that by the end of 1985 there would be more than forty channels available for lease, with overlapping 'footprints' from 'Euro-beams' and western and eastern beams. This internationalization of the supply of entertainment through trans-frontier satellite delivery to cable meant that neither the IBA nor the BBC could afford to ignore the possibility of a new kind of competition.

There were to be many fluctuations of mood concerning the future as cable plans were announced and financial prospects remained doubtful. The word 'crisis', which hit the headlines of the *Financial Times* on several occasions – as late, for example, as December 1984 – must be set alongside other headlines like that in the *Sunday Mirror* (14 April 1985): 'The Big Switch-on: Fun for all as Cable TV takes off.'

In fact, after the first eleven cable franchises had been announced by the Home Office in November 1983, the development of cable in 1984 was slow, 'down in the dumps' the *Sunday Times* described it (3 March 1985). Nor was enterprise quickened when the Government phased out 100 per cent capital allowances in the 1984 Budget. Yet after almost a year of official silence on the subject, Kenneth Baker's successor as Minister for Information Technology, Geoffrey Pattie, announced in March 1985 that '1985 would be the year of opportunity for cable.' There were then 400,000 British homes reported to be wired for the new cable services, with a projected doubling in 1986 and a singlefold increase by the end of 1988, and by 1990 it was hoped that about 4 million homes, 20 per cent of the total, would have access to multichannel cable.

The new Cable Authority, which began to operate in January 1985, with Richard Burton as Chairman, Paul Johnson, Professor James Ring, Peter Paine and Mrs Elizabeth Mac-Donald Baron as Members, and Jon Davey (from the Home Office) as Director General, had not found it easy to attract takers for the unallotted franchises which remained out of the first eleven, but it was planning in 1985 to announce five new areas for cable every four months. If such a rate of expansion were to prove possible, the roles of the IBA and the new Cable Authority might well become competitive rather than complementary.

They would not be competing, however, on equal terms. The new Authority's general programme obligations were more negative than positive and its guidance 'indicative'; and since the success of the cable companies would depend on the willingness of people in the locality where pay-TV was offered to pay a necessary subscription and take up the service, the new Authority was not to be called upon to demand wide range, balance or even high quality in programming. In such circumstances there would be obvious pressure on the IBA itself to relax its own monitoring requirements. How the Government would react to new forms of competition in the formulation of its own policies remained uncertain.

Once people are free to choose what they wish to see and hear from a wide range of different channels, the Government's White Paper had claimed in 1983, 'the idea that programmes can reflect points of view which may be unattractive to some is likely to be widely and readily accepted.' There was nothing self-evident about this, however. Nor was it obvious that an increase in the number of channels would reflect more 'points of view'. That would depend on the ownership and control of the channels.

Moreover, a neutral attitude in the future on the part of Government to controversial broadcasting from home or abroad could not be taken for granted, a point proved in August 1985 when the BBC was told to think again by the Home Secretary. Jon Davey, the Cable Authority's Director General, told an International Institute of Communications meeting in London in April 1985, in answer to a question, that, since all foreign channels would operate on terms authorized by their governments, he saw no reason why the Authority should in any way be concerned with their content. It was an optimistic comment. In the past minor deviations from what the Government considered to be 'responsible' television had on occasion provoked unnecessarily sharp criticism from governmental – and political – sources, and the limits to 'free publishing' had been all too evident, as they were to be in Summer 1985.

The story of direct broadcasting by satellite, linked as it has been and is at every point in the story of cable, has had other implications for the IBA and its franchising process since 1981. In February 1982, a few weeks before the Home Secretary awarded the first two United Kingdom DBS channels to the BBC and named United Satellites Ltd, a consortium formed for the purpose by British Aerospace, British Telecommunications and GEC/Marconi, as the satellite provider, the IBA had begun to show a more positive attitude towards DBS; and the Home Secretary's statement that the IBA might be authorized to operate two further channels when the necessary amendments to the 1981 Act could be made spurred it to claim, without bidding in detailed terms for specific channels, that it would place DBS 'centrally in plans for our future'. In 1983 it was brought even more into the picture as the BBC, faced with financial difficulties, was reluctant to meet exceptionally heavy DBS costs, possibly seven times larger than those originally anticipated. The Government's acceptance of a suggested DBS receiver standard different from that favoured by the BBC, and its zeal to support DBS without contributing to its costs, were additional factors of importance. Not surprisingly, therefore, in December 1983 official policy in relation to DBS was, in the words of the *Economist*, in such a state of disarray that 'the Government's hope of getting anybody to invest in hardware soon and fill the DBS channels' was now felt to rest with the IBA, 'the regulatory authority for commercial television, whose job it would be to coax investors into the open.'

The IBA had been accused of missing the boat in 1982; in 1983 it seemed to be joining the boat when the sky was dark with cloud. In May 1983 it published its own proposal for a phased development of two of the three UK channels available after the BBC's two. DBS, it claimed, should be part of its television operation so that in the first years it could be supported by ITV income or reserves, and the Authority should have responsibility for the first two channels, exercising similar functions as it already exercised for ITV and independent local radio – those of appointing and monitoring programme companies, arranging contracts and safeguarding services. The first channel should go to a consortium of the current ITV companies; the second should be offered for competition, as would be the first after the initial contract period. DBS services should conform to the programme requirements of the Broadcasting Act of 1981.

The ITV companies themselves remained split on a DBS project, with some of them inclined to wait for the BBC to take the initial risk, but they were united in the conviction that if they were to become involved – and the major companies thought that DBS could not get off the ground without them – the extension of their existing ITV regional contracts beyond 1989 was a necessary precondition. They put a formal proposal to the Authority, therefore, at a Standing Consultative Committee meeting in November 1983, that the 1982 franchises should be extended by three years to the end of 1992, arguing that they would face competition from cable systems – possibly from 1984, but certainly from 1989 – at a time when ITV revenue would be required to provide a necessary financial base for DBS.

In this way the franchise question became directly related to the advance of new technology. The IBA had already authorized such extensions of franchises in 1964, however, while it waited for the Government's decision on a second ITV channel, and three times during the 1970s, while it waited for a decision on Channel 4 and for the passing of the 1980 Act. Now a statutory amendment would be needed to extend the maximum contract period of eight years for ITV (section 19 (2)). It seemed perfectly possible. According to the chairman of Anglia, there was 'a sense of realism in the air and we feel sure that long before the next franchise affair comes around some sort of order and practical thinking will have been restored on the television scene.' Nonetheless, the first draft of the Cable and Broadcasting Bill, published in November 1983, made no substantial concessions on ITV franchises; it added only to this section that the maximum period for a DBS contract would be twelve years.

With increasing doubts about the viability of the DBS enterprise – and with newspaper reports, many of them exaggerated, about the increasing reluctance of the BBC to remain heavily involved – the Government, without at that stage making concessions, pressed hard for a partnership which would include both the IBA, which it knew might draw in private funds, and the BBC; and at a meeting in January 1984 of representatives of the BBC, the IBA, ITCA and United Satellites Ltd, chaired by Jeffrey Sterling, chairman of P&O and special advisor to the Secretary for Trade and Industry, Norman Tebbit (the Department of Trade and Industry was just as interested in the outcome as the Home Office), it was decided to set up a working party to hammer out an agreement.

Press reports of its private meetings suggested that the Government plan for two BBC and IBA DBS channels was dropped at the working party's first meeting and that what was on the table at this stage was a three-channel project, with one channel to be shared, one going to the BBC and one to the commercial companies. Two satellites would be launched with two channels each, the fourth channel to serve as a back-up. A close relationship between the IBA and the BBC was much in favour at this time and the BBC's Chairman, Stuart Young, spoke in public the same month, January, of the need for a noncompetitive market until an audience was built up and of the importance of subsidies and tax incentives to manufacturers to bring down the cost of DBS receivers. As continuing government pressure was reported on the BBC, the IBA and ITCA to agree on a workable project and there were ebbing and flowing semi-secret talks behind the scenes, a 'top civil servant' was quoted as saying that the ITV companies were 'the only ones who can save the BBC, and the pressure is on everyone to come up with a working solution enabling the two broadcasting authorities to share their commitments to DBS.'

But the ITV companies remained divided in mind, and in February 1984 no decision had yet been reached by ITCA even after a preliminary report of the working party was received. 'If there is a decision by the ITV companies it is literally months away,' observed ITCA's General Secretary David Shaw. 'The

205

boards and shareholders of individual companies will have to be consulted, and that could take a lot of time.' Instead, the decision was taken that the ITV companies would approach the Home Office for an amendment to the 1981 Broadcasting Act, to be made in the long-awaited Cable and Broadcasting Bill which had been introduced in the Lords, not the Commons, in November 1983 and which was then in its committee stage.

The Bill contained a Part II on broadcasting services, the provisions of which enabled the IBA to supply, by means of DBS, television services additional to those it provided under the 1981 Act; the proposed amendment would have had the effect of extending ITV franchises at least for the lifetime of the first satellite, and possibly longer through rolling contracts, unless the IBA found specific reasons for the advertisement of any contracts. It also allowed for DBS franchises up to fifteen years. 'The companies are not using the issue as blackmail: it is a business fact,' David Shaw stated.

In March 1984 *Broadcast*, with its customary ear to the ground, reported a DBS deal, accurately forestalling by two months the announcement made by the Home Secretary in the Commons on 8 May when he moved the second reading of the Cable and Broadcasting Bill. The wording of the draft had by now taken a sharp turn since the autumn of 1983, and many of the pressures had registered. A new joint venture company was to be formed for DBS of which the BBC would hold 50 per cent; and of the 50 per cent private sector share it was expected that ITV companies would hold at least half. No coercion or pressure, however, would be placed on them, and the Authority would invite other business participants, a third element, to apply to join the project, which would have a maximum life of ten years from the satellite launch. New arrangements would have to be made with Unisat, given that the normal life of a satellite was 7–10 years. The BBC would have to raise the finance for its share in the project in the private sector, and ITV costs could not be offset against the levy payable on ITV profits.

The Government, it was stated, wanted a competitive system to be introduced as soon as possible, and the Bill empowered the IBA to invite applications for two DBS commercial channels, additional to its television services under the 1981 Act. A

206

Satellite Broadcasting Board of six members, three from the BBC Board of Governors and three from among the members of the Authority, serving five years at a time, would be set up, with the task of providing television services 'of high quality (both as to the transmission and as to the matter transmitted)' by DBS to the United Kingdom, the Isle of Man and the Channel Islands. The BBC and IBA would have the duty to provide what supporting services the Board required, on commercial terms, and, unless previously dissolved, the Board would function for ten years from the start of the first television service. Programmes broadcast by satellite were to be provided not by the Board but by 'a programme provider' approved by the Secretary of State and under contract to the Board. All financial and other arrangements for the satellite were to be made by the programme provider, who would make appropriate payments to the Board for their outgoings. The programmes broadcast by the Board might include advertisements.

There was an important international development at the end of 1984 when, faced with its members' differences over varieties of DBS reception standards, the European Broadcasting Union, itself increasingly concerned with the impact of new technologies on 'traditional' broadcasting, approved a 'family of systems' for the three reception modes: DBS, low-power satellite reception by cable headends, and home reception of cable channels on existing receivers. The important objective now, the EBU argued, although it must have doubted that it could be achieved, was to design a single European receiver capable of operating in all three modes.

During the course of debate on the Cable and Broadcasting Bill the Government gave assurances that there would be no favoured position for existing ITV companies in applications for DBS programme contracts. When the IBA had its own DBS services it would be 'entirely independent in its choice of programme contractors, just as it is in the award of the terrestrial franchises' 'These services,' it went on, 'will compete with the joint project.'

In May 1984 the IBA invited applications for participation in the 'third force', in order to make recommendations to the Home Secretary by July. It would require of the participants 'financial soundness, adequate resources and the ability to make a positive contribution to the enterprise.' From fifteen applicants the Home Secretary chose five: Thorn-EMI, Granada TV Rentals, S. Pearson, Virgin Records Ltd and Consolidated Satellite Broadcasting, a group of independent UK producers, John Gau and Jeremy Wallington among them, who were to invest £80 million, roughly 20 per cent each. The completed consortium (dubbed the 21 Club) met at Broadcasting House on 7 August to deal with the joint venture structure, new negotiations with Unisat and a working timetable. Andrew Quinn from Granada Cable and Satellite was appointed coordinator in September, and by the end of the year the Home Secretary was being asked to let the DBS project go to international tender if Unisat's price could not be reduced.

Already after the *Broadcast* report on the future pattern of DBS in March 1984 there had been press criticism. There had been other press reports too during the same month that the IBA was proposing to recommend to the Home Office that 'in principle' future ITV regional contracts should be held on rolling contracts, and the *Financial Times*, echoing the strong doubts which had been expressed by Lord Thomson in April 1981, complained that 'such a system would mean that existing ITV companies could in theory hold their franchises indefinitely.' It added hopefully, however, that the change 'would also probably involve more vigorous annual assessments, and these could lead to the loss of a franchise at any time if a company's performance proved inadequate.' It is interesting to note that only 'performance' was picked out in this comment on extended monitoring powers; there was no longer mention of financial or structural restraints. There was a reference also in *Marketing Week* (16 March 1984) to 'a rolling review system whereby one or two TV contracts come up for review each year,' thus avoiding 'the horrors of the mass review, while ensuring openness and competition.'

The Home Secretary's reaction to the IBA's suggestion of a rolling-contracts system was said to be 'cool' (*Financial Times*, 12 March 1984), yet the Government was preparing to make a far more substantial concession – an extension of the life of the franchises which would otherwise expire at the end of 1989. It was clear that at this crucial point in official policy-making the chronology of new communications development mattered more than the chronology of the franchise-allotting system, for the Government, backed by its large 1979 majority, was increasingly anxious to see the commercial companies participating in the joint (then) £400 million DBS project with the BBC. For their part the companies were still maintaining – and it was a strong bargaining point independently of any point made by the IBA – that they could not invest in any such long-term project if their 'terrestrial franchises' – one of the first occasions on which this term was generally used – would be under threat soon after broadcasts from space began. Technology and finance could not be separated from each other.

There was immediate criticism, of course, from outside the system, along the lines of the Annan Committee's criticism that rolling contracts 'would entrench the existing companies' position still further.' Thus, Stuart Wilson, who had been a beneficiary of the 1967 franchise affair and an unsuccessful applicant in 1980 and who now declared himself a definite nonstarter in 1989, went back to the old games images and named the new game 'Happy Families'. Pushing talk of the new technology to one side, he added that 'the fact that the IBA made a mess of the exercise in 1981 does not affect the principle, simply the method.' 'An unparalleled carve-up taking place in broadcasting,' conducted with 'breath-taking haste and a lack of public debate,' was the verdict of *Campaign* (20 April 1984).

The *Times*, also talking of a 'carve-up', pointed out (12 April 1984) that the concession of seven years' extension to ITV companies was worth £7 billion in revenue, in contrast to the £200 million or so which would be the companies' share of DBS costs. The deal, the *Times* went on, in an unappealingly strident tone that was to run through all its future comments on communications policies, meant that 'much of British TV for the rest of the century would be dictated by an odd mixture of BBC paranoia, ITV greed and Government job creation'; it would be a move which would have 'more far-reaching effects than any amendment to television policy since the creation of ITV itself.' Its worst aspect, however, was that it had been subject 'to the barest scrutiny by Parliament and to no rigorous public inquiry.'

There were harsh criticisms of the Cable and Broadcasting Bill from other quarters also, and on other and quite different grounds. Five versions, 207 amendments and thirty-seven new clauses demonstrated that Ministers were 'making up television policy as they went along,' Denis Howell complained (*Hansard*, 9 July 1984), while for Austin Mitchell, another Labour MP, who had become known to the public through television, this was 'the messiest legislation . . . passed for years' and had been 'handled in a shambolic disorganized fashion.' One missing item in the debate was the whole question of franchise allotment. Not one word was uttered by government spokesmen on the IBA's experience – and that of the companies – in 1980 or earlier. History, it was clear, did not teach.

In the Act no new requirements at any level were laid on the Authority, and the subtitle of Part II, section 46, read with admirable simplicity, 'No need for IBA to invite applications before entering into certain contracts.' The section would await the Home Secretary's direction to come into force, however, and this was to be withheld if the project for the first DBS service of the Satellite Broadcasting Board did not succeed. Part II, sections 42–4, creating that Board with a life of ten years, would also await the Home Secretary's direction – although the six members of the Board were named in October 1984, with Lord Thomson as chairman for the first year. If the Board's project were to prove successful, the ITV franchise process need not be brought into force.

It is notable that during the debates on the 1984 Bill Members of Parliament spent far more time discussing cable than broadcasting – or DBS. Lords Hill and Howard, ex-IBA and ex-BBC, concentrated their forces on the point that the new Cable Authority, according to the *Economist* (7 April 1984) only the fifth quango to be created in five years, had no responsibility parallel to that of the IBA for programme balance or for 'proper proportions of British origin and performance' and no lifespan, while the IBA's future could be extended to the Arthur Clarkeian year, 2001. Moreover, while the IBA was given a consultative status in relation to the Cable Authority as far as advertising codes were concerned, the wording was vague; and it was emphasized that while some procedures were to be shared and some 'national events' were to be 'protected' for the IBA and the BBC, the new Authority was not to be conceived of as 'the third leg of a tripod'.

Some of the provisions relating to the new Cable Authority may have general long-term implications for the IBA. Thus, while the IBA with its far greater supervisory duties and powers has no restrictions on its power to revoke contracts, the Cable Authority has powers only to revoke them in cases of non-compliance, specifically if it considers it necessary to do so 'in the public interest'. Moreover, the Cable Authority's penalizing procedure for advance monitoring in detail of an official licence holder's progress and advertisements has no parallel within the IBA, which instead has the statutory duty to approve in advance the programme schedules for ITV and independent local radio. Given too that for its licensed services the Cable Authority has no mandate to maintain either range and quality or balance, as has the IBA, but only to ensure compliance with its 'guidance', it has more of the aspect of an ultimate police agency than of an independent agency in its own right. The areas of discretion and judgement traditionally left to the BBC and the IBA have been reduced, the limits of action defined. The new Authority will offer the kind of regulation, familiar in the United States, which is compatible with a substantial measure of 'deregulation'.

The IBA's public response to these aspects of the 1984 legislation was to insist through its Chairman that 'deregulation' was only a fashionable 'buzz-word' (*Airwaves*, Winter 1984–85). Moreover, although the IBA itself had by then relinquished some of its controls over independent local radio – for example, over technical standards and practices – and the contracting companies were now to be left to take their own decisions on such matters as hours of broadcasting for special events and, more significantly, diversification of interests, Lord Thomson was at pains to insist that the IBA, far from being 'in the deregulatory business', was 'committed firmly to its responsibilities as a regulator.' What was happening, he insisted, was adaptation. There would be no more monitoring of independent local radio programmes by IBA regional offices, and performance would be reviewed every four or five years in mid-contract, replacing the existing system of biennial reviews. Financial reasons, the need to save money, were cited for the change – 'streamlining the medium from the point of view of

211

cost effectiveness' – and one of the most important features of the new policy was the decision not to expand the number of local radio stations from fifty-one even though as many as sixty-nine were allowed under the law.

John Whitney, IBA Director General, touched on matters which went well beyond finance for sound and vision when he spoke of 'DBS just over the horizon' and of 'facing the challenges of the 1980s and beyond'; but in June 1985 UK DBS moved further over the horizon – and possibly out of sight – when the 21 Club, after eighteen months of facing the challenges, informed the Satellite Broadcasting Board that it withdrew from the project. Its reasons were government rigidity, restricting it to the high-cost Unisat system, a ten-year franchise and a reception system which would not be adopted in Europe outside the UK; heavy advance costs of satellite insurance; and the uncertainties introduced by Government licensing in May of direct reception of low-power satellites. In the background was the knowledge that the immediate way into European television markets was by the multiplying number of low-power satellites delivering channels to cable networks. The consortium concluded that the enormous costs of a national UK system could not be met without major governmental financial support.

The loss of its sole approved 'programme provider' left the shadow Board with no role. Early in July it wound itself up and Lord Thomson, its chairman, informed the Home Secretary of its voluntary dissolution. Sections 42 and 43 of the 1984 Act remained inoperative therefore. Indeed, the Act provides for their annulment by statutory order of either House. After the dissolution Stuart Young, BBC Chairman, said, 'Things won't stand still and I believe the BBC, with its rich programme resources, has a major role to play in developing the service for the nation which will eventually spring from the new technology.' But there was no return to talk of BBC DBS channels.

The DBS problem was back on the Home Office desk, and back to what Giles Shaw, Minister for Broadcasting, had called in March 'alternative options' (*Financial Times*, 20 March 1985). The Government had amended the IBA's power to invite applications for two DBS channels by delaying it until three years after the Board's channels had come into operation. That delay was removed and IBA action under the Act was now the unique option. The Act made no stipulations as to the satellite system. It appeared that the Authority could set its own technical conditions for the system which the applicant contractor had to provide (at an earlier stage in the story it had investigated the international market); it was as free to choose DBS contractors as it was to award ITV regional contracts. Under the 1981 and 1984 Acts it was now the single UK Authority responsible for both terrestrial and DBS Commercial television services. In August 1985 the Home Office invited it to test the extent of interest of potential investors in a DBS system which would have neither public subsidy nor government constraints.

With the disappearance of the 21 Club, ITV franchises were no longer linked to DBS prospects and, as with cable, the position of the Authority, which might find ITV companies among its DBS applicants, was to encourage their interest on condition that their primary function as programme contractors was fully performed. The question of procedures lost much of its element of novelty, therefore, and movement towards the 1990 regional contract awards started with an IBA mid-term review on not dissimilar lines to that of the 1970s; it was announced by the Director General to the companies in January 1985. Initial assessments were to be made of each company under the same headings as had been used for the 1979–80 contract procedures. They began in March 1985 and were generally reported by the companies to be low key, mostly conducted at regional officer level, although regular annual meetings with managing directors and programme controllers to deal with programme schedules were said to have been serious and searching. There were to be no public statements of the Authority's appraisals until the end of the year. This, Whitney stated, would avoid any dangers of awkward financial repercussions for the companies and any disturbance of the network. The companies may come through the review process without stress, but it remains to be seen whether the process will be more relevant to the 1988 decisions than the 'simultaneous appraisals' of 1974–75 were to those of 1980.

Whether or not the 1985 mid-term review is in fact more vigorous, the notion of a reappraisal of procedures (and perhaps of rolling contracts?) surfaced again on 4 June 1985 when Viscount Whitelaw, Lord President of the Council and leader of the House of Lords (and the previous Home Secretary), gave the IBA Robert Fraser Lecture in the Banqueting Hall, Whitehall. Speaking 'not in any way on behalf of the Government' – but surely not without Home Office sympathy – he argued that 'the increasing complexity of modern broadcasting' meant that the IBA would have to consider very carefully how contracts were to be awarded to companies in the future. 'I suspect,' he went on, 'that the advent particularly of satellite broadcasting and cable makes some change in the arrangements even more important,' adding that he wondered whether 'the wholesale replacement of one company with another totally different one will prove sensible in the future'. 'Perhaps in future,' he concluded, 'the law might be amended so that clear instructions from the IBA on crucial changes in the company leading to changes in direction might be thought sufficient sanction without causing wholesale disruption and indeed widespread uncertainty for some time before the date of the review.' Without any doubt the Authority's Chairman shared this view. The text of the Act was already under scrutiny by its lawyers to define precisely the extent of the action the IBA was required to take.

Lord Thomson, speaking at a *Financial Times* cable and satellite conference in March 1985, had already spelled out what he meant by the phrase 'the increasing complexity of modern broadcasting'. Describing DBS as an 'instrument of national policy', he argued that it would be successful only if there were 'confident' terrestrial broadcasters. On what did 'confidence' depend? Would existing companies choose to become involved in the satellite business? How would possible profits (and investment) affect the profits (and investment) in the terrestrial system? Should there be any erosion of TV audiences, it was likely that finance for ITV would be more difficult to attract; as Colin Shaw put it in *Broadcast* (22 August 1983), 'up to now . . . the rewards have been worth the gamble. But will that be true by the end of the decade?' The basis of the regional system might be in question. There could be an evolution of large companies each with a cluster of orbital stations rather than any significant development of small stations, cable or otherwise, geared to local audiences and their needs, and in such a situation some existing smaller contracting companies might lose their identity. There would be more rather than less massing of interests as ITV 'found ways to participate in new channels that would subsidize the terrestrial networks' (*TV Today*, September 1983).

Such new channels, whether ITV companies were to be part of them or not, were slow to come. Indeed, by August 1985 two only of the eleven 1983 franchised cable systems were in service with five expected to be in operation by the end of the year; and when in July the Cable Authority's Director General announced five new area contracts (for each of which only one application had been made), he admitted that the Authority's initial rapid development plan exceeded potential investment. Yet meanwhile powerful business interests, with strong press leadership, had crossed old boundaries, technological and national, in satellite broadcasting and new clusters of interests had formed. Brian Haynes's SATV, for example, was restructured in June 1983 when Rupert Murdoch's News International plc acquired 65 per cent of its shares at a cost of £5 million and substantial new investment capital was injected into the business then, in April 1984, and again in May 1985. The channel was renamed Sky and moved its programmes from the European Space Agency's preoperational satellite OTS to the first operational satellite Eutelsat 1. In the spring of 1985 Sky was claiming more than 3 million subscribers in eleven countries and was transmitting for seventy-three hours a week, and, with Belgium among countries entered, estimating 7 million viewers by the end of the year. There was talk of 'Sky Wars', too, when in 1984 Robert Maxwell acquired control of Rediffusion Cablevision for a reported £9 million, although Sky was one of five channels offered to Rediffusion subscribers. 'We are revolutionizing television,' claimed Ian Harkness, Rediffusion Cablevision's marketing executive (*Broadcast*, 12 April 1985); but there were fewer signs of revolution inside Britain than outside it.

Comparisons and contrasts with the United States were often being drawn, but across the Atlantic, where there is a different broadcasting tradition, satellite television was always a jump ahead (as Brenda Maddox claimed in the *Times*, 3 May

1985). There were already a million backyard dishes and a growing hard-sell operation to promote them, alongside cable and competing with it. Domestic satellite systems, the US entrepreneurs promise, can deliver a hundred satellite systems of 'obvious diversity'. 'When you buy your satellite system from the dealer,' the brochures proclaim, 'you are the cable company and you control what you watch.' There are enthusiasts in Britain who believe in consequence, as *Broadcast* put it (12 April 1985), that 'high-powered DBS, a vision of the 1970s, is becoming increasingly irrelevant as developments in receiving-dish technology move towards the point where home receivers will be able to pick up signals from the present generation of cheaper satellites carrying more channels.' There are other enthusiasts who question whether Britain can remain outside DBS when France and Germany, where the governments fund high-power DBS systems up to and including satellite launch, are inside.

Viscount Whitelaw's view on 5 June 1985 was that 'it would be a pity if Britain were to lag behind other countries in such major technological developments' and his hope was that 'all those concerned will come together in order to combine commercial success with the safeguarding of our British interests.' Like his colleagues, he offered no funds, however, and it is plain that UK DBS will not be a major competitor to the terrestrial broadcasters before or by 1990.

For all the stress on the free play of market forces, and the unwillingness of the Government to provide development finance on the scale of government investment in some other European countries, there is an unwillingness too to let market forces rip. As in dealing with many other contemporary problems in Britain, the balance between financial viability and social direction is left unresolved. Yet once decisions have been taken, the outcomes tend to be irreversible. This would surely be true of BBC finance by advertising, a more serious problem for the IBA, in the short run at least, than new technology.

Once the differences between national policies are considered within an international context, procedures seem less crucial than objectives. There is no place in Britain below Cabinet level where all the interconnected issues of broadcasting, 'dual system' cable and satellites, the role of the press,

216

international relations, technological and social options, can be considered, and there is no indication that at that high level they are being so considered in depth. Instead, there is a concentration on specific points along with a division of responsibility. Everything is piecemeal and subject to limited and defined inquiry, different in approach and method from the intermittent but wide-ranging inquiries into British broadcasting before and after the Second World War. Moreover, within this frame, British approaches to the media mix remain mixed. Thus, for Anthony Pragnell, retired from Brompton Road, the Government's new Cable Authority fits – and in his view rightly so – into a traditional pattern, offering the necessary kind of protection to the IBA (and the BBC) which Albert Scharf, the president of the European Broadcasting Union, had urged in a lecture of March 1983 (*EBU Review*, September 1983). 'One should pave the official road,' Scharf had said, 'before people make their way on their own on continuing and controversial paths across the meadow if one wished to keep broadcasting activities in the public interest within a framework of regulations.' That was what Pragnell thought that the British Government had done when it set up the Cable Authority. Meadows not skies. 'Later,' Scharf added, 'it will be much more difficult to undo deregulation.'

To people outside the circles of broadcasting policy and administration, such an approach, even if it is called safeguarding rather than protectionist, is far too negative. The case for public broadcasting rests on stronger grounds than tradition. In any discussion of broadcasting futures – and the franchise system within them – it is the programming core of broadcasting that should be the dominant concern, and it is this that is most vulnerable not only to the intrusion of new technology but to the pressures of Government. However internationalized broadcasting may become as a result of satellites, however multinational the programmes on offer, there should still be a place for 'unifying' broadcasting appealing to national, regional and local audiences and taking into account both cultural identity and programme balance. However packaged broadcasting may become, there should still be a place for the kind of independent producers who have contracted so effectively for Channel 4; they bring a necessary element of experiment into the system. However low the selling costs of the cheapest American programmes, there should still be a place for quality programmes made by, among others, network companies big enough to concentrate their strength and to foster and develop programme-making talent. A system which fails to offer an incentive to develop such talent would destroy the creative force of broadcasting.

This is probably the strongest argument in favour of public-service broadcasting within a pluralistic, multimedia communications context; and fortunately in Britain there is a stronger commitment to quality – and variety – than there is in most broadcasting systems, however many their channels. If, however, what Christopher Dunkley has called 'the programme quality spiral' (*Financial Times*, 19 December 1984) were to move downwards, for whatever reasons, it would be difficult, perhaps impossible, ever to reverse it. From a programming point of view the IBA and the BBC belong to the same system. The ITV companies can set relatively high tariffs for advertising because the BBC is not in competition with them for advertising, and they can – and do – use their monopoly of selling time to compete with the BBC not only for audiences but for quality programming, for 'brilliance' as Michael Grade, Controller BBC1, called it in a debate organized by the Institute of Practitioners in Advertising in April 1985.

In 1988, which seems likely to be something of an *annus mirabilis*, the varied themes of this chapter will converge. It is not only the year when the IBA must decide whether or in what terms to launch a third franchise affair, but the year when the Government will have to take decisions (near to a general election?) on the future financing of the BBC. If then or before then the latter were to be called upon to derive the whole or part of its revenue from advertising or sponsorship, the existing duopoly built on the relationship of the BBC, financed by licence fee, and the IBA, supervising a system based on advertising, would in effect be dissolved. Experience in Europe shows how a vestigial licence fee shrinks in face of inflation and currency instability. But this is only a part of the picture. These decisions will be taken in the light of satellite, cable and video development as it looks then.

218

The first long-running award of contracts by the ITA from 1954 to 1962 constructed the independent television system. In 1967–68 Lord Hill's Authority conducted the first franchise affair, the first simultaneous award of all contracts, demonstrating by the removal of two programme contractors that no franchise was a freehold, and regularizing and regulating the system, taking some account of the recommendations of the Pilkington Committee and more of the legislation which followed it. In the second, after fourteen years, the Authority's decisions for 1982 made no changes to the system or the network basis; it merely changed some of the contractors in an atmosphere of contrived drama. In January 1988, less than two years from the publication of this book, and subject in the meantime to any such statutory amendments as Viscount Whitelaw seemed to suggest, the Authority is due to publish its own decisions on the ITV contracts to be offered from 1990 to 1998. In three years' time light will have been thrown on some of the unresolved political and financial issues which are current ITV preoccupations – the Government's decision on the levy system; the Peacock Report, and the Government reception of it; the state of the advertising market; and ITV's revenue performance following the bad times of 1984 and 1985. A certain amount of further light will have been thrown too on the competitive scene – the extent of audience penetration by cable services, including channels based in other countries conveyed by low-power satellite, and by foreign-based DBS services; the offer for the perhaps twelve-year use of UK DBS channels by British or foreign entrepreneurs or combinations of both.

Whether the new light will be bright or dim – and given the tendency in Britain to blur issues the second is more likely – it is difficult to see how the Authority could offer a repeat version in 1988 of the 'charades' of 1979 and 1980. Whether the duopoly continues or not – and with it existing broadcasting institutions – it will not be easy to tolerate in the future the existence of an Authority which, however good its intentions, reaches decisions which are not clearly explained and which cannot be easily justified. Those who make judgements must always expect to be judged.

The IBA will have to make certain of the 'robustness' of the

219

ITV system and of financially strong contractors. Channel 4, still stirring in 1985 to reach its audience objective of a 10 per cent share, will have to be secured. Both the contracts the IBA offers and the process to obtain them will have to be such as to attract applicant companies. The arbitrariness of the 1980 affair – and the mystique which surrounded it – must go.

Arbitrariness must be replaced by criteria which are explicit, consistent and seen to be sustained from mid-term reviews to franchise awards and to final contracts. Decisions should be justified, even if reached and explained in private circumstances. When John Whitney obtained a coat of arms for the IBA in 1983 the motto chosen was '*Servire Populo*'.

Mystique was generated in 1980 by the Authority's distancing itself from applicants, by communication through questionnaires not through dialogue, and by public denouements dramatically arranged. Public accountability was not achieved by the 1980 façade of public relations exercises. These did not and could not plumb public opinion.

The ITV system survived the procedures of 1980 and 1981. Since then market forces have reshaped the finance, management and output of the new companies and some ITV programmes from old and new contractors have won honours and applause. But Lord Thomson's judgement in 1981 on the franchise process itself is firmly on the record: 'There must be a better way.'

Index

221

222

223